STUDIES
IN
MEANING
5

Also available from Pace University Press

Studies in Meaning:
Exploring Constructivist Psychology
(2002)

Studies in Meaning 2:
Bridging the Personal and Social
in Constructivist Psychology
(2004)

Studies in Meaning 3:
Constructivist Psychotherapy in the Real World
(2008)

Studies in Meaning 4:
Constructivist Perspectives on Theory, Practice, and Social Justice
(2010)

www.pace.edu/press

STUDIES IN MEANING 5: PERTURBING THE STATUS QUO IN CONSTRUCTIVIST PSYCHOLOGY

Edited by
Jonathan D. Raskin
State University of New York at New Paltz

Sara K. Bridges
The University of Memphis

and

Jack S. Kahn
Palomar College

Pace University Press
2015

Table of Contents

PART III
CONSTRUCTIVIST PSYCHOTHERAPY

PART IV
LOOKING FORWARD

Contributors

Michael Basseches, Department of Psychology, Suffolk University, Boston, Massachusetts, USA

Sara K. Bridges, Department of Counseling, Educational Psychology and Research, The University of Memphis, Tennessee, USA

Jonah N. Cohen, Department of Psychology, Temple University, Philadelphia, Pennsylvania, USA

Jay S. Efran, Department of Psychology, Temple University, Philadelphia, Pennsylvania, USA

Amanda El-Hashem, Department of Counseling, Developmental and Educational Psychology, Boston College, Boston, Massachusetts, USA

Mark Freeman, Department of Psychology, College of the Holy Cross, Worcester, Massachusetts, USA

Jack S. Kahn, School of Social and Behavioral Sciences, Palomar College, San Marcos, California, USA

Michael F. Mascolo, Department of Psychology, Merrimack College, North Andover, Massachusetts, USA

Donald Meichenbaum, Department of Psychology, University of Waterloo, Waterloo, Ontario, Canada; and The Melissa Institute for Violence Prevention and Treatment, Miami, Florida, USA

Robert A. Neimeyer, Department of Psychology, The University of Memphis, Tennessee, USA

Jelena Pavlović, Institute for Educational Research, Belgrade, Serbia

Jonathan D. Raskin, Department of Psychology and Counseling Graduate Program, State University of New York at New Paltz, New York, USA

Alexander Riegler, Center Leo Apostle for Interdisciplinary Studies (CLEA), Vrije Universiteit Brussel (Free University of Brussels), Brussels, Belgium

Caroline M. Stanley, Department of Psychology, Bridgewater State University, Bridgewater, Massachusetts, USA

Tom Strong, Division of Applied Psychology, Faculty of Education, University of Calgary, Alberta, Canada

David A. Winter, Department of Psychology, University of Hertfordshire, Hertfordshire, UK

Preface: Is Constructivist Psychology Still Relevant?

Is constructivist psychology still relevant? Was it ever? Is it merely an obtuse cluster of theories bogged down in obscure epistemological debates of little to no relevance for most people? Why is it that constructivism is so often referenced in the clinical literature, yet organizationally it counts only a small number of people among its identifiable adherents and struggles to sustain itself as a coherent movement within the field?

Do constructivist theories offer genuinely practical and scientifically grounded models for conducting psychological research and psychotherapy? If constructivist approaches are firmly rooted in pragmatism's notion of ideas as useful, why do they so often seem ensconced in the ivory tower, aloof from the practical demands of everyday researchers and practitioners? Why is it that personal construct psychology, perhaps the original constructivist perspective in psychology, is all but extinct in the United States (its country of origin)? At the same time, how is it that the narrative and dialogical approaches, both deeply rooted in constructivist principles, seem to have infused the wider culture to such a degree that even politicians and pundits speak of the "dominant" narratives and discourses driving understanding of world events?

Finally, to what extent has constructivism simply become an ill-defined buzzword for "meaning" (as in the very title of this series, *Studies in Meaning*), with the result that many people call their work "constructivist" without understanding the theoretical bases from which the term emerges?

The rest of this volume takes up these issues by having prominent constructivist theorists put aside the usual topics of their scholarship and instead directly grapple with the very questions posed above. Borrowing the language of radical constructivism, the resulting contributions are intended to "perturb" the status quo and get constructivists and non-constructivists alike thinking about constructivism's past, future, strengths, weaknesses, and overall utility.

On a personal note, we would like to thank Emily Brown for her extensive assistance with name indexing. Her work in this regard was indispensable and we are so grateful to her for the time and care she gave to such a thankless task. We also wish to thank Alex Grover at Pace University Press for his tireless work on page proofs—especially in light of the seemingly endless litany of corrections we sent his way.

Finally, it has been a difficult few years for the constructivist community when it comes to the passing of important colleagues. We have lost many seminal figures since the last *Studies in Meaning* was published in 2010. Many of them were contributors to previous volumes (Stephanie Lewis Harter, Ernst von Glasersfeld, Donald Granvold, and Thomas Szasz), while others influenced the work found in those volumes (Hans Bonarius, Peggy Dalton, Joe Doster, Fay Fransella, Ted Hazelton, Dennis Hinkle, Bill Lyddon, Miller Mair, Peter Pisgrove, and Linda Viney). Each of these people perturbed the status quo in their own unique ways and for that we are forever grateful. We dedicate this volume to them.

Jonathan D. Raskin
State University of New York at New Paltz

Sara K. Bridges
The University of Memphis

Jack. S. Kahn
Palomar College

January 2015

PART I

CONSTRUCTIVISM

○8 1 ○

An Introductory Perturbation:
What Is Constructivism and Is There a
Future in It?

Jonathan D. Raskin

In discussing the future of "constructivism," it helps to begin by defining the term. Unfortunately, this is not an easy task. Sometimes constructivism is used quite loosely, as an umbrella catch-all covering any approach to studying people that focuses on how they individually and socially construct understandings. Other times, the term is applied more narrowly, referring to a particular theory or set of closely related theories with specific epistemological assumptions about what people know and how they know it (Chiari & Nuzzo, 1996, 2010; Hayes & Oppenheim, 1997; Neimeyer, 2009; Raskin, 2002). Unfortunately, it is rare for those who call themselves or are called constructivists to be explicit about how they are using the term. This yields a great deal of confusion, which impacts discussions about constructivism's future.

The *Studies in Meaning* series has, in certain respects, amplified this confusion. The original idea behind the volumes was to provide a home for scholarship examining meaning and its role in psychology, counseling, and related fields. My co-editors and I purposely cast a wide net in order to include as many people as possible in the conversation. The only litmus test for considering a contribution was, "Does this material effectively address research and practice related to how people make meaning?"

Those calling themselves personal construct psychologists, radical constructivists, social constructionists, dialogical self theorists, and narrative psychologists—among other self-identifications—were invited into the tent. In personal construct terms (Kelly, 1955/1991a, 1955/1991b), we made a conscious choice to construe "constructivism" *loosely*, in hopes that doing so might yield new and interesting possibilities. In many respects, doing so has proved fruitful. Contributions to past *Studies in Meaning* volumes have traversed a wide-range of topics from a variety of perspectives, ranging from exploring theoretical horizons (Raskin & Bridges, 2002) to integrating the personal with the social (Raskin & Bridges, 2004) to surveying psychotherapeutic theory and practice (Raskin & Bridges, 2008) to examining social justice (Raskin, Bridges, & Neimeyer, 2010).

The downside to our approach has been that the term "constructivism" has, at times, perhaps been employed too loosely. Concern about this was clearly evident in Kenny's (2010a) thoughtful yet unsubtly titled review of *Studies in Meaning 4*, "Can We Award a Medal for 'Vaguery in the Field'?" He criticized the volume for what he perceived to be its overly inclusive definition of constructivism:

> The book sets out to be about "constructivist perspectives" on "theory," "practice" and "social justice" but in effect what we find are many examples of different areas of professional practice, many of them very interesting to read about, but few of them falling within the term "constructivist." (Kenny, 2010a, p. 161)

From Kenny's (2010a) perspective, too many of the contributors failed to ground their ideas in proper constructivist theory. He lamented that

> these varied authors reference very different models and approaches, often ones incompatible with a constructivist stance. These include the cognitive-behavioral approach, old-style psychodynamics, the narrative approaches, deconstructionism, liberation psychology, objectification theory, and others. (p. 161)

4

Though occasionally adopting what I consider to be an overly narrow view, Kenny (2010) is on to something when expressing concern about carelessly using "constructivism" in reference to any approach vaguely invoking meaning. The root of the problem (and an issue grappled with throughout the current volume) seems to be that how we employ the term "constructivism" in professional circles—where we are concerned with organizing conferences and bringing those sharing common interests together as part of a burgeoning constructivist "movement"—is often different from how we use the term in scholarly contributions—where complex and precise theories and methods are explicitly posited, explicated, and applied to issues. This volume of *Studies in Meaning* continues the series' long-time emphasis on constructivism as both "theory" and "movement" by keeping the big umbrella open so that people from a variety of perspectives can gather under it. At the same time, contributors are challenged to clarify and question their preferred perspectives. What counts as constructivism? How effectively have scholars of different constructivist "varieties" tried to advance (or resisted advancing) constructivism as an organized movement?

Given its small but dedicated cadre of adherents, what does the future hold for constructivism? In this introductory contribution, I spend the bulk of my time presenting *four premises of an integrative constructivism* as a way to orient readers to different varieties of constructivism discussed in the volume and make clear ways in which I see these different constructivisms as capable of being subsumed under one broad constructivist banner. I then warn against the dangers of *careless constructivism* (the tendency to equate constructivism with simplistic platitudes such as "people invent reality") and *parochial constructivism* (the rigid insistence that one's own preferred perspective is the only truly "constructivist" one). Carelessness and parochialism complicate efforts to effectively move constructivism forward. Finally, I set the stage for the rest of the book with an *attempt to perturb the status quo by posing questions about constructivism's future.* It is these questions that are taken up by contributors throughout the remainder of the volume.

TOWARD AN INTEGRATIVE CONSTRUCTIVISM

Constructivism has many "varieties" (Neimeyer & Raskin, 2001), and it is sometimes difficult to discern what they share in common. When introducing newcomers to constructivism, I typically highlight three specific constructivist theories: personal construct psychology, radical constructivism, and social constructionism (Raskin, 2002). George Kelly's (1955/1991a, 1955/1991b) *personal construct psychology* (PCP) focuses on how people create individual systems of "bipolar" constructs, each consisting of something and its perceived opposite; experiential reality therefore is a product of the construct dimensions one devises and applies to the world. Similarly, *radical constructivism*—associated with thinkers such as Ernst von Glasersfeld (1995), Heinz von Foerster (1984), and Humberto Maturana (Maturana & Poerksen, 2004; Maturana & Varela, 1992)—emphasizes how knowledge is a private and personal product shaped by an organism's biological and psychological structure; the purpose of knowledge is survival rather than replication of a presumed external world. Finally, *social constructionism*, rooted in the work of people like Kenneth Gergen (1994, 2009a, 2009b) and John Shotter (1993), stresses how knowledge is generated communally through dialogue and relational coordination; people develop "discourses" that they use to construct shared understandings, which often are mistaken for truth itself (Burr, 2003).

Yet if we take seriously Kenny's (2010a) criticism that those calling themselves constructivists often use the term too loosely, it becomes important to delineate a set of common premises that more clearly capture what is meant by "constructivism." The premises I offer may not satisfy everyone (some social constructionists, for example, might object to the first two premises). However, with these premises I attempt to provide a "tighter" construction of constructivism, one that I believe to be helpful in weaving a more inclusive but cohesive constructivist tapestry.

Premise 1: People Are Informationally Closed Systems

Premise 1 assumes that people are *informationally closed systems only in touch with their own processes* (Glasersfeld, 1995; Raskin, 2011; Raskin & Debany, 2012). What an organism knows is personal and private. In adhering to such a view, constructivism does not conceptualize knowledge in the traditional manner, as something moving from "outside" to "inside" a person. Instead, what is outside sets off, triggers, or disrupts a person's internal processes, which then generate experiences that the person treats as reflective of what is outside. Sensory data and what we make of it are indirect reflections of a presumed outside world (Glasersfeld, 1995; Quale, 2008). This is why different organisms experience things quite differently. How Jack's backyard smells to his dog is different from how it smells to him because he and his dog have qualitatively different olfactory systems. Of course, how Jack's backyard smells to him may also differ from how it smells to Sara because not only is each of them biologically distinct but each has a unique history that informs the things to which they attend and attribute meaning. The world does not dictate what it "smells" like; it merely triggers biological and psychological processes within organisms, which then react to these triggers in their own ways. The kinds of experiences an organism has depend on its structure and history (Maturana & Poerksen, 2004; Maturana & Varela, 1992). Therefore, what is known is always a private and personal product of one's own processes.

Premise 1 and Radical Constructivism

Premise 1 is consistent with radical constructivism's view that all that people ever come into direct contact with is their experiential reality (Glasersfeld, 1995; Poerksen, 2004; Quale, 2008). While people affectively believe in an external reality and take its existence for granted in the course of daily life, there is no way to ever cognitively know with certainty that such a reality does indeed exist (Glasersfeld, 1995; Quale, 2008). Because we are only in direct touch with our internal processes, we are precluded from proving beyond a shadow of a doubt that the outside world is there. Despite this, most of us proceed with our lives as if it is. We emotionally believe in external reality, even if we cannot rationally confirm it (Quale, 2008).

Premise 1 is also consistent with radical constructivism's *myth of instructive interaction*, which maintains that systems can never be directly instructed (Efran & Greene, 1996; Efran, McNamee, Warren, & Raskin, 2014). This is why constructivist approaches to teaching emphasize developing a variety of activities for students, with the idea that one never knows in advance which activity might trigger a student to reorganize his or her understandings in new ways—in the more common vernacular, to learn (Quale, 2008)! Jay Efran nicely described the myth of instructive interaction and its concomitant notion of people as informationally closed systems:

> [Radical constructivist Humberto] Maturana asserts that from the point of view of a biologist living systems are informationally closed—that is, things don't get in and they don't get out. From the outside, you can trigger a change, but you cannot directly instruct. Think of it as having a toaster and a washing machine. And, the toaster is going to toast no matter what you do. And, the washing machine is going to wash no matter what you do. And they both can be triggered by electricity. But the electricity doesn't tell the toaster what to do. The toaster's structure tells the toaster what to do. So similarly, we trigger organisms, but what they do has to do with their internal structure—including their nervous system—and the way it responds to various perturbations. (Efran, McNamee, Warren, & Raskin 2014, p. 3)

Premise 1 and Personal Construct Psychology

In personal construct psychology, Kelly's (1955/1991a, p. 32) *fundamental postulate* holds that people's processes are "psychologically channelized" by the ways in which they anticipate events. This paints construing as a psychological process in which people's internal experience is "channelized . . . through a network of pathways" (p. 34). What one knows is always organized and constrained within these pathways, so even though a person "ultimately seeks to anticipate real events" (p. 34), he or she only knows these events indirectly through a channelized network of constructive processes (Raskin, in press). Thus, PCP and Premise 1 fit nicely together.

Premise 1 and Social Constructionism

Premise 1 is more difficult to reconcile with social constructionism, which explains why social constructionists like Gergen (1994) often see their approach as distinctly different from constructivism. Gergen (1994) acknowledges that "both constructivism and constructionism are skeptical of foundational warrants for an empirical science" and that both also challenge "the traditional view of the individual mind as a device for reflecting the character and conditions of an independent world" (p. 68). However, Gergen (1994) objects to what he views as constructivism's (a) tendency to grant "mind" and "world" ontological status, (b) reduction of the world to mental construction, and (c) overemphasis on individuality and knowledge as personal. As he puts it:

> The constructionist concurs with the constructivist in both the rejection of subject-object dualism and the related presumption that knowledge is an accurate representation of the world. However, while constructivists tend to replace the dualism with a form of cognitive monism, constructionists move from the mental world to the domain of the social. . . . World construction takes place not within the mind

9

of the observer but within forms of relationship. (Gergen, 1994, pp. 242–243)

Reducing world to mental construction. Gergen (1994) also expresses concern that constructivism reduces the world to mental construction and in doing so is too individualistic. I disagree with this view because, in my interpretation of constructivism, the world is not a construction; only our experience of it is. This may not satisfy social constructionists, who do not view experience as private and personal in the same way that constructivists often do, but it is an important distinction because distinguishing experiential reality from external reality (even a hypothetical, impossible-to-prove-for-sure external reality) is important in maintaining a coherent constructivist stance (Raskin & Debany, 2012). Again, more on this in Premise 4.

The discourse of individualism. Admittedly, Premise 1 does defend the discourse of individualism, which social constructionists often dismiss. This discourse is worth defending because at times it proves itself to be pragmatically valuable. After all, *the relationships that social constructionists so thoughtfully posit as generating constructed understandings are, implicitly, relationships between individuals.* Therefore, distinguishing people as discrete entities worthy of study in their own right remains vital—even when incorporating social constructionism's critical insight that the personal has too often been privileged at the expense of the social in Western psychology. An integrative constructivism attempts to build on the best that constructivism and constructionism have to offer, combining traditionally constructivist notions about knowledge as personal and private with social constructionism's emphasis on knowledge as generated within a social domain.

Taken on its own, Premise 1 can be seen as exemplifying Gergen's (1994) portrayal of constructivism as a form of solipsistic individualized mental monism that overlooks relational and social aspects of meaning construction. However, the remaining three premises speak to Gergen's concerns in ways that permit social constructionism to be subsumed, along with personal construct psychology and radical constructivism, under a general, integrative constructivist label.

PREMISE 2: PEOPLE ARE ACTIVE MEANING MAKERS

Premise 2 maintains that *people are active meaning makers, drawing distinctions as they construct ways of understanding* (Glasersfeld, 1995; Kelly, 1955/1991a, 1955/1991b; Raskin, 2011; Raskin & Debany, 2012). This expands on Premise 1 in that once people's internal systems are triggered, they organize their experiential responses into something meaningful and coherent. That is to say, they actively construe. Events alone do not dictate what people know; constructive processes play a central role as people impose meaning and order on sensory data.

Premise 2 and Personal Construct Psychology

In personal construct psychology, active meaning-making involves building bipolar construct dimensions, the "transparent patterns or templets" people create and then "fit over the realities of which the world is composed" (Kelly, 1955/1991a, p. 7). Kelly criticized American psychology for ignoring the private and personal nature of knowing (i.e., Premise 1). He felt that overlooking this prevents psychologists from viewing people as active meaning makers (i.e., Premise 2). Along these lines, he remarked:

> If a man's private domain, within which his behavior aligns itself within its own lawful system, is ignored, it becomes necessary to explain him as an inert object wafted about in a public domain by external forces, or as a solitary datum sitting on its own continuum. (Kelly, 1955/1991a, p. 28)

By contrast, Kelly's personal construct psychology advances a view of people as active and agentic meaning constructors. This is evident in the *choice corollary*, which asserts that "a person chooses for himself that alternative in a dichotomized construct through which he anticipates the greater possibility for extension and definition of his system" (Kelly, 1955/1991a, p. 45). It also is evident in Kelly's (1958/1969) notion that *behavior is an experiment.* Instead of seeing people as mere byproducts of numerous determining variables, personal construct psychology portrays them as active devisers and testers of constructs. By testing their constructs in the course of daily living, people come to actively examine, evaluate, and revise them.

Premise 2 and Radical Constructivism

Radical constructivism also endorses an active model of the person. Von Glasersfeld (1995) rooted his radical constructivism in the assertion that knowledge is *actively* built up by the cognizing subject, adding that the purpose of this knowledge is not to replicate a presumed outside world but to help the organism survive. Additionally, von Glasersfeld (1995) appropriated Jean Piaget's constructivist theory of knowing to make the case for an active construer, contending that the English-speaking world has long misinterpreted Piaget as putting forward an empirically passive model of the person and a view of knowledge as ever more closely approximating reality. However, von Glasersfeld (1995) argued that for Piaget "knowledge arises from the active subject's activity, either physical or mental, and that it is goal-directed activity that gives knowledge its organization" (p. 56). He continued:

> The concept of "action scheme" is central in Piaget's theory of knowledge. . . . That it was widely misunderstood, is due above all to the fact that he derived it explicitly from the biological notion of "reflex". Action schemes were therefore tacitly interpreted by many readers as stimulus-response mechanisms. This made traditional psychologists comfortable because it allowed them to classify Piaget's theory as an "interactionist" one. (p. 56)

English-speaking psychologists therefore misunderstood Piaget as saying that people "accommodate" whenever their constructions get closer to matching reality:

> This misinterpretation simply confirmed the notion that inter-action provides the intelligent organism with knowledge, and that this knowledge, through further interaction, becomes better, in the sense that it comes to reflect the environment more accurately. Thus, although Piaget frequently spoke of "construction", he could be accepted as a somewhat idiosyncratic developmental theorist, and the psychologists' peace of mind was saved. (p. 56)

This construal of Piaget was, in von Glasersfeld's (1995) view, erroneous because constructions never come into contact with (or "match") reality; experiential reality is not dictated by the world but by people's active construction processes. The criterion for evaluating constructions is not reality correspondence (which can never be known), but viability.

Premise 2 and Social Constructionism

Despite some areas of tension, Premise 2 can work in conjunction with social constructionism. Yes, social construc-tionists often speak of shared "discourses" that determine how people experience and understand themselves, and this appears to challenge an active and/or agentive view of the person (Burr, 2003; Gergen, 1991, 1995, 2009). However, social constructionists also often portray *people as discourse users,* able to mix and match from discourses they encounter in different areas of their lives (Burr, 2003; Gergen, 1991). Vivien Burr (2003) suggests that social constructionism "demands an agentic person at least in some respects, in the person's ability to manipulate discourse and use it for their own ends" (p. 146). In other words,

> narrative and relational views of the person seem relatively easy to align with personal agency. Although our own narratives may be to some degree moulded by cultural narrative form and content, we are

nevertheless the authors of our own stories. Even where the self and self-narratives are jointly produced, we must at least have as much agency in their production as our co-authors. (Burr, 2003, p. 147)

Thus, an integrative constructivism offering the premise that people are active meaning-makers can effectively assimilate personal construct psychology, radical constructivism, and social constructionism.

PREMISE 3: PEOPLE ARE SOCIAL BEINGS

Premise 3 places people squarely within the social realm by asserting that *people are social beings, using their intersubjective experiences to confirm the utility of their constructions* (Glasersfeld, 1995; Kelly, 1955/1991a; Raskin, 2011; Raskin & Debany, 2012). Construing always happens within a context. How people meaningfully build understandings is intimately tied to the social situation and their relationships with others.

Premise 3 and Personal Construct Psychology

Premise 3 ties in nicely with personal construct psychology, especially Kelly's (1955/1991a) idea of sociality, which states that when people construe one another's constructions, they are able to adopt roles in relation to each other. The more effectively two people do so, the more intimate the resulting role relationship can be (Leitner & Faidley, 1995). Building on Premises 1 and 2, Kelly (1955/1991a) insisted that psychologists must never forget that people are social beings who bring their private worlds to bear within a shared public domain:

If a man's existence in a public domain is ignored, our painstakingly acquired knowledge of one man will not help us understand his younger brother, and our daily psychological efforts will yield no increment to the cultural heritage. (p. 28)

Sociality means that people's constructions are not experienced as simply private and personal; worries about solipsism are lessened because PCP introduces the idea of role relationships based on effectively construing one another's constructions.

Premise 3 and Radical Constructivism

Premise 3 also owes much to the notion of *intersubjective experience*, which grows out of von Glasersfeld's (1995) work. Von Glasersfeld held that people create a subjective internal environment that they populate with "repeatable objects." These repeatable objects are experienced as "external and independent" by the person constructing internal representations of them (Glasersfeld, 1995, p. 24). Certain repeatable objects—those we identify as sentient, primarily other people—are treated as if they have the same active meaning-making abilities that we attribute to ourselves. Consequently, we are able to experience an *intersubjective reality* whenever other people respond to us in ways that we interpret as indicating they experience things the same way we do. Once again, this alleviates concerns about constructivism being solipsistic because people do relationally coordinate with one another in confirming and maintaining their constructions.

Premise 3 and Social Constructionism

Premise 3, with its emphasis on knowledge as a product of shared relational coordination, is most compatible with social constructionism. When operating from a social constructionist frame, the truths people take for granted are constituted through how they talk, interact, and behave together (Burr, 2003; Gergen 1991, 2004, 2009). Knowledge becomes a social and relational, rather than individual, endeavor. As such, human understanding is embedded within and emerges from local relationships, which are in turn nested within a larger cultural context (Gergen, 1991, 1994, 2009). Out of this intertwined matrix materialize socially constructed discourses—the often taken-for-granted ways of acting, speaking, and living together that yield particular experiential realities for people; socially constructed discourses shape how people come to see themselves, others, and the wider world (Burr, 2003). For instance, selfhood, romantic love, democracy, and the American Dream are examples of shared discourses that people have socially constructed (Burr, 2003; Gergen, 1991). These discourses shape how those within a given relational setting (e.g., family, community, country) experience themselves and their lives.

Whereas Premise 1 contends that knowledge is personal and private, Premise 3 counters that it is equally social. This need not be seen as contradictory. Kelly's sociality and von Glasersfeld's intersubjective reality carve out a significant place for social interaction in the development of meaning systems. Both account for ways in which human constructions inevitably occur within settings that involve other people and shared ways of life. For Kelly (1955/1991a, 1955/1991b), this means that how people engage one another is tied to how effectively they construe each other's construction processes. For von Glasersfeld (1995), it means that people construe one another as active meaning makers and consequently treat their personal understandings as communally shared when others' behavior is interpreted as affirming those understandings. As I stated elsewhere, "when experiencing sociality or an intersubjective reality, we come to experience our constructions as socially shared to the extent that they appear to be (and, for all functional purposes, can be treated as if they are) also held by others" (Raskin & Debany, 2012, p. 16).

Another way of thinking about this is to suggest that Premise 1 and Premise 3 constitute a form of "double aspectism." That is, they are two sides of the same coin. When operating from Premise 1, we emphasize the ways in which constructions are personal and private, delving into understanding the psychological and physiological structure of the person and how that structure forms the basis for constructing understandings. When we shift to Premise 3, we stress how a person's constructions are generated within a social context in which people presume others are no different from themselves in being active meaning constructors. In terms of sociality, "each person construes the constructions of others and, in so doing, comes to coordinate with others in ways that subjectively feel like shared understandings—or social constructions" (Raskin & Debany, 2012, p. 16). Thus, constructivists can readily shift back and forth between Premises 1 and 3—alternatively studying the personal and social sides of meaning construction by seeing them as two aspects of a unified whole.

PREMISE 4: PEOPLE CONSTRUE ONTOLOGICALLY AND EPISTEMOLOGICALLY

Premise 4 marks an effort to counter characterizations of constructivism as a form of "anything goes" relativism by maintaining that *sometimes people construe ontologically, focusing their constructions on what is experienced as an external and independent real world; other times they construe epistemologically, focusing on how and why they construe as they do* (Raskin & Debany, 2012). When construing ontologically, people believe certain things to be true. For example, when a psychologist construes using the *ontological mode*, concepts such as mind, self, behavior, cognition, and emotion are typically treated as real entities about which assertions can be made. Even though these entities may also be seen as humanly invented understandings, when construing ontologically they are taken for granted as having an independent existence and are functionally treated as such.

Despite critics' claims to the contrary (Boghossian, 2006; Cobern & Loving, 2008; Gillett, 1998; Held, 1995, 1998; Mackay, 2003, 2011; M. R. Matthews, 2002; W. J. Matthews, 1998; Slife & Richardson, 2011a, 2011b), when a constructivist psychologist conducts an empirical experiment, the variables she operationally defines are construed ontologically—that is, they are granted ontological status and claims about their truth value are readily asserted and believed. When taking leave of the laboratory for a discussion about philosophy of science, that same constructivist psychologist likely shifts to the *epistemological mode*, examining how it is she came to experience the variables she was studying as ontologically distinct. An important shift occurs from understanding the world to "understanding one's understandings" (Raskin & Debany, 2012, p. 17). Ontological and epistemological modes of construing allow us to unproblematically tack back and forth from assertion and belief to reflection and reconsideration—as we all do throughout the course of daily life. When it comes to PCP, radical constructivism, and social constructionism, perspectives may be relative to the extent that ontological claims are always inevitably tied to time, place, and position. However, "anything goes" does not apply. What goes is tied to ontological and epistemological modes of construing. There is nothing inconsistent in constructivists speaking of "minds," "worlds," and "discourses" because when doing so they are operating from the ontological mode. Nor do they slide into incoherence when they deconstruct these very same terms that they previously treated as real. All they have done is shift to an epistemological mode in order to accommodate a different set of questions.

THE DANGERS OF CARELESS AND PAROCHIAL CONSTRUCTIVISM

Clarifying constructivist assumptions is important because being constructivist is often equated with being relativistic, antiscientific, and philosophically incoherent (Boghossian, 2006; Cobern & Loving, 2008; Gillett, 1998; Held, 1995, 1998; Mackay, 2003, 2011; M. R. Matthews, 2002; W. J. Matthews, 1998; Slife & Richardson, 2011a, 2011b). If it is to have a future, constructivism must counter these claims. Unfortunately, constructivists themselves often inadvertently encourage these criticisms by talking carelessly or parochially about their work.

Careless Constructivism

    Careless constructivism is marked by a tendency to make broad and admittedly crazy-sounding claims (e.g., "Reality is invented," "People can change reality by changing their constructions"). While most self-identified constructivists grasp the more subtle theoretical implications that are presumably implied when people make such offhand statements, the wider world likely scratches its collective head at such bizarre and imprecise claims. Saying that "reality is invented" grossly simplifies—and even ignores—the previously discussed constructivist distinction about people only being in touch with their private worlds. Therefore, it fails to differentiate experiential from external reality. Its provocative endorsement of invention over discovery coarsely oversimplifies constructivist arguments about people as active meaning devisers operating within a social realm. It trades subtlety for shock value, turning a potentially nuanced theoretical and scientific discussion about the strengths and limitations of human knowing into one where anyone wanting to sound reasonable is likely to side against the constructivists. As a result, constructivists become similar to the talk show guest set up for derision and booing by both audience and host in a rigged debate, with the latter already assumed to be on the side of all that is true, right, and good.

    On the other hand, nuance is often boring and usually doesn't get one invited to be on a talk show in the first place. Consider the following more expansive alternative to saying that "reality is invented":

> Experiential reality results from processes set in motion when a presumed external event disrupts an organism's internal equilibrium; this generates a variety of psychophysiological meaning-generation processes that yield viable understandings, which in turn help the organism predict and navigate events.

This statement, while clearly more thoughtful and thorough, is a lot less sexy than "reality is invented." Others may not be responsive to it, either because it requires them to learn more or because, compared to its shorter and punchier alternative, it does not seem particularly provocative or in need of refutation. Not only may others potentially fail to understand this longer assertion, they also may not care to understand it. The appeal of careless constructivism thus becomes apparent: what it lacks in subtlety, it makes up for in shock value. The question is whether the shock value has come at too great a cost. I urge constructivists to be careful in their use of careless constructivism.

Parochial Constructivism

Parochial constructivism is exemplified by an insistence that one's own particular view of constructivism is the only proper view. Difficulty reconciling parochial constructivism with Kelly's (1955/1991a) constructive alternativism is tinged with a great deal of irony. People engage in parochial constructivism more or less intentionally. Sometimes they actively shun approaches they believe are not "really" constructivism, whereas other times they are simply unaware of commensurate perspectives worthy of attention.

Several years ago I became embroiled in a protracted debate over whether the personal construct psychology community had become parochial in its suspicion of the wider constructivist movement (Butt, 2006; Chiari & Nuzzo, 1996; Fransella, 1995, 2007; Raskin, 2004, 2006). My argument was that personal construct psychologists should be open to radical constructivist, social constructionist, and narrative perspectives because these perspectives might prove theoretically and scientifically generative in addition to providing a potentially receptive new audience for Kelly's theory (Raskin, 2004). Ignoring these perspectives struck me as intellectually and strategically shortsighted. Unfortunately, this point seemed to get overshadowed because I mischievously (but perhaps unwisely) suggested that PCP'ers might be behaving parochially due to Kellyian threat (Raskin, 2004). In the ensuing exchange (Butt, 2006; Fransella, 2007; Raskin, 2006), my main point—that engaging with like-minded others operating from somewhat different constructivist theoretical bases was a good idea—may have been lost. I wasn't saying that people should abandon PCP or stop doing PCP work. I was merely saying don't be parochial; pay attention to other interesting constructivist perspectives—scientifically because they can enhance PCP work and pragmatically because we're a small group and it makes sense to gather friendly allies under one big tent. Like careless constructivism, parochialism may come at too great a cost.

Yet the parochial pull remains strong. Kenny's (2010a) aforementioned review of *Studies in Meaning 4* offers a recent and overt example. His main lament was that too many contributors failed to sufficiently reference the accepted constructivist canon: "Half of the 14 chapters make no reference to the work of George Kelly . . . . Of the seven that do mention Kelly, three merely mention his name without actually recounting anything of his work" (Kenny, 2010a, p. 161). He also complained that many of the authors advance perspectives both inconsistent with constructivism and "long past their sell-by date" (p. 165), concluding that "Kelly is largely ignored or forgotten or even unknown to the various authors . . . many of whom are busily working within totally different frames to that of constructivism" (p. 165). I'm not sure how Kenny came by the authority to stamp "sell-by" dates on ideas or to definitively declare, without providing much in the way of argument or justification, which ones are suitably consistent with constructivism. It appears that for Kenny, if one does not discuss and cite Kelly or von Glasersfeld sufficiently, then one's work cannot be of interest to a proper constructivist.

Kenny applies his "insufficiently constructivist" criticism not just to newcomers or PCP outsiders but also to card-carrying club members, who—he earnestly informs us—are getting it all wrong. He is appalled, for instance, that long-time personal construct psychologist Larry Leitner (2010) integrates terms such as "reverence" and "awe" into Kellyian theory, an unforgivable offense that clearly "would not have gone down very well with Kelly himself" (p. 164). He also takes Robert Neimeyer (2010), arguably today's best-known constructivist, to task for "completely" omitting "Kelly from his list of references"—leading him to take an ad hominem swipe at Neimeyer's judgment: "[I]s this another slip of his Freud?" (Kenny, 2010a, p. 165). Failing to properly genuflect before Kenny's view of constructivism inevitably means one is ignorant of or has purposely forsaken the constructivist bandwagon, at least from the vantage point of Kenny's procrustean bed. This is parochial constructivism at its worst.

The irony is that despite his parochialism, Kenny (2010b) simultaneously has expressed worry about the viability of personal construct psychology due to what he sees as its intellectual isola-tionism. He has accused personal construct psychologists of parochially separating themselves in ways that he believes have doomed them to irrelevancy. That is, his concerns about the future of constructivism match up nicely with those put forward for discussion in the present volume. While I am sympathetic to his concern that we grapple to identify and debate premises uniting different constructivist approaches (hence avoiding careless constructivism), I remain wary of becoming so parochial that we insult, alienate, and drive away most of our prospective conver-sation partners before the discussion begins.

CONSTRUCTIVISM: IS THERE ANY FUTURE IN IT?

Now that the four premises of an integrative constructivism have been outlined and I have warned against the hazards of careless and parochial constructivism, we can shift to the main issue to be taken up by contributors to the present volume: Is there a future for constructivism and, if so, what is it? This is more than an academic exercise. Consider these sobering facts about the personal construct psychology community: (a) only 50 people purchased a 2013 membership in the Constructivist Psychology Network (CPN); (b) the 2013 personal construct psychology congress drew fewer than 40 attendees; (c) the European Personal Construct Association no longer maintains a website ("The Psychology of Personal Constructs," n.d.); (d) many of the most prominent members of the PCP community are retired, on the cusp of retiring, or deceased; and (e) the only place in the United States where one can currently enter a psychology doctoral program and study with a full-time professor rooted in personal construct psychology is The University of Memphis. Based on this data, one could easily conclude that PCP is on the verge of extinction in the United States.

The news is not all grim. As has been historically the case (Neimeyer, 1985), PCP remains on stronger footing in Europe than North America. The University of Hertfordshire, despite delays in implementation, has approved a master's training program in personal construct psychology ("Personal Construct Psychology MSc", n.d.). On the publication front, there is a great deal of activity: two Italian-language online journals have recently been launched; Joern Scheer and Trevor Butt's online journal, *Personal Construct Theory & Practice*, remains a vital presence; and the *Journal of Constructivist Psychology* continues to generate many online downloads and a solid citation index for a journal of its size and scope.

The picture beyond PCP also shows promise. Alexander Riegler's online radical constructivist journal, *Constructivist Foundations*, continues to be successful, its contents now cata-logued in EBSCO's Education Research Complete—an important achievement for an online publication. The social constructionist community enjoys tremendous success with its Taos Institute. Among Taos' many ongoing initiatives are book publishing, continuing education workshops, and a doctoral program in social constructionism ("The Taos Institute," n.d.). Further, its associates program allows constructionist scholars and practitioners scattered across the world to come together under one umbrella and participate in existing Taos initiatives or develop their own.

When it comes to the current organizational success of various constructivist approaches, it seems—at least on the surface—as if PCP is struggling, radical constructivism is hanging in there, and social constructionism is doing a great deal to foster a worldwide network providing opportunities for those interested in it. However, that is merely my impression. What do prominent members of the constructivist community think about the current status of the field and its prospects for the future? The remainder of this volume offers constructivist, social constructionist, and narrative scholars an opportunity to share their thoughts on the current status and future prospects of their respective perspectives.

REFERENCES

Boghossian, P. A. (2006). *Fear of knowledge: Against relativism and construc-tivism*. Oxford: Clarendon Press.

Burr, V. (2003). *Social constructionism* (2nd ed.). London, England: Routledge.

Butt, T. (2006). Reconstruing constructivism [Review of the book, *Studies in meaning 2: Bridging the personal and social in constructivist psychology*]. *Journal of Constructivist Psychology, 19*, 91–96. doi: 10.1080/10720530590948863

Chiari, G., & Nuzzo, M. L. (1996). Personal construct theory within psychological constructivism: Precursor or avant-garde? In B. M. Walker, J. Costigan, L. L. Viney, & B. Warren (Eds.), *Personal construct theory: A psychology for the future* (pp. 25–54). Melbourne, Australia: Australian Psychological Society Imprint Series.

Cobern, W. W., & Loving, C. C. (2008). An essay for educators: Epistemological realism really is common sense. *Science & Education, 17*, 425–447. doi: 10.1007/s11191-007-9095-5

Efran, J. S., & Greene, M. A. (1996). Psychotherapeutic theory and practice: Contributions from Maturana's structure determinism. In H. Rosen & K. T. Kuehlwein (Eds.), *Constructing realities: Meaning-making perspectives for psychotherapists* (pp. 71–113). San Francisco, CA: Jossey-Bass.

Efran, J. S., McNamee, S., Warren, B., & Raskin, J. D. (2014). Personal construct psychology, radical constructivism, and social constructionism: A dialogue. *Journal of Constructivist Psychology, 27*, 1–13.

Foerster, H. von. (1984). On constructing a reality. In P. Watzlawick (Ed.), *The invented reality: How do we know what we believe we know? Contributions to constructivism* (pp. 41–61). New York, NY: Norton.

Fransella, F. (1995). *George Kelly*. London, England: Sage.

Fransella, F. (2007). PCP: A personal story. *Personal Construct Theory and Practice, 4,* 39–45. Retrieved from http://www.pcp-net.org/journal/pctp07/fransella07.html

Gergen, K. J. (1991). *The saturated self: Dilemmas of identity in contemporary life.* New York, NY: Basic Books.

Gergen, K. J. (1994). *Realities and relationships: Soundings in social construction.* Cambridge, MA: Harvard University Press.

Gergen, K. J. (2009). *An invitation to social constructionism* (2nd ed.). London, England: Sage.

Gergen, K. J. (2009). *Relational being: Beyond self and community.* Oxford, England: Oxford University Press.

Gillett, E. (1998). Relativism and the social-constructivist paradigm. *Philosophy, Psychiatry, and Psychology, 5,* 37–48. doi: 10.1353/ppp.1998.0006

Glasersfeld, E. von. (1995). *Radical constructivism: A way of knowing and learning.* London, England: The Falmer Press.

Hayes, R. L., & Oppenheim, R. (1997). Constructivism: Reality is what you make it. In T. L. Sexton & B. L. Griffin (Eds.), *Constructivist thinking in counseling practice* (pp. 19–40). New York, NY: Teachers College Press.

Held, B. S. (1995). *Back to reality: A critique of postmodern theory in psychotherapy.* New York: Norton.

Held, B. S. (1998). The many truths of postmodernist discourse. *Journal of Theoretical and Philosophical Psychology, 18,* 193–217. doi: 10.1037/h0091185

Journal of Constructivist Psychology. (n.d.). Retrieved from http://www.tandfonline.com/toc/upcy20/current#.UizLgcasjlM

Kelly, G. A. (1969). Man's construction of his alternatives. In B. Maher (Ed.), *Clinical psychology and personality: The selected papers of George Kelly* (pp. 66–93). New York, NY: Wiley.

Kelly, G. A. (1991a). *The psychology of personal constructs: Vol. 1. A theory of personality.* London, England: Routledge. (Original work published 1955)

Kelly, G. A. (1991b). *The psychology of personal constructs: Vol. 2 . Clinical diagnosis and psychotherapy.* London, England: Routledge. (Original work published 1955)

Kenny, V. (2010a). Can we award a medal for "vaguery in the field"? *Constructivist Foundations, 5*(2), 161–165. Retrieved from http://www.univie.ac.at/constructivism/journal/5/2/161.kenny

Kenny, V. (2010b). Exile on mainstream. Constructivism in psychotherapy and suggestions from a Kellian perspective. *Constructivist Foundations*

6(1), 65–76. Available at http://www.univie.ac.at/constructivism/journal/6/1/065.kenny

Leitner, L. M. (2010). The integral universe, experiential personal construct psychology, transpersonal reverence, and transpersonal responsibility. In J. D. Raskin, S. K. Bridges, R. A. Neimeyer (Eds.), *Studies in meaning 4: Constructivist perspectives on theory, practice, and social justice* (pp. 227–245). New York, NY: Pace University Press.

Leitner, L. M., & Faidley, A. F. (1995). The awful, aweful nature of role relationships. In R. A. Neimeyer & G. J. Neimeyer (Eds.), *Advances in personal construct theory* (Vol. 3, pp. 291–314). Greenwich, CT: JAI Press.

Mackay, N. (2003). Psychotherapy and the idea of meaning. *Theory and Psychology, 13*, 359–386. doi: 10.1177/0959354303013003004

Mackay, N. (2011). On some accounts of meaning and their problems. In N. Mackay & A. Petocz (Eds.), *Realism and psychology: Collected essays* (pp. 548–596). Leiden, The Netherlands: Brill.

Matthews, M. R. (2002). Constructivism and science education: A further appraisal. *Journal of Science Education and Technology, 11*(2), 122–134. doi: 10.1023/A:1014661312550

Matthews, W. J. (1998). Let's get real: The fallacy of post-modernism. *Journal of Theoretical and Philosophical Psychology, 18*, 16–32. doi: 10.1037/h0091169

Maturana, H. R., & Poerksen, B. (2004). *From being to doing: The origins of the biology of cognition* (W. K. Koek & A. R. Koek, Trans.). Heidelberg, Germany: Carl-Auer.

Maturana, H. R., & Varela, F. J. (1992). *The tree of knowledge: The biological roots of human understanding* (R. Paolucci, Trans. rev. ed.). Boston, MA: Shambhala.

Neimeyer, R. A. (1985). *The development of personal construct psychology.* Lincoln, NE: University of Nebraska Press.

Neimeyer, R. A. (2009). *Constructivist psychotherapy.* London, England: Routledge.

Neimeyer, R. A. (2010). Reconstructing the continuing bond: A constructivist approach to grief therapy. In J. D. Raskin, S. K. Bridges, & R. A. Neimeyer (Eds.), *Studies in meaning 4: Constructivist perspectives on theory, practice, and social justice* (pp. 65–91). New York, NY: Pace University Press.

Neimeyer, R. A., & Raskin, J. D. (2001). Varieties of constructivism in psychotherapy. In K. S. Dobson (Ed.), *Handbook of cognitive-behavioral therapies* (2nd ed., pp. 393–430). New York, NY: Guilford.

Personal Construct Psychology MSc. (n.d.). Retrieved from http://www.herts.ac.uk/courses/personal-construct-psychology

Poerksen, B. (2004). *The certainty of uncertainty: Dialogues introducing constructivism* (A. R. Koeck & W. K. Koeck, Trans.). Exeter, England: Imprint Academic.

The Psychology of Personal Constructs. (n.d.). Retrieved from http://www.pcp-net.de/epca/

Quale, A. (2008). *Radical constructivism: A relativist epistemic approach to science education.* Rotterdam, The Netherlands: Sense Publishers.

Raskin, J. D. (2002). Constructivism in psychology: Personal construct psychology, radical constructivism, and social constructionism. In J. D. Raskin & S. K. Bridges (Eds.), *Studies in meaning: Exploring constructivist psychology* (pp. 1–25). New York, NY: Pace University Press.

Raskin, J. D. (2004). The permeability of personal construct psychology. In J. D. Raskin & S. K. Bridges (Eds.), *Studies in meaning 2: Bridging the personal and social in constructivist psychology* (pp. 327–346). New York, NY: Pace University Press.

Raskin, J. D. (2006). Don't cry for me George A. Kelly: Human involvement and the construing of personal construct psychology. *Personal Construct Theory and Practice, 3,* 50–61. Retrieved from http://www.pcp-net.org/journal/pctp06/raskin06.html

Raskin, J. D. (2011). On essences in constructivist psychology. *Journal of Theoretical and Philosophical Psychology, 31,* 223–239. doi: 10.1037/a0025006

Raskin, J. D. (in press). Personal construct psychology in relation to an integrative constructivism. In D. A. Winter & N. Reed (Eds.), *The Wiley-Blackwell handbook of personal construct psychology.* Chichester, England: Wiley-Blackwell.

Raskin, J. D., & Bridges, S. K. (Eds.). (2002). *Studies in meaning: Exploring constructivist psychology.* New York, NY: Pace University Press.

Raskin, J. D., & Bridges, S. K. (Eds.). (2004). *Studies in meaning 2: Bridging the personal and social in constructivist psychology.* New York, NY: Pace University Press.

Raskin, J. D., & Bridges, S. K. (Eds.). (2008). *Studies in meaning 3: Constructivist psychotherapy in the real world.* New York, NY: Pace University Press.

Raskin, J. D., Bridges, S. K., & Neimeyer, R. A. (Eds.). (2010). *Studies in meaning 4: Constructivist perspectives on theory, practice, and social justice.* New York, NY: Pace University Press.

Raskin, J. D., & Debany, A. E. (2012). The inescapability of ethics and the impossibility of "anything goes": A constructivist model of ethical meaning-making. In S. Cipolletta & E. Gius (Eds.), *Ethics in action: Dialogue between knowledge and practice* (pp. 13–32). Milan, Italy: LED.

Shotter, J. (1993). *Cultural politics of everyday life: Social constructionism, rhetoric and knowing of the third kind.* Toronto, Canada: University of Toronto Press.

Slife, B., & Richardson, F. (2011a). Is Gergen's *Relational Being* relational enough? *Journal of Constructivist Psychology, 24,* 304–313. doi: 10.1080/10720537.2011.593470

Slife, B., & Richardson, F. (2011b). The relativism of social constructionism. *Journal of Constructivist Psychology, 24,* 333–339. doi: 10.1080/10720537.2011.593475

The Taos Institute. (n.d.). Retrieved from http://www.taosinstitute.net/

❧ 2 ❧

What Does the Future Hold for Personal Construct Psychology?

David A. Winter

George Kelly was way ahead of his time when, in 1955, he published his two-volume magnum opus, *The Psychology of Personal Constructs*. This work was no less than a presentation of a whole new psychology, radically departing from the mechanistic, reductionist, and deterministic assumptions of the dominant approaches of the day. It clearly anticipated the trends that have occurred in psychology over the following half-century or so, as reflected in the debts that proponents of subsequent approaches have acknowledged that they owe to Kelly (Mischel, 1980). However, nowadays it is a rare psychology student who has even heard of personal construct psychology. Why is this so? Has personal construct psychology outlived its usefulness? What does its future hold? These are the questions that will be explored herein. A brief summary of personal construct theory is presented, followed by a review of developments in, and applications of, the theory. The current status of personal construct psychology is then considered, together with its links with other approaches. Finally, anticipations of the future of personal construct psychology are explored.

Personal Construct Theory

The psychology of personal constructs is based upon the philosophical assumption of "constructive alternativism," which states that "all of our present interpretations of the universe are subject to revision or replacement" (Kelly, 1955, p. 15). The existence of a real universe is not questioned, but it is assumed that no one can experience this universe directly, instead viewing it "through transparent patterns or templets which he creates and then attempts to fit over the realities of which the world is composed" (Kelly, 1955, pp. 8–9). These transparent patterns or templates are personal constructs.

Kelly's theory was unusual in being set out very formally in terms of a fundamental postulate with eleven corollaries. The fundamental postulate, stating that a "person's processes are psychologically channelized by the ways in which he anticipates events" (Kelly, 1955, p. 47), essentially reflects Kelly's metaphor of the person as a scientist, whose primary concern is the prediction of the world. Personal constructs are the basis of the individual's predictions of those events to which they are applicable, and since constructs are, in Kelly's view, bipolar (e.g., "constructivist" versus "realist"), each provides a choice in the way in which an event is construed. A person's choices are, for Kelly, directed towards maximizing his or her ability to predict the world.

An individual's predictions may or may not be validated by his or her construing of subsequent events. Optimally, invalidation will lead the person to reconstrue, formulating new predictions, but people vary in the extent to which they are able to do this, which also depends upon the nature of the constructs involved in the predictions. Each person's constructs are organized in a hierarchical system, in which some are more superordinate than others, and constructs also vary in the extent to which they can be applied to new events. The construct system generally consists of various subsystems, although these are not necessarily entirely consistent with each other.

People not only differ in their constructs, but also in the way in which these are organized into systems. However, there is also some commonality in people's construing, especially with others in the same cultural group. For Kelly (1955), the essence of social interaction is sociality, the attempt to construe another person's construction processes, or to see the world through his or her eyes.

DEVELOPMENT AND APPLICATIONS OF PERSONAL CONSTRUCT PSYCHOLOGY

The Theory

There have been few attempts to develop Kelly's theory in the years since it was first put forward, although some new corollaries have been proposed in the areas of the development of construing and social construing, in which the theory has been regarded by some writers as insufficiently elaborated (Katz, 1984; Procter, 1981; Thomas, 1979). Extensions have also been proposed to Kelly's taxonomy of emotions (Cummins, 2006; McCoy, 1981).

The dearth of theoretical developments in the psychology of personal constructs perhaps reflects the comprehensiveness of Kelly's original vision. It may also indicate research evidence that has been provided in support of aspects of the theory (Adams-Webber, 1979, 2003), for example the relative importance of personal as opposed to supplied constructs; the resistance to change of superordinate constructs (Hinkle, 1965); and the bipolarity of construing (Millis & Neimeyer, 1991; Riemann, 1990).

Methodology

Of the two major methods for the assessment of construing developed by Kelly, the self-characterization and the role construct repertory test, it was the grid form of the latter that originally most captured the imagination of researchers and practitioners, being used in over 90 percent of personal construct research studies (Neimeyer, 1985; Neimeyer, Baker, & Neimeyer, 1990). Indeed, the repertory grid probably was, and is, better known than the theory from which it was derived, although it has been argued that it is most productively used in conjunction with that theory (Fransella, Bell, & Bannister, 2004). This popularity of the grid is in part due to the burgeoning of methods of grid analysis, mostly supported by computer software. Amongst other aspects of construing, these allow investigation of similarities and differences in the individual's view of particular aspects of his or her world; relationships between, and thus the meaning of, constructs; structural features of the construct system; conflicts in construing; and the content of personal constructs (Caputi, Bell, & Hennessy, 2012; Feixas, Geldschlager, & Neimeyer, 2002). The grid is an extremely flexible procedure, adaptable to innumerable areas of investigation and use in different cultural settings (e.g., Goins, Winter, Sundin, Patient, & Aslan, 2012). It can be used to analyze an individual's construing, can allow comparison of the construct systems of two or more people, or elucidate shared features of construing within a group of people. With its amenability to both quantitative and qualitative analysis, and its applicability in both nomothetic and idiographic investigations, it can be regarded as one of the first "mixed methods" approaches in psychology.

In recent years, the growth of narrative approaches in psychology has been conducive to renewed interest in story-telling methods, including the self-characterization and elaborations of this. There has also been the development of numerous alternative personal construct assessment techniques, ranging from interviews to non-verbal methods (Caputi et al., 2012).

Clinical Applications

The clinical field is the "focus of convenience" of personal construct psychology, the area in which it was originally developed and has been most extensively applied. Kelly's (1955, p. 831) view of psychological disorder as "any personal construction which is used repeatedly in spite of consistent invalidation" was in contrast to the traditional psychiatric view. Indeed, Kelly regarded psychiatric diagnosis as "all too frequently an attempt to cram a whole live struggling client into a nosological category" (p. 775). His alternative approach of "transitive diagnosis" mapped the client's pathways of movement in terms of a set of "diagnostic constructs" which were "neither good nor bad, healthy nor unhealthy, adaptive nor maladaptive" (p. 453). In Kelly's view, "it is not complete until a plan for management and treatment has been formulated" (p. 180). This, in effect, is the currently fashionable approach of formulation, often claimed as deriving from the cognitive-behavioral tradition (Bruch, 1998), with no apparent awareness that formulation was the term that Kelly used to describe his approach in 1955. Although it can be refined somewhat (Winter, 2003a, 2009; Winter & Procter, 2013), it still provides a necessarily radical alternative to the cramming of ever larger numbers of the population into the nosological categories ingeniously developed by the authors of successive editions of the *Diagnostic and Statistical Manual of Mental Disorders* and other such systems.

The work of personal construct psychologists in the clinical field has included the elucidation of processes of construing in a range of client groups, throughout the life cycle, and the development and evaluation of treatment methods (Winter, 1992a; Winter & Viney, 2005). The latter range from approaches that focus on particular aspects of the client's construing, such as dilemmas (Feixas & Saúl, 2005), to those, such as Leitner's (1988) "experiential personal construct psychotherapy," that are more concerned with the therapeutic relationship. There is also now a growing evidence base for personal construct psychotherapy, which has generally been found to be as effective as alternative, including cognitive-behavioral, approaches (Holland et al., 2007; Metcalfe, Winter, & Viney, 2007; Viney, Metcalfe, & Winter, 2005; Winter, 2003b).

Educational Applications

George Kelly himself ran a traveling psychological service to schools, and later personal construct psychologists have considered the development of children's construing (e.g., Mancuso, 2003; Salmon, 1970) and extended the application of personal construct psychology in educational settings. This work has included the development of novel techniques tailored for the exploration of children's views of the world (Ravenette, 1997). Of particular importance has been a stance that when children are presented as problems, this is often because they invalidate the construing of adults, whose response to this, including reaching for diagnostic labels, may be less than useful (Mancuso, Yelich, & Sarbin, 2002; Ravenette, 1997). It follows that problem resolution is likely to necessitate reconstruing by adults as much as by the "problem child."

Other applications of personal construct psychology in the educational setting have focused on the learning process, including increasing both students' and teachers' awareness of their own processes (Pope & Denicolo, 2001; Thomas & Harri-Augstein, 1985), and facilitating learning that is lifelong (Kompf, in press). One area of concern has been the development of a pedagogical relationship that is inviting and fosters creativity (Novak, 1990).

Organizational Applications

A further major area of application of personal construct psychology has been consultancy in the organizational or business setting. Some of this work has simply involved assisting individuals in organizations by such means as vocational guidance, counseling, and coaching (Brophy, Fransella, & Reed, 2003; Fransella, Jones, & Watson, 1988; Savickas, 1997). The other focus is on aspects of the organization itself, such as market research (i.e., others' construing of the organization), employee selection, team building, decision making, and conflict resolution (Brophy et al., 2003; Coopman, 1997; Jankowicz, 1990). It has included the use of methods to explore an organization's "corporate construing," which may then be compared with the construing of its major stakeholders (Balnaves & Caputi, 2000).

Social Applications

Although Kelly's theory has sometimes been criticized for over-emphasizing the individuality of construing, it has been counter-argued that it is a social psychology, as evidenced in its consideration of commonality, sociality, dependency, and people being "validating agents" for others' construing (Walker, 1996; Walker & Winter, 2007). In his later work, Kelly (1962) extended these concerns by focusing upon the "cultural matrix" of construing, and there have been numerous further elaborations and applications of personal construct psychology in relation to social and cultural issues (Kalekin-Fishman & Walker, 1996; Stringer & Bannister, 1979). Initial research on a personal construct model of friendship formation (Duck, 1979), which produced consistent findings, was followed by work on the development and deterioration of personal relationships (Neimeyer & Hudson, 1985; Neimeyer & Neimeyer, 1985). However, perhaps the development of greatest significance was Procter's (1981) family construct psychology, in which families were viewed as having construct systems with similar properties to personal construct systems. This has now been extended to a "relational construct psychology" (Procter, 2014).

Other Applications

The very extensive range of convenience of personal construct psychology (those areas to which it is applicable) is indicated by the diversity of the fields to which it has been applied since the publication of Kelly's magnum opus (Fransella, 2003a; Winter & Reed, in press). To name but a few, these include the arts (Scheer

& Sewell, 2006), politics (Scheer, 2008), anthropology (Orley, 1976), religion (Todd, 1988), forensic psychology (Horley, 2003), restorative justice (Tschudi, 2008), sport (Savage, 2003), accounting (Purdy, 2000), and environmental issues (Reed & Page, in press).

STATUS OF PERSONAL CONSTRUCT PSYCHOLOGY

Reflexive Evaluation

Kelly's (1955) ten "design specifications" for a psychological theory provide a means of evaluating personal construct psychology reflexively, in its own terms. The first of these, that it should have an *appropriate focus and range of convenience*, can be considered, as indicated above, to be well met in view of its demonstrated utility in the clinical setting (its focus of convenience) and its extraordinarily broad range of other applications (its range of convenience). These latter applications also demonstrate the *fertility* of the theory, another of Kelly's design specifications, as do the various new approaches, techniques, and research programs developed from it. As we have seen, the theory has also fulfilled two further specifications in that it has produced *testable hypotheses*, the testing and general confirmation of which have shown it to be *valid* (Adams-Webber, 2003). The theory's *generality* is also demonstrated by its applicability well beyond the setting and historical context in which it was developed, and is enabled by the abstract way in which the theory is presented. The theory's concepts have been shown to be amenable to *operational definition*, particularly in terms of measures derived from personal construct assessment procedures such as the repertory grid (Fransella, Bell, & Bannister, 2004). It has *avoided the problems associated with the assumptions of mental energy*, which had no place in Kelly's theory, without any consequent diminution of its explanatory power. It has also been *able to account for the choices that people make*, there being some empirical support for its view of choice, which has even provided some understanding of choices that are apparently destructive to the self or others (Fransella, 1972; Neimeyer & Winter, 2006; Winter, 2006). It also goes without saying that the theory *recognizes individuality.*

Paradoxically, the only one of Kelly's design specifications that his theory fails to meet is that it should be *modifiable and ultimately expendable.* Although there have been numerous modifications and developments in approaches derived from it, the theory itself remains largely unmodified, perhaps being a victim of its own success in meeting Kelly's other specifications. Nevertheless, its integration with other models has been proposed—although, as we shall see, this remains a subject of debate.

Sociohistorical Analysis

Personal construct theory can therefore be considered to have met the "test of time" in its own terms, but what is its status from a more external perspective? Neimeyer's (1985) sociohistorical analysis indicated that personal construct theorists met Mullins' (1973) criteria for a cohesive scientific group, namely "a theoretical break from its parent discipline," "the emergence of a social organizational leader," "the establishment of research and training centers," and "the publication of intellectual materials" (Neimeyer, 1985, pp. 94-5). Neimeyer also charted the theory's development through the stages delineated by Mullins, namely a "normal stage" of piecing the theory together up to 1955; a "network stage" up to 1966, in which personal construct psychologists discussed their work amongst themselves; a "cluster stage" up to 1972, in which groups were formed around leaders at different research centers; and a "specialty stage," from then onwards, in which the primary concern has been the institutionalization of the group's work. This development proceeded at different rates in different countries, and, for example at a faster pace in the United Kingdom than in personal construct theory's country of origin. There have been separate analyses of the theory's development in particular continents or countries (e.g., Feixas, 1989; Viney, 2006; Winter, 1992b).

Neimeyer (1985) went on to consider four problems facing the theory, namely its intellectual isolationism, extending occasionally to disdain for theorists of other persuasions; the crisis of methodology associated with an overreliance on repertory grid technique; the theory's relationship to the cognitive therapies; and differing views concerning the formation of an international organization. We shall return to some of these issues when considering current choices facing personal construct theorists and anticipations of the future.

Neimeyer's own explorations of the future of personal construct psychology involved conducting a Delphi poll, in which 130 members of the "Clearing House for Personal Construct Theory" (which regularly circulated reference lists on the theory) were asked to respond to questions concerning predictions about developments in the theory, methods, research, psychotherapy, and the social organization of the theory group (Neimeyer, Davis, & Rist, 1986). The questions were then repeated, but with respondents knowing the identities and aggregate views of their fellow panelists. In terms of theory, panelists predicted refinement of models of construct interrelationships, incorporation of cognitive psychology concepts, and a more social emphasis to the theory, but little revision of the basic theory itself. In regard to methods, refinement and extension of repertory grid technique was predicted, including use of interactive software for eliciting data. The development of non-grid, and particularly qualitative, methods was also predicted. Increases in research were anticipated in various areas, including models of particular disorders and psychotherapy, particularly in relation to the therapeutic process, with the use of rigorous research designs but also a focus on idiographic research. Further research output in the areas of social, educational, vocational, and developmental psychology were also considered likely. Developments in personal construct family, couple, group, and child psychotherapy were considered particularly likely, but, although it was expected that the therapy would become more technically eclectic, there was little anticipation of integration with other approaches. Panelists also tended to predict the establishment of formal personal construct organizations and a journal, as well as an increase in adherents, the impact of the theory, and training programs. Just as in Neimeyer's sociohistorical analysis, national differences between personal construct psychologists were very apparent, but in general most of the panelists' predictions (although not, for example, the incorporation of cognitive psychology concepts, and not a substantial increase in the theory's adherents) have been confirmed in subsequent years.

Neimeyer, Baker, and Neimeyer (1990) subsequently updated Neimeyer's (1985) analysis, concluding that "construct theory's rate of development has been dramatic" on the basis of such findings that "*the number of personal construct publications has more than doubled in the last eight years*" (p. 12). Although they still accounted for the majority of these publications, the percentage of repertory grid-based publications had dropped, with a corresponding increase in publications relating to theoretical and therapeutic issues, as well as other areas of application. The situation described by Neimeyer et al. (1990) was one of exponential growth, and "an international base of support enjoyed by few psychological theories" (p. 17). A later review, conducted at the time of the fiftieth anniversary of the publication of Kelly's magnum opus, saw little reason to change this assessment of the status of personal construct psychology (Walker & Winter, 2007).

CHOICES

Subsuming or Being Subsumed

The intellectual isolationism and insularity of personal construct theory noted by Neimeyer (1985) was regarded by him as an adaptive stage in the theory group's early development. However, he and others have argued that in order for personal construct psychology to survive and maintain its vitality, this stage should be followed by more openness to integration with other approaches. For example, while personal construct psychotherapy was always technically eclectic (Lazarus, 1967) in borrowing techniques from other theoretical persuasions but conceptualizing their mode of action in personal construct theory terms, Neimeyer (1988, p. 290) encouraged it to move on to a "Theoretically Progressive Integrationism," including an integrative dialectic with other theories that share a comparable metatheory. Such integrative directions in the therapeutic sphere could extend to treatment services with an overall constructive alternativist philosophy and view of the healing process (Harter, 1988) while employing therapists from a range of different traditions (Winter, 1985, 1990).

Attempts to classify personal construct theory, and align or integrate it with other approaches, have resulted in numerous different labels being applied to it over the years, for example in personality textbooks. While, from the perspective of constructive alternativism, this is only to be expected, Kelly (1969a) himself found some of the labels (e.g., "cognitive") puzzling, and others (e.g., that he was a "learning theorist") so "patently ridiculous" as to provide him with "no end of amusement" (p. 216). In the view of Bannister and Fransella (1986), such labels are no more than an attempt to put a revolutionary "in his place." Since the theory is still very commonly presented as cognitive, we shall consider the arguments concerning its integration with cognitive approaches, particularly in the therapeutic sphere, before going on to discuss its positioning within the constructivist movement.

Personal Construct Psychology and Cognitive Approaches

Despite Kelly's own position on this matter, based on his holistic view of the person, typical descriptions of him are that he was "perhaps the first cognitive-behavioral theorist" (Ivey, Ivey, & Simek-Downing, 1987, p. 302) and "the first truly cognitive personologist" (Wiggins & Pincus, 1992, p. 496). Interestingly, there is some evidence that authors who classify personal construct theory as cognitive tend to show the most misinterpretations of Kelly's ideas (Walker, 1991).

A particular area of debate, as noted in Neimeyer's (1985) socio-historical analysis, has been the relationship of personal construct psychotherapy to the cognitive therapies. Whereas leading cognitive therapists acknowledged debts to Kelly (Beck et al., 1979; Ellis, 1977), and some personal construct theorists were also able to see compatibilities between the two approaches (Neimeyer, 1985), others (particularly those whose sympathies were more with humanistic psychology) eschewed any such linkages, largely on the basis of differences at a metatheoretical level. For example, Leitner regarded cognitive approaches as "essentially behavioristic positions in sheep's clothing" and "in a sense very antithetical to construct theory when you look at the image of man implicit in them" (Neimeyer, 1985, p. 125). Mancuso made his position even clearer: "These people who call themselves cognitive psychotherapists are full of hogwash. There is nothing cognitive about their work. They're very mechanistic" (Neimeyer, 1985, p. 125).

More recently, there has been empirical investigation of differences between personal construct and cognitive approaches to therapy. Viney (1994) demonstrated more acknowledgement of the client's negative emotions in the former approach than in rational-emotive therapy, but her study only examined sessions of one therapist for each form of therapy. Winter and Watson (1999) found that transcripts of personal construct psychotherapy and rationalist cognitive therapy could be blindly identified with considerable accuracy by a leading personal construct psychotherapist and a leading rationalist cognitive therapist. The two types of therapy were also differentiated on a range of therapy process measures, tapping therapist and client behavior in sessions, client perceptual processing, and therapist facilitative conditions. This study therefore indicated that personal construct and cognitive therapies are different not just in theory but also in practice. Arguably, though, there may be greater similarities between personal construct psychotherapy and some of the more contemporary, "third wave" (Hayes, 2004) cognitive-behavioral therapeutic approaches.

However, it was when behavior therapy was in the throes of its "second wave," namely the "cognitive revolution," that personal construct psychologists perhaps missed a major opportunity. During this period, addressing the first gathering of personal construct psychologists to be labeled an international congress, Fay Fransella, referring to the cognitive revolution, asserted that *"If behaviour therapy is up for grabs—we must be in there doing the grabbing!"* (Fransella, 1978, p. 6), and that "We must not allow" personal construct psychology "to be incorporated within existing psychological frameworks—if we had to we must do the incorporating" (p. 6). That her ambitions did not cease with grabbing behavior therapy was indicated when she went on to say that *"We are making a take-over bid for the discipline of psychology"* (p. 6, italics in original). The mixed reaction to her address brought into sharp focus differences within the personal construct movement concerning its direction, and, in particular, the stance towards integration with other approaches. For many of the audience, Fransella's position was regarded as too aggressive, and one leading personal construct theorist went so far as to want to stop speaking to her for years as a result (Fransella, 1996). There was also the formation of a "subsuming group," which, albeit not with the greatest seriousness, met regularly to consider what other approaches personal construct psychology might be able to subsume. Twenty-two years later, Fransella returned to a similar theme at an international congress on personal construct psychology when invited to speculate on the future: "Why integrate, to some common approach, that will swamp one of the most powerful and useful psychological theories that has ever been created?" (Fransella, 2000a, p. 444). She also expressed similar anticipations to those at the 1977 congress: "Perhaps it will become THE mainstream psychology taught and practiced around the world?" (p. 447).

Fransella's underlying message in 1977 and thereafter, namely that personal construct psychology was faced with a choice between subsuming other approaches or being subsumed, has proved prophetic. In subsequent years it has not been personal construct psychology but the cognitive-behavioral approach that has been "doing the grabbing," not even Buddhism or existentialism being safe from its rapacious clutches. As Aaron Beck is reported to have said, "if it works, it's CBT," and it is instructive to note that even in reviews of psychotherapy research that acknowledge that there is an evidence base for personal construct psychotherapy, this evidence is included under a general heading of cognitive-behavioral therapies (Carr, 2009; Cooper, 2009). In health services that are increasingly dominated by short-term cognitive behavioral therapies, with little opportunity to practice alternative approaches, personal construct psychotherapists are therefore increasingly confronted with the dilemma of either facing marginalization and possible extinction or "selling their souls" and jumping on the bandwagon by accepting the cognitive-behavioral label (Winter, 2008, 2010).

Personal Construct Psychology and Constructivism

At first glance, the alignment of personal construct psychology with the constructivist movement would seem much less problematic than that with cognitive approaches (although a report of Kelly using the term constructivist to describe his approach [Priest & Nishimura, 2008] appears to be a complete misquote). Thus, one might think that there is little doubt that personal construct theory is one of "*a family of theories that share the assertion that human knowledge and experience entail the (pro)active participation of the individual*" (Mahoney, 1988, p. 27), and is therefore constructivist rather than realist. However, although Kelly was regarded as a "critical constructivist" by Mahoney because he acknowledged the existence of a real world, with which constructions differ in their goodness of fit, for others this implies that he was a "limited realist" (Stevens, 1998). Finer tuned analyses of constructivism than that of Mahoney have generally positioned personal construct psychology with epistemological constructivism, again because of its emphasis on constructions of an external reality (Chiari &

Nuzzo, 1996; Raskin, 2002), although claims have also been made for it being regarded as a hermeneutic constructivism (Warren, 1998), emphasizing subject/object interdependence. Furthermore, while personal construct psychology has been generally contrasted with social constructionism because of its emphasis on personal knowing, these approaches have also been considered "two sides of the same coin" (Paris & Epting, 2004).

For our present purposes, the question of what type of constructivism best characterizes personal construct psychology is of less interest than how the future of personal construct psychology may be affected by its relationship with constructivism. To consider this question, we shall return to Fransella and her concerns about personal construct psychology being subsumed. Her views on this matter appeared to change over the space of a page in her book on George Kelly, where she wrote that "I see no problem at all in personal construct theory being subsumed under the label *constructivist*" (Fransella, 1995, p. 130, italics in original), but then that if "personal construct theory is allowed to be subsumed under the umbrella of constructivism as if it were *nothing but* constructivist, Kelly's philosophy may well survive, but his theory will sink without trace" (p. 131, italics in original). Subsequently, she seemed to acknowledge that this latter anticipation was probably unfounded, writing that

> I thought the constructivist movement might result in Kelly's psychological theory being lost sight of. But I now think that unlikely. . . . It is now clear to me that the constructivist movement and interest in qualitative methods have paved the way for a much wider acceptance of personal construct theory and repertory grid method, and I see no reason why they will not continue to be accepted and used. (Fransella, 2001, p. 379)

Nevertheless, she later asserted that "it is certainly an issue that is not going away" (Fransella, 2007, p. 44).

Fransella's views on this matter appear to be based upon her construal of personal construct psychology as a theory and associated methodology, and of constructivism as a philosophy that can lead to atheoretical eclecticism—albeit a construal that has been challenged by Raskin (2004). This is not dissimilar to earlier debates concerning the relationship between personal construct and humanistic psychologies. While these approaches share various basic assumptions about human nature (Bugental, 1964; Epting, 1984), their differences are exemplified by Kelly's (1969, p. 135) statement that "humanistic psychology needs a technology through which to express its humane intentions" and by his criticism of the eschewal of diagnostic constructs by person-centered therapists. Carl Rogers in turn viewed Kelly's approach as too intellectual, but Epting (1984, p. 187) regards it as having "both a heart and a head." In Rychlak's (1977) terms, it can be viewed as a "rigorous humanism," and similarly it can perhaps also be construed as a "rigorous constructivism." This does not imply that it is the only constructivist approach that merits this label, although in my view none, including the examples provided by Raskin (2004) in countering Fransella's views, share the degree of rigor in both theory and methodology that characterizes personal construct psychology.

At an organizational level, Fransella's concern that personal construct psychology might "sink without trace" in a sea of constructivism has perhaps received some validation by developments initiated by North American personal construct psychologists. For example, the *International Journal of Personal Construct Psychology* metamorphosed into the *Journal of Constructivist Psychology*, while the North American Personal Construct Network became the Constructivist Psychology Network. By contrast, in Europe and Australia, there are still associations devoted purely to personal construct psychology (albeit in some European countries together with some associations and training courses with a more broadly constructivist base), together with a journal and newsletters edited by personal construct psychologists from these continents. Given Neimeyer's (1985) analysis of the development of personal construct psychology, such international differences need not surprise us.

Fransella's views regarding personal construct theory and constructivism were interpreted by Raskin (2004) as reflecting the threat and anxiety experienced by the personal construct psychology community in the face of change. In his view,

> If we turn hostile in response to our threat and anxiety by insisting that PCP is the only bet for successfully transporting meaning making from our fragile suburban neighborhood into the larger metropolis of psychology, then I am afraid we risk our standing in city and suburb alike. . . . it won't be long before the bank forecloses on our house and we wind up homeless and irrelevant, wandering aimlessly around what will by then have evolved into a PCP-less constructivist neighborhood. (p. 330)

Raskin's alternative solution to the threat and anxiety posed by the impact of constructivism is for the personal construct community to increase the permeability of their constructs so as to embrace constructivism.

While threat and anxiety would be understandable responses to awareness of the possibility of imminent and fundamental changes to personal construct psychology when that psychology has been, as for Fransella, one's way of life (Winter, 2013), she did not accept this interpretation of her views about constructivism. Nor was there any real evidence of impermeability in her use of the theory's professional constructs, which extended to subjects as varied as mathematics, cancer, and the construing of plants (Fransella, 2000b, 20003b). The concerns that she and some other personal construct theorists have expressed were less about the evolution of the theory (which, as we have seen, should be welcomed as it is one of Kelly's design specifications for a psychological theory) than about it being seen as just one amongst many approaches to the study of meaning, the precise and elaborate details of which can be ignored, diluted, or misunderstood. The extent and nature of these latter misunderstandings, which we shall now consider, perhaps indicate the importance of the role that Fransella and others have taken as "guardians" of personal construct theory and the purity of its concepts.

Individuality, Commonality, and Sociality

In view of personal construct theory's emphasis on the individuality of construing, it is perhaps not surprising that many personal construct psychologists highlight the individuality of their approach and de-emphasize its commonality with other approaches. The importance of stressing the distinctiveness of personal construct concepts is indicated by the frequent misunderstanding of these concepts in psychology textbooks (Walker, 1991), as also occasionally in the personal construct literature. For example, Kelly's (1955) diagnostic construct of hostility, which he defined as *"the continued effort to extort validational evidence in favor of a type of social prediction which has already proved itself a failure"* (p. 510, italics in original), is often presented simply—including seemingly to some extent in the passage quoted from Raskin (2004) above—as continuing to assert one's failed predictions and ignoring evidence that disconfirms these. Such descriptions effectively view Kellian hostility as no more than a cognitive process of selective attention, and fail to acknowledge that it involves actively manipulating social events to generate evidence in support of predictions that are being challenged. A further example is provided by accounts of fixed-role therapy that indicate that the authors have failed to grasp key, theory-based aspects of this technique (Adams-Webber, 1981), which involves the client being asked to experiment with playing a new role for a short period of time. Kelly carefully incorporated into the fixed-role therapy procedure features that were designed to minimize the threat and guilt (in Kelly's sense of the client feeling dislodged from his or her core role) experienced by the client. For example, the sketch of the new character whose role the client is asked to play should demonstrate acceptance of the client, and experimentation with dimensions orthogonal to the client's major construct dimensions rather than simply "slot rattling" the client to the opposite poles of these dimensions (Bonarius, 1970). It is also made clear in introducing the procedure that the client's old self is not being sent into permanent exile but is merely going on a two-week vacation, on the return from which "we will . . . see what we can do to help him" (Kelly, 1955, p. 385). These aspects of fixed-role therapy are mostly conspicuous by their absence in descriptions of its use by cognitive-behavioral therapists, which generally involve the client being required to role play being a person who is the complete opposite of someone with their particular symptoms: for example, inorgasmic women being asked to role play having orgasms (Lobitz & LoPiccolo, 1972), and clients who are viewed (by rational-emotive therapists) as irrational being asked to role play being rational (Dryden, 1987)!

It is therefore entirely appropriate for personal construct psychologists to disavow commonalities with other approaches when these are claimed on the basis of less than accurate understanding of the concepts and techniques concerned. However, it also behooves personal construct psychologists to acknowledge commonalities at a superordinate level with certain approaches, including but not limited to several that fall under the constructivist umbrella. As the personal construct literature on friendship formation (e.g., Duck, 1973) indicates, a lack of perceived commonality may leave the personal construct community alone and friendless, as described in the previously mentioned scenario presented by Raskin (2004).

Another central feature of the personal construct view of relationships is sociality, the construing of the other person's construction processes, essentially in an attempt to see the world through that person's eyes. In addition, Kelly (1955) emphasized the importance of taking a "credulous attitude," involving an acceptance of (although not necessarily agreement with) the other person's view of the world, but strangely this is sometimes less than evident in the views expressed by personal construct psychologists, including Kelly himself, about the work of theorists of other persuasions. As Neimeyer (1985) has indicated, this may have been necessary in the early stages of the development of personal construct theory to emphasize its distinctiveness, but it is now only likely to lead to further intellectual isolationism.

Showing sociality and being credulous should enable one to speak the language of the other person, but a problem arises when that language is based on assumptions that are at variance with one's own. This is a particular issue for personal construct theory since Kelly (1955) considered that "a different approach calls for a different lexicon" and "many old terms are unhitched from their familiar meanings" (p. xi). A common complaint of newcomers to personal construct writings is that they are couched in rather obscure terms—impermeability, constriction, suspension, and so forth, not to mention such tongue-twisters as the circumspection-preemption-control cycle—with little attempt to use more familiar psychological language. Furthermore, even when the reader derives some comfort from finding an everyday term like guilt, this soon disappears when it is discovered that this term has an entirely different meaning from that to which he or she is accustomed. Arguably, the need to learn a new language also arises when studying many other psychological theories (including other constructivist approaches, with their use of such terms as autopoeisis and structural coupling), but is perhaps less so with those, such as psychoanalysis, whose terms have entered common parlance.

Dilemmas faced by personal construct psychologists in the use of language are particularly evident in the clinical sphere. For example, although, as we have seen, conventional psychiatric diagnostic terms were eschewed by personal construct theory, paradoxically the theory became widely known in the 1960s because of a diagnostic grid test of schizophrenic thought disorder (Bannister & Fransella, 1967) and the research that this generated. Although Fransella (2001, p. 375) subsequently wrote that she was "not proud of having used the repertory grid in that nomothetic way," the test and associated research served an important purpose in demonstrating that people diagnosed as thought disordered schizo-phrenic were characterized by the same processes of construing as anyone else, albeit using one of these—loose construing—to a greater degree. This also resulted in greater receptiveness to, and a burgeoning of research on, personal construct perspectives on other psychological disorders. While some reports of clinical applications of personal construct theory (e.g., Button, 1985) have been structured in terms of psychiatric diagnostic categories in order better to communicate with clinicians who used this language, others have been structured in personal construct terms, reserving psychiatric categories for the index (e.g., Winter, 1992a).

Such issues are of particular relevance to the future of personal construct psychology because of the increasing requirement from funders of health services (but not limited to this domain) that interventions should be "evidence-based" or "empirically supported." This demand was initially resisted by some personal construct psychotherapists, who, together with leading humanistic therapists, regarded it as an "empirical violation" of their approach (Bohart, O'Hara, & Leitner, 1998). However, it was clear that such a stance would only be likely to lead to the extinction of personal construct psychotherapy since, in the words of a policy document from the English National Health Service, "it is unacceptable . . . to continue to provide therapies which decline to subject themselves to research evaluation" (Parry & Richardson, 1996, p. 43). Therefore, as we have seen, other personal construct psychotherapists have now produced not inconsiderable evidence of the effectiveness of personal construct psychotherapy. However, this evidence still fails to appear in most guidelines for health service providers and commissioners (such as those published in the U.K. by the National Institute for Health and Care Excellence), largely because most of the research concerned was conducted on heterogeneous client groups, not diagnosed in terms of traditional psychiatric categories.

A further reason for much of this research being discounted has been its tendency to use less conventional designs and outcome measures. Thus, there has been an unfortunate tendency by some personal construct psychologists not only to regard "natural science methodology" (Bohart et al., 1998)—such as the albeit flawed gold standard of the randomized controlled trial—as anathema, but to view qualitative research as the only approach compatible with the basic assumptions of their theory. This is despite the ability of methods such as the repertory grid to quantify, as well as allow qualitative examination of, highly personal processes of meaning-making. A similar resistance to the use of symptom-focused outcome measures, in addition to those viewed as more compatible with personal construct theory, displays a singular lack of sociality with clients as well as commissioners of health services. After all, these individuals, in selecting which of the over 500 available types of psychological therapy are likely to be helpful, are generally most concerned with whether a particular therapy will reduce the symptoms of their psychological distress, whatever else it might also have to offer. To quote Kelly (1955, p. 831, italics in original), "*We may say, simply, that the goal of psychotherapy is to alleviate complaints.*" As Roth and Fonagy (2005) remark concerning these issues and the consequent lack of coverage of personal construct psychotherapy in their influential review of psychotherapy research commissioned by the English Department of Health:

> This compounds the fact of a small evidence base with the problem that what is available is philosophically at variance with a conventional review such as this one. This latter point could be used to argue that the absence of reports of evidence for PCT in this book reflects our selection bias rather than a real absence of evidence. (p. 492)

ANTICIPATIONS

So what *does* the future hold for personal construct psychology? In my own university environment, it is not difficult to convince myself (perhaps with the aid of a little Kellian hostility, manufacturing some of the evidence) that this future is bright. The university houses the Centre for Personal Construct Psychology, founded by Fay Fransella and now directed by Nick Reed, as well as the archives of Fransella and another leading personal construct psychologist, Miller Mair. Its Doctorate in Clinical Psychology is highly influenced by personal construct psychology, its under-graduate psychology course has a personal construct psychology module, and an MSc in Personal Construct Psychology has been validated, as has a top-up Doctorate in Psychotherapy which will allow personal construct psychotherapists to carry out major research projects in this area. It is also looking forward to hosting the International Congress in Personal Construct Psychology in 2015. A new handbook of personal construct psychology has been commissioned (Winter & Reed, in press), and there are plans for publication of collected works of various personal construct psychologists (e.g., Winter & Reed, 2015), including Kelly himself.

Although there are some other pockets of personal construct psychology activity in academic institutions worldwide, these are few and far between. Nevertheless, the breadth of application of personal construct psychology and its methodology, as in the various examples presented above, is hardly indicative of an approach that is in terminal decline. In summary, to ensure that their approach continues to flourish, I would suggest that personal construct psychologists take heed of the following.

1. Show Aggressiveness

Kelly (1955) viewed aggressiveness as the active elaboration of one's perceptual field. It is displayed by personal construct psychologists in extending their applications of Kelly's theory and methods to an ever broader range of domains (Walker & Winter, 2007). In my own work, when faced with problems in relatively uncharted territory that has seemed to defy any understanding or possibility of constructive intervention, I have invariably turned to personal construct psychology and have not found it wanting. Such problems have included serial killing (Winter, 2007; Winter et al., 2007), mass murder (Winter & Tschudi, in press), and the aftermath of a brutal African civil war, many of the psychological casualties of which were kept in chains (Goins et al., 2012; Winter et al., 2011; Winter & Wood, 2013).

2. Be Open to Dilation, but Resist Dilution, of Personal Construct Theory

Broadening of the perceptual field may lead to its reorganization "on a more comprehensive level," as Kelly (1955, p. 476) described in his notion of "dilation." For example, as Raskin (2004) remarks, if personal construct psychology shows the permeability to new approaches that he regards as necessary for its evolution and survival, "our constructions of PCP will change" (p. 332). While thoughtful evolution of personal construct psychology is to be welcomed, as we have seen, Kelly's intricate theory has often been misrepresented when attempts have been made to subsume it within other approaches. If the precision and distinctiveness of personal construct concepts are not upheld in the face of such careless misunderstanding, the theory is indeed in danger, as Fransella (1995) feared, of sinking without trace. Its dilution should not be equated with, and indeed is in marked contrast to, its evolution. Correction of misrepresentations of core features of the theory therefore goes beyond mere fruitless quibbling about what Kelly "really meant" (Raskin, 2006).

3. Celebrate Personal Construct Psychology's Individuality and Distinctiveness

While the complexity of its language and its over-reliance on repertory grid technique in research have been viewed as barriers to the development of personal construct psychology (e,g., Neimeyer, 1985), these unique features of personal construct theory should, in my view, be celebrated rather than relinquished. Lessons may be learnt from the plight of clinical psychology, at least in the U.K., in which a once flourishing National Health Service profession is now faced with significant reductions in posts, at least at senior levels, and their replacement in many cases by less highly paid thera-pists. Arguably, one reason for this has been that, in embracing psychological therapies, clinical psychologists have ignored and deemphasized other, particularly more quantitative and psycho-metric, areas in which they could claim to be uniquely qualified. Similarly, if personal construct psychology regards features such as repertory grid technique as dispensable quantitative encum-brances rather than innovative and unique jewels in its crown that still have great potential to attract newcomers to the approach, it is likely to consign itself to being just another, not particularly remarkable, psychology of human meaning-making.

4. Acknowledge Commonalities at a Superordinate Level with Other Approaches

Where commonalities exist with other approaches, these need pose no threat to personal construct psychology, but should instead be welcomed as offering fertile possibilities for collaboration rather than continuing to engage in sterile arguments, for example concerning which, if any, branch of constructivism best charac-terizes Kelly's theory. Although personal construct psychologists, seeing themselves as radical outsiders, have often seemed to take Groucho Marx's (1959) view that they would not want to belong to any club that would accept people like them as members, they are likely to find that some clubs offer more congenial company and support than do others. Such solidarity is perhaps particularly necessary in a world in which pronouncements by politicians and policy makers tend to be couched in rationalist terms, far removed from constructive alternativism, as in the following quote from a British Secretary of State for Health, introducing a new initiative to expand (almost exclusively cognitive-behavioral) psychological therapy services: "Successful psychological therapies ensure that the **right number** of people are offered a choice of the **right services** at the **right time** with the **right results**" (Hewitt, 2007, p. 2, bold in original).

5. Display Sociality

To extend the influence of their approach, personal construct psychologists may occasionally need to display greater sociality, construing the construction processes of those whom they wish to influence and adapting their message accordingly. This may include, for example, presenting the "evidence base" for applications of the theory in a manner that is understandable by colleagues and policy-makers; publishing in journals read by a wider audience, and adapting the language accordingly; and greater attention to marketing of personal construct psychology and its applications. Although occasionally a degree of compromise and adaptation may be required, this need not extend to core aspects of construing. The alternative may be the equivalent of Kelly's (1961) notion of suicide as a "dedicated act," in which the individual chooses death rather than an anticipated relinquishing of cherished beliefs. In this case, while personal construct theory may be maintained in a pure, unsullied form, the result is likely to be professional suicide where applications of the theory, such as personal construct psychotherapy, being starved of support from funders and interest by potential clients.

In short, the prescription for a healthy future for personal construct psychology is no different from that for any individual, namely, without necessarily abandoning core constructs, to seek out experiences, experiment, and be open to reconstruction, all the while attempting to understand the construing of others. As Kelly (1977, p. 9) put it, "The cycle of human experience remains incomplete unless it terminates in fresh hopes never before envisioned. This, as I see it, is no less true for the puzzled scientist" (or personal construct psychologist) "than for the distraught person who seeks psychotherapeutic escape from the psychological redundancies that he has allowed to encompass him." If such an approach is taken, there is no reason why anticipations for personal construct psychology cannot be of fresh hopes rather than extinction.

REFERENCES

Adams-Webber, J. (2003). Research in personal construct psychology. In F. Fransella (Ed.), *International handbook of personal construct psychology* (pp. 51–58). Chichester, England: John Wiley.

Adams-Webber, J. R. (1979). *Personal construct theory; Concepts and applications.* Chichester, England: John Wiley.

Adams-Webber, J. R. (1981). Fixed role therapy. In R. Corsini (Ed.), *Handbook of innovative psychotherapies* (pp. 333–343). New York: John Wiley.

Balnaves, M., & Caputi, P. (2000). A theory of social action: why personal construct psychology needs a superpattern corollary. *Journal of Constructivist Psychology, 13,* 117–134.

Bannister, D., & Fransella, F. (1986). *Inquiring man.* London, England: Croom Helm.

Beck, A. T., Rush, A. J., Shaw, B. F., & Emery, G. (1979). *Cognitive therapy of depression.* New York, NY: Guilford.

Bohart, A. C., O'Hara, M., and Leitner, L. M. (1998). Empirically violated treatments: disenfranchisement of humanistic and other therapies. *Psychotherapy Research, 8,* 141–157.

Bonarius, J. C. J. (1970). Fixed role therapy: a double paradox. *British Journal of Medical Psychology, 43,* 213–219.

Brophy, S., Fransella, F., & Reed, N. (2003). The power of a good theory. In F. Fransella (Ed.), *International handbook of personal construct psychology* (pp. 329–338). Chichester, England: John Wiley.

Bruch, M. (1998). The development of case formulation approaches. In M. Bruch and F.W. Bond (Eds.), *Beyond diagnosis: Case formulation approaches in cognitive-behavioural therapy* (pp. 1–17). Chichester, England: John Wiley.

Bugental, J. (1964). The third force in psychology. *Journal of Humanistic Psychology, 4,* 19–26.

Button, E. (Ed.). (1985). *Personal construct theory and mental health.* London, England: Croom Helm.

Caputi, P., Bell, R., & Hennessy, D. (2012). Analyzing grids: new and traditional approaches. In P. Caputi, L.L. Viney, B.M. Walker & N. Crittenden (Eds.), *Personal construct methodology* (pp. 159–181). Chichester, England: Wiley-Blackwell.

Caputi, P., Viney L. L., Walker, B. M., & Crittenden, N. (2012). *Personal construct methodology.* Chichester, England: Wiley-Blackwell.

Carr, A. (2009). *What works with children, adolescents, and adults? A review of research on the effectiveness of psychotherapy.* London, England: Routledge.

Chiari, G., & Nuzzo, M. L. (1996). Psychological constructivisms: a metatheoretical differentiation. *Journal of Constructivist Psychology, 9,* 163–184.

Cooper, M. (2008). *Essential research findings in counselling and psychotherapy: The facts are friendly.* London, England: Sage.

Coopman, S. J. (1997). Personal constructs and communication in interpersonal and organizational contexts. In G. J. Neimeyer & R. A. Neimeyer (Eds.), *Advances in personal construct psychology* (Vol. 4, pp. 101–147). Greenwich, CT: JAI.

Cummins, P. (2006). The construction of emotion. In P. Cummins (Ed.), *Working with anger: A constructivist approach* (pp. 1–12). Chichester, England: John Wiley.

Dryden, W. (1987). *Counselling individuals: The rational-emotive approach.* London, England: Taylor and Francis.

Duck, S. W. (1973). *Personal relationships and personal constructs: A study of friendship formation.* London, England: John Wiley.

Ellis, A. (1977). The basic clinical theory of rational-emotive therapy. In A. Ellis & R. Grieger (Eds.), *Handbook of rational-emotive therapy* (Vol. 1, pp. 3–34). New York, NY: Springer.

Epting, F. R. (1984). *Personal construct counseling and psychotherapy.* New York, NY: Wiley.

Feixas, G. (1989). Personal construct psychology in Spain: a promising perspective. *International Journal of Personal Construct Psychology, 2,* 433–442.

Feixas, G., Geldschlager, H., & Neimeyer, R.A. (2002). Content analysis of personal constructs. *Journal of Constructivist Psychology, 15,* 1–20.

Feixas, G., & Saúl, L.A. (2005). Resolution of dilemmas by personal construct psychotherapy. In D. A. Winter and L. L. Viney (Eds.), *Personal construct psychotherapy: Advances in theory, practice and research* (pp. 136–147). London, England: Whurr.

Fransella, F. (1972). *Personal change and reconstruction.* London, England: Academic Press.

Fransella, F. (1978). Personal construct theory or psychology? In F. Fransella (Ed.), *Personal construct psychology 1977* (pp. 1–6). London, England: Academic Press.

Fransella, F. (1995). *George Kelly.* London, England: Sage.

Fransella, F. (1996). Whither personal construct psychology in Europe? How might such an organisation as EPCA contribute to its development? In J.W. Scheer & A. Catina (Eds.), *Empirical constructivism in Europe: The personal construct approach* (pp. 22–38). Giessen, Germany: Psychosozial-Verlag.

Fransella, F. (2000a). Personal construct psychology by the year 2045. In J. W. Scheer (Ed.) *The person in society: Challenges to a constructivist theory* (pp. 440–448). Giessen, Germany: Psychosozial-Verlag.

Fransella, F. (2000b). George Kelly and mathematics. In J. W. Scheer (Ed.) *The person in society: Challenges to a constructivist theory* (pp. 114–121). Giessen, Germany: Psychosozial-Verlag.

Fransella, F. (2001). The making of a psychologist: A late developer. In G. C. Bunn, A. D. Lovie, & G. D. Richards (Eds.), *Psychology in Britain: Historical essays and personal reflections* (pp. 372–380). London, England: BPS Books and Science Museum.

Fransella, F. (Ed.) (2003a). *International handbook of personal construct psychology.* Chichester, England: John Wiley.

Fransella, F. (2003b). New avenues to explore and questions to ask. In F. Fransella (Ed.), *International handbook of personal construct psychology* (pp. 447–454). Chichester, England: John Wiley.

Fransella, F. (2007). PCP: A personal story. *Personal Construct Theory and Practice, 4,* 39–45.

Fransella, F., Bell, R., & Bannister, D. (2004). *A manual for repertory grid technique.* Chichester, England: John Wiley.

Fransella, F., Jones, H., & Watson, J. (1988). A range of applications of PCP within business and industry. In F. Fransella & L. Thomas (Eds.), *Experimenting with personal construct psychology* (pp. 405–417). London, England: Routledge and Kegan Paul.

Goins, S., Winter, D., Sundin, J., Patient, S., & Aslan, E. (2012). Self-construing in former child soldiers. *Journal of Constructivist Psychology, 25,* 275–301.

Harter, S. (1988). Psychotherapy as a reconstructive process: Implications of integrative theories for outcome research. *International Journal of Personal Construct Psychology, 1,* 349–367.

Hayes, S. C. (2004). Acceptance and commitment therapy, relational frame theory, and the third wave of behavioural and cognitive therapies. *Behavior Therapy, 35,* 639–665.

Hewitt, P. (2007). Foreword. *Commissioning a brighter future: Improving access to psychological therapies positive practice guide* (p. 2). London, England: National Health Service.

Hinkle, D. (1965). *The change of personal constructs from the viewpoint of a theory of construct implications.* (Unpublished doctoral dissertation). Ohio State University, Columbus, OH.

Holland, J. M., Neimeyer, R. A., Currier, J. M., & Berman, J.S. (2007). The efficacy of personal construct therapy: a comprehensive review. *Journal of Clinical Psychology, 63,* 93–107.

Horley, J. (Ed.) (2003). *Personal construct perspectives on forensic psychology.* Hove, England: Brunner-Routledge.

Ivey, A. E., Ivey, M. B., & Simek-Downing, L. (1987). *Counselling and psychotherapy: Integrating skills, theory and practice.* Englewood Cliffs, NJ: Prentice-Hall International.

Jankowicz, D. (1990). Applications of personal construct psychology in business practice. In G. J. Neimeyer & R. A. Neimeyer (eds.), *Advances in personal construct psychology* (Vol. 1, pp. 257–287). Greenwich, CT: JAI.

Kalekin-Fishman, D., & Walker, B.M. (Eds.) (1996). *The construction of group realities: Culture, society and personal construct psychology.* Malabar, FL: Krieger.

Katz, J. O. (1984). Personal construct theory and the emotions: An interpretation in terms of primitive constructs. *British Journal of Psychology, 72,* 315–327.

Kelly, G. A. (1955). *The psychology of personal constructs* (2 vol.). New York, NY: Norton.

Kelly, G. A. (1961). Theory and therapy in suicide: the personal construct point of view. In M. Farberow & E. Schneidman (Eds.), *The cry for help* (pp. 255–280). New York, NY: McGraw-Hill.

Kelly, G. A. (1962). Europe's matrix of decision. In R.M. Jones (Ed.), *Nebraska Symposium on motivation* (pp. 82–123). Lincoln, NE: University of Nebraska Press.

Kelly, G. A. (1969a). The psychotherapeutic relationship. In B. Maher (Ed.), *Clinical psychology and personality: The selected papers of George Kelly* (pp. 216–223). New York, NY: John Wiley.

Kelly, G. A. (1969b). Humanistic methodology in psychological research. In B. Maher (Ed.), *Clinical psychology and personality: The selected papers of George Kelly* (pp. 133–146). New York, NY: John Wiley.

Kelly, G. A. (1977). The psychology of the unknown. In D. Bannister (Ed.), *New perspectives in personal construct theory* (pp. 1–19). London, England: Academic Press.

Kompf, M. (in press). Lifelong learning. In D.A. Winter & N. Reed (Eds.) *Wiley-Blackwell handbook of personal construct psychology.* Chichester, England: Wiley-Blackwell.

Lazarus, A. A. (1967). In support of technical eclecticism. *Psychological Reports, 21,* 415–416.

Leitner, L. M. (1988). Terror, risk, and reverence: experiential personal construct psychotherapy. *International Journal of Personal Construct Psychology, 1,* 299–310.

Lobitz, W. C., & LoPiccolo, J. (1972). New methods in the behavioral treatment of sexual dysfunction. *Journal of Behavior Therapy and Experimental Psychiatry, 3,* 265–271.

McCoy, M. M. (1981). Positive and negative emotions: a personal interpretation. In H. Bonarius, H. Holland, & S. Rosenberg (Eds.), *Personal construct psychology: Recent advances in theory and practice* (pp. 95–104). London, England: Macmillan.

Mahoney, M. J. (1988). Constructive metatheory: 1. Basic features and historical foundations. *International Journal of Personal Construct Psychology, 1,* 1–35.

Mancuso, J. C. (2003). Children's development of personal constructs. In F. Fransella (Ed.), *International handbook of personal construct psychology* (pp. 275–282). Chichester, England: John Wiley.

Mancuso, J. C., Yelich, G. A., & Sarbin, T.R. (2002). The poetic construction of AD/HD: a diagnostic fable. In R. A. Neimeyer & G. J. Neimeyer (Eds.), *Advances in personal construct psychology: New directions and perspectives* (pp. 233–257). Westport, CT: Praeger.

Marx, G. (1959). *Groucho and me.* New York, NY: Da Capo Press.

Metcalfe, C., Winter, D. A., & Viney, L. L. (2007). The effectiveness of personal construct psychotherapy in clinical practice: a systematic review and meta-analysis. *Psychotherapy Research, 17,* 431–442.

Millis, K. K., & Neimeyer, R. A. (1990). A test of the dichotomy corollary: Propositions versus constructs as basic cognitive units. *International Journal of Personal Construct Psychology, 3,* 167–181.

Mischel, W. (1980). George Kelly's anticipation of psychology. In M. J. Mahoney (Ed.), *Psychotherapy process: Current issues and future directions* (pp. 85–87). New York, NY: Plenum Press.

Mullins, N.C. (1973). *Theories and theory groups in contemporary American sociology.* New York, NY: Harper and Row.

Neimeyer, G. J., & Hudson, J. E. (1985). Couples' constructs: personal systems in marital satisfaction. In D. Bannister (Ed.), *Issues and approaches in personal construct theory* (pp. 127–141). London, England: Academic Press.

Neimeyer, R. A. (1985). *The development of personal construct psychology.* Lincoln, NE: University of Nebraska Press.

Neimeyer, R. A. (1988). Integrative directions in personal construct theory. *International Journal of Personal Construct Psychology, 1,* 283–297.

Neimeyer, R. A., Baker, K. D., & Neimeyer, G. J. (1990). The current status of personal construct theory: some scientometric data. In G. J. Neimeyer & R. A. Neimeyer (Eds.), *Advances in personal construct psychology* (Vol. 1, pp. 3–22). Greenwich, CT: JAI.

Neimeyer, R. A., Davis, K., & Rist, P. (1986). The future of personal construct psychology: A Delphi poll. *British Journal of Cognitive Psychotherapy, 4,* 37–44.

Neimeyer, R. A., and Neimeyer, G. J. (1985). Disturbed relationships: A personal construct view. In E. Button (Ed.), *Personal construct theory and mental health* (pp. 195–223). London, England: Croom Helm.

Neimeyer, R. A., & Winter, D.A. (2006). To be or not to be: personal construct perspectives on the suicidal choice. In T. Ellis (Ed.), *Cognition and suicide: The science of suicidal thinking* (pp. 149–169). Washington, DC: American Psychological Association.

Novak, J. M. (1990). Advancing constructive education: a framework for teacher education. In R. A. Neimeyer & G.A. Neimeyer, *Advances in personal construct psychology* (Vol. 3, pp. 233–255). Greenwich, CT: JAI.

Orley, J. (1976). The use of grid technique in social anthropology. In P. Slater (Ed.), *The measurement of intrapersonal space by grid technique. Vol. 1: Explorations of intrapersonal space* (pp. 219–232). London, England: John Wiley.

Paris, M. E., & Epting, F. (2004). Social and personal construction: Two sides of the same coin. In J. D. Raskin & S.K. Bridges (Eds.), *Studies in meaning 2: Bridging the personal and social in constructivist psychology* (pp. 3–35). New York, NY: Pace University Press.

Parry, G., & Richardson, A. (1996). *NHS psychotherapy services in England: Review of strategic policy.* London, England: NHS Executive.

Pope, M. L., & Denicolo, P.M. (2001). *Transformative education: Personal construct approaches to practice and research.* London, England: Whurr.

Priest, R., & Nishimura, N. (2008). Counseling multiracial clients in context: a constructivist approach. In J. D. Raskin & S.K. Bridges (Eds.), *Studies in meaning 3: Constructivist psychotherapy in the real world* (pp. 253–271). New York, NY: Pace University Press.

Procter, H. G. (1981). Family construct psychology: An approach to understanding and treating families. In S. Walrond-Skinner (Ed.), *Developments in family therapy* (pp. 350–366). London, England: Routledge and Kegan Paul.

Procter, H. G. (2014). Qualitative grids, the relationality corollary, and the levels of interpersonal construing. *Journal of Constructivist Psychology*, in press.

Purdy, D. (2000). The principles of financial reporting in the UK and personal construction. In J. M. Fisher & N. Cornelius (Eds.), *Challenging the boundaries: PCP perspectives for the new millennium* (pp. 140–155). Farnborough, England: EPCA Publications.

Raskin, J. D. (2002). Constructivism in psychology: Personal construct psychology, radical constructivism, and social constructionism. In J. D. Raskin & S.K. Bridges (eds.), *Studies in meaning: Exploring constructivist psychology* (pp. 1–25). New York, NY: Pace University Press.

Raskin, J. D. (2004). The permeability of personal construct psychology. In J. D. Raskin & S.K. Bridges (Eds.), *Studies in meaning 2: Bridging the personal and social in personal construct psychology* (pp. 327–343). New York, NY: Pace University Press.

Raskin, J. D. (2006). Don't cry for me George Kelly: Human involvement and the construing of personal construct psychology. *Personal Construct Theory and Practice, 3*, 50–61. Retrieved from http://www.pcp-net.org/journal

Ravenette, A. T. (1997). *Tom Ravenette: Selected papers. Personal construct psychology and the practice of an educational psychologist.* Farnborough, England: EPCA Publications.

Reed, N., & Page, N. (in press). Changing behaviour to be more environmentally friendly: A PCP perspective. In D. A. Winter & N. Reed (Eds.) *Wiley-*

Blackwell handbook of personal construct psychology. Chichester, England: Wiley-Blackwell.

Riemann, R. (1990). The bipolarity of personal constructs. *International Journal of Personal Construct Psychology, 3,* 149–165.

Roth, A., & Fonagy, P. (2005) *What works for whom? A critical review of psychotherapy research* (2nd ed.). New York, NY: Guilford.

Rychlak, J. F. (1977). *The psychology of rigorous humanism.* New York, NY: John Wiley-Interscience.

Salmon, P. (1970). A psychology of personal growth. In D. Bannister (Ed.), *Perspectives in personal construct theory* (pp. 197–221). London, England: Academic Press.

Savage, D. (2003). A sporting use of personal construct psychology. In F. Fransella (Ed.), *International handbook of personal construct psychology* (pp. 439–441). Chichester, England: John Wiley.

Savickas, M .L. (1997). Constructivist career counselling: Models and methods. In G. J. Neimeyer & R.A. Neimeyer (Eds.), *Advances in personal construct psychology* (Vol. 4, pp. 149–182). Greenwich, CT: JAI.

Scheer, J. W. (2008). Construing in the political realm—reflections on the power of a theory. *Personal Construct Theory and Practice, 5,* 76–85. Retrieved from http://www.pcp-net.org/journal

Scheer, J.W. & Sewell, K.W. (Eds.). (2006). *Creative construing: Personal constructions in the arts.* Giessen, Germany: Psychosozial-Verlag.

Stevens, C. D. (1998). Realism and Kelly's pragmatic constructivism. *Journal of Constructivist Psychology, 11,* 283–308.

Stringer, P., & Bannister, D. (Eds.) (1979) , *Constructs of sociality and individuality.* London, England: Academic Press.

Thomas, L. (1979). Construct, reflect and converse. In P. Stringer & D. Bannister (Eds.), *Constructs of sociality and individuality* (pp. 49–71). London, England: Academic Press.

Thomas, L., & Harri-Augstein, S. (1985). *Self-organised Learning: Foundations of a conversational science for psychology.* London, England: Routledge and Kegan Paul.

Todd, N. (1988). Religious belief and PCT. In F. Fransella & L. Thomas (Eds.), *Experimenting with personal construct psychology* (pp. 483–492). London, England: Routledge and Kegan Paul.

Tschudi, F. (2008). Dealing with violent conflict and mass victimization: A human dignity approach. In I Aertsen, J. Arsovska, H.-C. Rohne, M. Valinas, and K. Vanspauwen (Eds.), *Restoring justice after large-scale violent conflicts* (pp. 46–69). Uffculme, England: Willan Publishing.

Viney, L. L. (1994). Sequences of emotional distress experienced by clients and acknowledged by therapists: are they associated more with some therapists than others? *British Journal of Clinical Psychology, 33,* 469–481.

Viney, L. L. (2006). Small steps against the tyranny of distance in isolated communities. In P. Caputi, H. Foster, & L. L. Viney (Eds.), *Personal construct psychology: New ideas* (pp. 71–80). Chichester, England: John Wiley.

Viney, L. L., Metcalfe, C., & Winter, D.A. (2005). The effectiveness of personal construct psychotherapy: A meta-analysis. In D. A. Winter & L. L. Viney (Eds.), *Personal construct psychotherapy: Advances in theory, practice and research* (pp. 347–364). London, England: Whurr.

Walker, B. M. (1991). *The accounts of George Kelly's personal construct psychology in undergraduate psychology textbooks.* Paper presented at 9th International Congress on Personal Construct Psychology, Albany, New York.

Walker, B. M. (2006). A psychology for adventurers: an introduction to personal construct psychology from a social perspective. In D. Kalekin-Fishman & B. M. Walker (Eds.), *The construction of group realities: Culture, society, and personal construct theory* (pp. 7–26). Malabar, FL: Krieger.

Walker, B. M., & Winter, D. A. (2007). The elaboration of personal construct psychology. *Annual Review of Psychology, 58,* 453–477.

Warren, B. (1998). *Philosophical dimensions of personal construct psychology.* London, England: Routledge.

Wiggins, J. S., & Pincus, A. L. (1992). Personality structure and assessment. *Annual Review of Psychology, 43,* 473–504.

Winter, D. (2013). Personal construct psychology as a way of life. *Journal of Constructivist Psychology, 26,* 3–8.

Winter, D. A. (1985). Personal styles, constructive alternativism, and the provision of a therapeutic service. *British Journal of Medical Psychology, 58,* 129–136.

Winter, D. A. (1990). Therapeutic alternatives for psychological disorder: personal construct psychology investigations in a health service setting. In G. J. Neimeyer & R.A. Neimeyer (Eds.), *Advances in personal construct psychology* (Vol. 1, pp. 89–116). Greenwich, CT: Jai Press.

Winter, D. A. (1992a). *Personal construct psychology in clinical practice: Theory, research and applications.* London, England: Routledge.

Winter, D. A. (1992b). Personal construct theory in Europe: How do the spectacles fit? In A. Thomson & P. Cummins (Eds.), *European perspectives in personal construct psychology: Selected papers from the inaugural conference of the EPCA. York, England. 1992* (pp. 1–26). Lincoln, NE: European Personal Construct Association.

Winter, D. A. (2003a). Psychological disorder as imbalance. In F. Fransella (Ed.), *International handbook of personal construct psychology* (pp. 201–209). Chichester, England: John Wiley.

Winter, D. A. (2003b). The evidence base for personal construct psychotherapy. In F. Fransella (Ed.), *International handbook of personal construct psychology* (pp. 265–272). Chichester, England: John Wiley.

Winter, D. A. (2006). Destruction as a constructive choice. In T. Mason (Ed.), *Forensic psychiatry: Influences of evil* (pp. 153–177). Totowa, NJ: Humana.

Winter, D. A. (2007). Construing the construction processes of serial killers and other violent offenders: 2. The limits of credulity. *Journal of Constructivist Psychology, 20,* 247–275.

Winter, D. A. (2008). Personal construct psychotherapy in a National Health Service setting: does survival mean selling out? In J. D. Raskin & S.K. Bridges (Eds.), *Studies in meaning 3: Constructivist psychotherapy in the real world* (pp. 229–252). New York, NY: Pace University Press.

Winter, D. A. (2009). The personal construct psychology view of psychological disorder: did Kelly get it wrong? In L. M. Leitner & J. C. Thomas (Eds.), *Personal constructivism: Theory and applications* (pp. 279–295). New York, NY: Pace University Press.

Winter, D. A. (2010). Personal construct psychotherapy under threat. In D. Bourne & M. Fromm (Eds.), *Construing PCP: New contexts and perspectives* (pp. 52–65). Norderstedt, Germany: Books on Demand GmbH.

Winter, D., Bridi, S., Urbano Giralt, S., & Wood, N. (2011). Loosening the chains of preemptive construing: constructions of psychological disorder and its treatment in Sierra Leone. In D. Stojnov, V. Džinović, J. Pavlović, & M. Frances (Eds.), *Personal construct psychology in an accelerating world* (pp. 95–108). Belgrade, Serbia: Serbian Constructivist Association/EPCA.

Winter, D., Feixas, G., Dalton, R., Jarque-Llamazares, L., Laso, E., Mallindine, C., & Patient, S. (2007). Construing the construction processes of serial killers and other violent offenders: 1. The analysis of narratives. *Journal of Constructivist Psychology, 20,* 1–22.

Winter, D. A., & Procter, H. G. (2013). Formulation in personal and relational construct psychology: seeing the world through clients' eyes. In R. Dallos & L. Johnstone (Eds.), *Formulation: Making sense of people's problems* (2nd ed.). London, England: Brunner-Routledge.

Winter, D. A., & Reed, N. B. (Eds.) (2015). *Wiley-Blackwell handbook of personal construct psychology.* Chichester, England: Wiley-Blackwell.

Winter, D. A., & Reed, N.B. (2015). *Towards a radical redefinition of psychology: The selected papers of Miller Mair.* Hove, England: Routledge.

Winter, D. A., & Tschudi, F. (in press). Construing a "perfect knight": A personal construct investigation of mass murder. *Journal of Constructivist Psychology.*

Winter, D. A., & Viney, L. L. (Eds.) (2005). *Personal construct psychotherapy: Developments in theory, practice and research.* London, England: Whurr.

Winter, D. A., & Watson, S. (1999). Personal construct psychotherapy and the cognitive therapies: different in theory but can they be differentiated in practice? *Journal of Constructivist Psychology, 12,* 1–22.

Winter, D. A., & Wood, N. (2013). *Reconstructing life as a one-foot man: Reflections on the role of football.* Paper presented at 20th International Congress of Personal Construct Psychology, Sydney, Australia.

ℭ 3 ℬ

What Does the Future Hold for Radical Constructivism?[1]

Alexander Riegler

In the light of its heterogeneous nature, radical constructivism (RC) was recently referred to as a tool for problem solving. Can it re-invent itself to have a future as a major paradigm? To answer this question, RC is defined in terms of three increasingly larger sets of theoretical core principles and then aligned with possible empirical, methodological, and programmatic content to check its applicability for Gerhard Schurz's definition of paradigms. Based on Peter Cariani's list of intellectual, organizational, and social factors that help intellectual movements to sustain themselves and grow, it is pointed out which elements are already present and which still need to be developed. I argue that RC must be defined as a paradigm rather than as a problem-solving tool in order to attract the researchers necessary to make it a self-sustaining community. As such, I believe it has a future in a variety of disciplines, including those that are traditionally linked with it such as communication science and family therapy, as well as new research domains such as quantum mechanics and computational theory.

[1] I would like to thank Peter Cariani, Dewey Dykstra Jr., Vincent Kenny, Andreas Quale, and Armin Scholl for their critical comments, which contributed greatly to writing this paper.

The Past

History is full of examples where a movement seeks to dominate others. If successful, this group defines mainstream thought, thereby establishing an intellectual hegemony that suppresses plurality. Penalties for disbelieving in reigning orthodoxies have ranged from execution and exile, to public ridicule, exclusion from particular professions, and loss of funding.

Radical constructivism has always followed a different and inclusive strategy that forgoes "absolutism." It was never meant to be another "grand narrative" seeking to indoctrinate others. Rather, it is a constructive and—as I will point out—pluralistic proposal to think about crucial aspects in a different way, and then leave it to others to make up their minds.

> Radical constructivism is a subversive way of thinking that might change a person's ways of being in the world—but never a truth for all to adopt and apply to all circumstances, and especially not an instrument for the oppression of non-believers. (Tobin 2007, p. 295)

It is subversive because it calls into question "how we are in the world, how we relate to others, what we regard as worth knowing, and how we can come to know and assist others to know" (Tobin, 2007, p. 297).

So what is the future of a philosophical position that despite its sophistication does not insist on being the explanation for everything? Has history not shown that any such non-aggressive group eventually perishes under the pressure of others who violently fight non-believers? I suggest an answer to the question of how RC should comport and organize itself going into the future by drawing on insights I have gained as the editor-in-chief of the journal *Constructivist Foundations* (at http://www.constructivistfoundations.info). In particular, I draw on the papers Andreas Quale and I collected for a special issue on "Can Radical Constructivism Become a Mainstream Endeavor?"

(Quale & Riegler, 2010), which appeared three days after the death of Ernst von Glasersfeld, who founded the term "radical constructivism" in 1974.

WHICH RADICAL CONSTRUCTIVISM?

There are at least three ways to understand the term "radical constructivism:" (a) as the specific philosophy of Ernst von Glasersfeld; (b) as an extended interdisciplinary paradigm; and (c) as a pluralistic paradigm.

In its most narrow version, RC refers to the theoretical edifice von Glasersfeld had been building since 1974 (cf. Glasersfeld, 1974). He understood it as a conglomerate of various predecessors including, among others, the cognitive constructivism of Jean Piaget, the philosophical skepticisim of George Berkeley, the fictionalism of Hans Vaihinger, the transcendental philosophy of Immanuel Kant, and the Renaissance philosophy of Giambattista Vico.

The theoretical core of von Glasersfeld's original radical constructivism can be defined by two principles (Glasersfeld, 1995, p. 18). The first principle maintains that knowledge cannot be passively received but is actively built up by the cognizing subject. According to the second, less intuitive and readily acceptable principle, the function of cognition is adaptive, and it serves the organization of the experiential world rather than the discovery of ontological reality. Since these are *conjunctive* principles, he rejected the idea of any non-radical or "trivial constructivism" that embraces only the first principle but rejects the second. He insisted on calling his constructivism "radical" because reality construction is ubiquitous, and there is nothing in one's reality that is not the result of a construction process.[2] This is in sharp contrast to any

---

[2] While in everyday use the word "construction" may allude to the idea of arbitrarily fabricating something out of thin air, for von Glasersfeld, experiences (and empirical evidence) are at the root of reality construction, which therefore cannot be arbitrary (see also the "non-arbitrary" principle below).

"traditional theory of knowledge," which for so many is difficult to give up, i.e., the idea that our conceptual constructions represent in some way a mind-independent external reality, that "knowledge ought to be a veridical 'representation' of a world as it 'exists' prior to being experienced (that is, ontological reality)" (Glasersfeld, 1991, p. 15).

Unfortunately, von Glasersfeld never founded any larger research group (cf. Müller, 2010) that would assemble under the RC label. So although his impact on other disciplines, educational research in particular, was immense (Quale, 2008; Tobin, 2007), philosophically RC was marginalized. This did not even change after the Siegen school of radical constructivism in Germany, headed by Siegfried J. Schmidt, masterfully enlarged the definition of radical constructivism to include related approaches in an effort to introduce RC as a "new paradigm in the interdisciplinary discourse" (Schmidt, 1987, p. 11, my translation).

These related approaches are Heinz von Foerster's second-order cybernetics and Humberto Maturana and Francisco Varela's theory of autopoietic systems. They derived from different premises but overlapped in many details, most notably in the emphasis on cognitive closure. In Riegler (2001), I characterized the theoretical core of this *extended version of radical constructivism* as a set of *conjunctive* principles: (a) cognitive systems are organizationally closed systems[3]; (b) because they are closed, cognitive systems entertain an agnostic perspective with regard to an external reality, and any statement about the latter is mere metaphysical speculation[4]; (c) also, due to the organizational closure, cognitive

---

[3] In the radical constructivist sense, closure refers to the quality of a cognitive system in which the changes of its states are propagated solely within the network of processes that constitutes them. As such, it is related to the notion of closure in mathematics and does not mean that cognitive systems are isolated from the environment and thus unresponsive to environmental perturbations.

[4] In other words, RC cannot deny the existence of an external reality to the observer any more than it can confirm it; rather it denies that it is knowable in some sort of absolute sense that is independent of the observer and her senses or measuring devices.

processes are circular such that they form a network of relations; and (d) reality construction is not arbitrary because constraints arise from inherent properties of the relational network. In particular, the last principle is a clear refutation of solipsism, with which RC has sometimes been reproached.[5]

When amalgamating the respective theories of von Glasersfeld, von Foerster, and Maturana and Varela, Schmidt focused on a rather small subset of related approaches. Historically, the second-order cybernetics movement included many more theoreticians such as Gordon Pask and Stafford Beer (see also below). Also, in more recent years a variety of new approaches has emerged, such as Varela's neurophenomenology, or first-person approaches, as well as enactivism, certain flavors of embodiment, non-dualism, and so on. In an effort to embrace all these approaches as variations of radical constructivism, the theoretical core of *radical constructivism in a broad pluralistic sense* was described in the inaugural issue of *Constructivist Foundations* (Riegler 2005) in terms of *weakly disjunctive* principles: (a) it rejects the separation between objective world and subjective experience; (b) the observer must always be included in explanations; (c) it rejects representationalism, i.e., the idea that there is a mapping of the states of the external reality onto the states of the cognitive system; (d) it maintains an agnostic relationship with reality; (e) the focus of research is moved from the world that consists of *matter* to the world that consists of *what matters*[6]; (f) it emphasizes that it is the cognitive system that organizes her experiences, resulting in an "individual

---

[5] Unfortunately, a great deal of the radical constructivist literature keeps itself busy with refuting this and similar allegations. Perhaps this should not be its primary goal. Instead, demonstrating the effectiveness of the RC paradigm in scientific practice may prove more fruitful. Already, Thomas Kuhn has pointed out that in times of normal science, researchers are not bothered with epistemological questions. For example, the initial upheaval Niklas Luhmann's constructivist theory created in sociology has ebbed away to "business as usual" and his followers are now busy with the details of his theory in sociological settings.

[6] This, however, does not mean that RC abandons "theories of matter" such as physics. Quite on the contrary, many physicists such as Heinrich Hertz, Ernst

as personal scientist" approach; (g) it focuses on self-referential and organizationally closed systems that strive for control over their inputs rather than their outputs; (h) process-oriented explanations are preferred over substance-based ones; and (i) it asks for an open and undogmatic approach to science. Applied disjunctively, these principles can be used to define a wider range of acceptable radical constructivist theories. It is my conviction that this diversity makes RC stronger, not weaker, as long as the core ideas are made explicit.

So if we want to talk about the future of RC, its three versions should be considered differently. Defining RC in terms of core principles also raises the question of whether these principles portray RC as a paradigm or as a more or less loose set of insights and methodological patches. In other words, how cohesive and mutually supporting are the various intellectual components of RC? The more we see RC as a coherent set of interrelated beliefs, the more it is like a paradigm. The more we see it as a collection of tools, the less it seems like a coherent, unified way of thinking.

IS RADICAL CONSTRUCTIVISM A PARADIGM OR A TOOL?

Some authors may argue that radical constructivism is a mere style of thinking, an efficient instrument, and a tool that lends itself to solving very specific problems only. Such a revised understanding of RC may appear interesting because it seems easier to defend the future of RC if it is not considered a paradigm. For example, Schmidt (2010), in contrast to his writings in the 1980s, is no longer convinced that RC is a new paradigm because it has been branching out of the one original RC into different versions (cf. also his description of RC as "multiply differentiated/refined discourse without systematic center" [Schmidt, 1993, p. 330, my translation]). Similarly, Vincent Kenny (2010) compares the unfolding development of constructivist approaches with a river delta. He is concerned at the way constructivism continually and inevitably

Mach, Percy Bridgman, and Nils Bohr held epistemological positions that are compatible with RC, i.e., that any mind-independent reality is inaccessible.

splits and divides, making a mainstream constructivism impossible. As listed in Riegler (2005), this plurality includes not only the approaches mentioned so far (von Glasersfeld, von Foerster, and Maturana and Varela) but also Jean Piaget's genetic constructivism, Ulrich Neisser's cognitive theory, Kevin O'Regan and Alva Noë's theory about sensorimotor dependencies, Rudolfo Llinas's and Gerhard Roth's neurophysiology, Herbert Müller's epistemic structuring of experience, Varela's enactivism and neurophenomenology, Olaf Diettrich's constructivist epistemology, Paul Watzlawick's therapeutic theory, George Kelly's personal construct psychology, Niklas Luhmann's operational constructivism, and so on.

In view of this plurality, instead of calling it a paradigm, Schmidt argued in favor of defining RC as a tool, a "problem-solving instrument" that has been demonstrating its usefulness in various disciplines.[7] Can this demotion be justified by the fact that RC is heterogeneously spread over various disciplines (rather than constituting a focused paradigm on its own that is represented in university faculties)? Can the relatively small size of its community be used as a reason to refrain from defining it in terms of a paradigm, much as Pluto is no longer considered a planet? Clearly, much of radical constructivism's future depends on which weight class it is in when it enters the prize ring: tools come and go while paradigms usually have a much longer lifespan.

The answer also depends on the definition of "paradigm." Ever since it was popularized by Thomas Kuhn, it has always been a problematic notion. Many sought to replace it with similar theoretical structures such as Imre Lakatos's "research program" or Ludwik Fleck's "Denkkollektiv." A rather stringent characterization was provided by Schurz (1998), who defined a paradigm as a "multi-component cognitive system" consisting of (a) the theory core; (b) an empirical component, i.e., exemplars; (c) a method-

---

[7] Schmidt does not provide any explicit list of problems RC-as-a-tool has solved and remains rather vague: "in the fields of ontology, truth theory or ethics" (Schmidt, 2010, p. 10).

ological component, i.e., tools; and (d) the explanatory promises as its programmatic component.[8]

Can this definition of a paradigm be applied to RC? Above, we have already established various *theoretical* cores of the radical constructivist paradigm. So it seems appropriate to turn to the other components that are indispensible for the *practical* success of RC in the future.

THE SECRET OF SUCCESS

In his commentary, Cariani (2010) provided a list of components an intellectual movement needs in order to be successful in terms of persistence and growth. Many of them apply directly to radical constructivism so they can be regarded as ingredients of its future.

The first issue is the assertation that a theory must be intellectually acceptable and accessible and provide for certainty. For RC in particular, this can be a major obstacle as some of its basic assumptions are counterintuitive and therefore difficult to understand and to embrace. So what can be done to prevent new generations of scholars turning their back on RC just because it refers to concepts such as "the cognitive system is organizationally closed" and "reality is a construction"?

Volker Gadenne (2010) identified both concepts as problematic because they contradict the beliefs of many scholars. The closed-

---

[8] Examples of the theoretical component are operant conditioning in behaviorism, mutation and selection in Darwinian evolutionary theory, and the existence of the unconscious in Freud's theory. The empirical content of a theory is the set of successful explanations and anomalies as well as the prognostic excess of theory, i.e., whether more or fewer of its prognoses can actually be empirically observed. For example, Schurz referred to behaviorism as being "empirically progressive" until it was observed that learning problem solutions does not occur incrementally, as predicted by behaviorism, but that it occurs saltatorily, as predicted by the cognitive paradigm. Methodologically, behaviorism refrained from hypotheses about the internal mind, Darwinism used standard empirical natural science, and Freud a hermeneutic-interpretative approach.

system hypothesis implies epistemological solipsism, which many people seem to conflate with ontological solipsism, and this makes radical constructivism utterly unattractive for them. The rejection of realism means not only parting company with naïve and common sense realism but also with the great number of sophisticated versions of realism in the history of philosophy, which in turn does not sit well with professional philosophers, who have carefully reflected upon them.

In order to secure the future of RC, it is important to depict these counterintuitive concepts not as truths in themselves but rather as *inevitable* consequences of intuitively acceptable and intelligible situations. For example, von Glasersfeld tried to derive the statement that we must remain agnostic about any mind-independent reality (something most philosophers, let alone scientists, find too eccentric to accept) from the intuitive argument that whatever our senses supposedly report on, such a reality cannot be independently verified. Compare this with the situation in a legal context, where such a requirement makes a great deal of sense: there, one has to prove a statement by independent means. In the case of human senses, there are no such independent channels and hence no ways of independently verifying the existence of that which the sense organs supposedly perceive. There is no means of verifying anything except through some measurement process that involves sensors, be they human senses or human senses augmented by artificial sensors. Even a consensual construction of reality is at first a consensual construction rather than the proof of the existence of an external world. As a consequence, epistemological realism can be considered an over-interpretation of a conclusion from the consensual construction of reality to the ontological existence of this reality. This and similar strategies that allow reasoning from the intuitive to the counterintuitive must be applied to all concepts used by RC in order to find acceptance in terms of comprehension and certainty.

Furthermore, a theory should be open to new ideas and lend itself to enlargement. It is probably a weakness of many non-mainstream schools that they rather tend to secure their intellectual heritage and try to defend it from attempts to change and expand it. This is a risky strategy because while it keeps the idea pure it also means being unwilling to adapt dynamically to changes. Radical constructivism must not make this mistake for it must not be at odds with its own principles, i.e., the central role the concept of adaptation plays in von Glasersfeld's second principle. Dynamic adaptation motivates the pluralistic definition of RC. It is implemented in *Constructivist Foundations*, where von Glasersfeld's heritage is taken beyond its original boundaries to include movements such as enactivism and neurophenomenology, which each on their own terms may complement and expand the original ideas of RC. Also, it keeps the door open for new generations of researchers who are willing to sail under the constructivist flag, provided they are granted the latitude necessary to formulate their own ideas, conduct their own experiments, and arrive at their own conclusions, which are not determined by any narrow constructivist paradigm. However, this does not mean that just anything goes. Some flavors of radical constructivism such as social constructionism or Roth's neurophysiological approach may run into difficulties as they accept ontological premises. This makes it indispensable to sharpen the radical constructivist profile in terms of an all-embracing set of principles.

Further on the list is the requirement that a theory should be measured in terms of being able to attend to, clarify, and solve problems, whether intellectual ones or problems with regard to society. Radical constructivism has shown its usefulness in a variety of contexts, including education research (e.g., Dykstra, 2005), sociology (e.g., Riegler & Scholl, 2012), literature, communication, and media science (e.g., Scholl, 2010), and family therapy and psychotherapy (e.g., Kenny, 2010). However, it has had little or no impact on what Karl Müller (2010) calls its "core domains," i.e., cognitive science and neuroscience, biology and evolutionary theory, and organizational theory. Still, RC's impact so far is by no means a mediocre success: which other philosophical movement has had so much influence on and has proven its usefulness in so many disciplines?

In any scientific discipline, the number of publications is a measure of its practitioners. In the radical constructivist literature, many references relate to first generation constructivists, most of whom have already passed away. Their importance has been recognized in many publications and festschrifts. However, in order to stay alive, RC needs to replenish its member pool. This goal is severely hampered by the fact that there are no official institutions that could take care of that. While university departments are the life-lines of academia, we do not find any radical constructivist departments in universities today, no radical constructivist curricula, and no organization in general that would provide the means necessary for teaching new generations of scientists and philosophers. While part of the blame goes to the disciplinary structure of academia that makes it difficult for cross-cutting transdisciplines such as cybernetics, systems theory, semiotics, and constructivism to establish themselves, there was only one larger institute in recent academic history, Heinz von Foerster's Biological Computer Laboratory at the University of Illinois at Urbana-Champaign (cf. Müller & Müller, 2007), that provided a home for the *predecessors* of constructivist thought. However, it was disbanded before the radical constructivist movement could take off (Müller, 2010). Neither of the other, now aging luminaries founded departments at universities or other academic organizations that would have, by now, attracted and taught a larger number of young radical constructivists.

An important first step to attract new generations of radical constructivists and keep the community together are events and platforms in which to participate. Over recent years, a constant number of constructivists have been gathering at the Heinz von Foerster conferences in Vienna and the conferences of the American Society of Cybernetics. In addition to that, radical constructivism needs many more avenues and focal events that help participants to create a sense of belonging to the radical constructivist community. There are mainly two publication platforms that help radical constructivists publish their ideas and insights, i.e., *Constructivist Foundations* and *Cybernetics and Human Knowing*. However, there is little done in the area of social media, which has become so important not only for private purposes but also for commercial and even academic ends. Here, much more engagement is needed from radical constructivists, not only to draw attention to the field and coordinate its future, but also simply to increase its recognizability among the vast number of other philosophical and interdisciplinary movements. While in the past, the first generation of radical constructivists, most notably von Foerster and Maturana, had ingenious ideas for how to summarize key concepts in distinctly recognizable phrases, recently there has been little "branding" of that sort. Examples of those early slogans were Maturana's "Everything said is said by an observer," von Foerster's "Truth is the invention of a liar," and Piaget's "The mind organizes the world by organizing itself." They not only helped to draw attention to radical constructivism but also served as exemplars of the paradigm. Naturally, there are drawbacks with slogans that at first sight seem to contradict the uninitiated's intuition: How can everything said be said by an observer? How can the truth be a lie? How can the mind organize the world? These thus create misunderstandings, which discredit the scholarly nature of radical constructivism if presented out of context.

Still, exemplars such as these serve an important function, i.e., to counter the tendency of RC to dissolve into various flavors. While such plurality is certainly important and must not be suppressed, a movement that is divided into various small sub-movements easily falls prey to other competing theories to the point of becoming entirely marginalized, non-mainstream groups. An equilibrium has to be established that does not undercut the independence of movements summarized under radical constructivism while at the same time defends the common theoretical core, methodology, exemplars, and predictive promises against competing movements. This, however, defines RC as a (pluralistic disjunctive) paradigm rather than a tool. Being a paradigm not only strengthens the reputation of radical constructivism as a serious scientific movement but also helps to create a strong identity pulling together researchers whose research has always had a constructivist foundation without them knowing it. As Cariani writes, "as it turns out, I have long agreed with all of the fundamental tenets of RC . . . However, I did not realize this complete agreement until I recently saw that simple list of core principles" (Cariani 2010, p. 129).

Providing such core principles is as important as describing radical constructivism in extended texts, in particular in books in which the reader can explore the details of the theory. Unfortunately, such books are rare among radical constructivists: von Foerster, for example, has never published a monograph on this topic, and von Glasersfeld wrote just one book. Here, the talent of radical constructivists is in high demand as books are needed in greater numbers, both at the level of introductory texts and books for the advanced expert in which new problems and their solutions are explored in great detail. While not all these books will ever get the same amount of attention, a high number of book publications serves an important aspect, i.e., forestalling the impression RC is an unproductive and thus negligible movement with little scientific output.

Books and publications in general, as well as events and educational efforts, all contribute to helping radical constructivists grow the necessary internal motivation to go on with their research. Only if they can develop for themselves the feeling of being able to express their insights in front of and discuss them in a larger group of peers will they have the incentive to make the necessary efforts. This has two dimensions: an individual one and a social one.

On the individual level, self-generated reinforcement is of utmost importance. Von Glasersfeld (1983) explained its importance in the context of education. For the constructivist, instructionally designed education is plainly wrong and pupils must rather be taken to situations where they can discover the rewarding nature of increasing their knowledge on their own, comparable to the "mathematician's satisfaction in doing mathematics." It is not by rewarding their success with "certain well-known commodities, such as cookies, money, and social approval" that they develop this attitude but with "one thing that is often by far the most reinforcing for a cognitive organism: to achieve a satisfactory organization, a viable way of dealing with some sector of experience" (Glasersfeld, 1983, p. 65). This can be greatly facilitated by providing radical constructivists with a helpful environment of peers. Without it, radical constructivism is doomed to stagnate, being self-satisfied with the insights reached so far and unwilling to take the baton any further.

On the social level, groups and networks can easily provide concrete and pressing incentives that both encourage and discourage authors. An example of the latter may be Alan Gross. In the early 1990s, he became well-known for his anti-realist criticism claiming that "the end product of science was a web of words and that its claims were secured by the various means of persuasion" (Gross, 2013). This led to the publication of his book *The Rhetoric of Science* (Gross 1990). Back then, he was in the company of social constructivists[9] who brought forward similar claims, most notably Steve Woolgar and Bruno Latour's (1979) *Laboratory Life*. By the time of his 2013 article, however, he had undergone an "alteration" in his course. As he frankly writes in this article, the many criticisms his book received from realists made him change his views such that he now claims that "some theories of science seem beyond argument," i.e., that some parts of scientific reality are not constructed but independently verifiable elements in science (including diseases caused by bacteria and viruses, the periodicity of the elements, and the conversion of mass and energy as described by Albert Einstein). While cognitive flexibility, adaptability, and the ability to reflect academic opinions in one's own

---

[9] It is important to note, though, that radical constructivism should not be confused with social constructivism as they differ significantly with respect to their theoretical principles. For RC, reality construction starts in the cognitive being while the premise of SC is that it is society that fabricates scientific truths.

theories is certainly appreciated, one may wonder what result a supportive and encouraging constructivist surrounding might have yielded instead?

It clearly shows the necessity for radical constructivism to create and fill institutional anchors where "ideas can be developed, refined, and written about endlessly," and where students "can be educated, earn degrees, find jobs in academia" (Cariani, 2010, p. 130) in order eventually to provide the intellectual support for each other such that radical constructivists do not need to succumb to pressure from realists for fear of ridicule and/or their career. In other words, the future of RC goes hand in hand with its ability to create faculty positions at university and scholarly institutions. Some remedy can be expected from the permeation of academic structures by radical constructivists, as is the case with communication science in Germany. Even though there are no dedicated radical constructivist research facilities, RC is already so widespread that candidates with a constructivist background stand a chance in appointment procedures (Armin Scholl, personal communication).

In Müller's (2010) analysis, in its "early years" radical constructivism failed to create the widespread network among scientists that would guarantee a self-sustaining expansion in the 1970s. According to Müller, this applies to all main RC proponents back then. None of the relevant actors involved in von Glasersfeld's personal network had the necessary means to promote network formations, and he therefore never assembled a larger research group (and it did not help that von Glasersfeld never obtained a Ph.D.). Von Foerster, who retired in 1976, was too late to assemble a number of scientists "to work on second-order cybernetics in a normal research environment" (Müller, 2010, p. 34). On the autopoietic front, Maturana, Uribe, and Varela stopped their collaboration in the 1980s. Other relevant proponents were Gordon Pask, who had developed a constructivist conversation theory but failed "to create a sufficiently strong research environment," and Stafford Beer, who introduced second-order concepts in organization and management theory but confined himself to teamwork with small groups only. A rather unfortunate strategy was pursued by Kelly, who tried to form a movement in the UK even though he lived in the US, where not even he taught his theory in his own classes in clinical psychology. As a result, he was never recognized by the American Psychological Association (Vincent Kenny, personal communication). Müller concluded that due to its weak network back then (which was in stark contrast to its strong theoretical output), RC failed to become mainstream in cognitive science, artificial intelligence or complexity science. Clearly, this had a major impact on the further development of the movement. Not being part of the mainstream meant being excluded from the intellectual security offered in academic and other research institutions and networks. RC found itself in a situation where it "has not been involved in any serious activities in mainstream journals or in debates with mainstream groups" (Müller, 2010, p. 37).

So another conclusion to be drawn from Gross's alteration of epistemological perspective is that for many authors, if not for an entire movement, the question is often whether to go with the mainstream of the scientific community and entertain the reader with popular topics or whether it pays to swim against the tide and cling to core principles. In the case of radical constructivism, one conviction on this is von Glasersfeld's claim that you either have to take the idea of reality construction seriously at all levels (hence the adjective "radical," meaning making no exceptions) or you "are still caught up in the traditional theory of knowledge" (Glasersfeld, 1991, p. 16) because you believe that at least a few of our ideas and theories "represent an independent, 'objective' reality" (Glasersfeld, 1991, p. 16). Considering only some of our theories "constructions" while others are "true representations of reality" means giving up RC altogether.

While the scientific community is certainly a major target for radical constructivism, there is a still bigger community, i.e., that of human society. RC (or any scientific or philosophical movement) must ask itself the question: What are the implications for society? Does it help to make society better? Can it create "killer apps" that attract the attention of the masses and of funding? Cariani (2010) names a few such targets within the reach of RC, including enhanced educational technologies and autonomous robots, as well as better psychological and social theories. Another important field could be that of knowledge management. It is the transformation from an information-based to a knowledge-based society that results in an increased need for knowledge discovery and knowledge management. In this context, RC replaces the concept of absolute and mind-independent information "out there" in favor of asking how knowledge comes about. It therefore provides a framework for alternative forms of knowledge management that excel traditional approaches that have proven insufficient as solution strategies for complex problems and the demands of a faster moving global economy, science, and culture. Such a radical constructivist knowledge society would be characterized by its ability and willingness to revise knowledge continuously rather than to cling to traditional habits.

THE FUTURE

As stated at the beginning, the future of radical constructivism should be considered for each of its three versions.

The future of von Glasersfeld's original radical constructivism is certainly assured in educational research (Tobin 2007). In addition, as von Glasersfeld always emphasized that his theory is a theory of rationality, the question arises of whether it can account for a wide spectrum of cognitive processes, including non-conscious and emotional aspects. Questions such as "Who does the reality constructing?" must be attended to in the light of recent insights in consciousness research, in particular Benjamin Libet's (1985) claim that what we call free will is but an illusion as all our deliberate decision-making is dictated by the non-consciousness. Given the nature of the limbic system, which not only works outside conscious control but in fact may be the ultimate authority for any conscious action, the relationship between cognition and emotion needs to be addressed in radical constructivism.

The future of the extended interdisciplinary version of radical constructivism has recently been boosted by attempts to rejuvenate the research program of the 1960s and 1970s. The main proponent is the group around Karl Müller on Second-Order Science (see also a forthcoming issue of *Constructivist Foundations*). The goal is to re-invent its "rich cognitive tradition for the emerging science landscapes of the 21st century" (Müller 2010, p. 37). Six steps are proposed including the accommodation and adaption of early years RC to fit the current research landscape; the promotion of RC in new areas such as situated cognition, computer-mediated learning environments, self-reflexive economic modeling or cognitive psychology; and a "small number of highly active research nodes within the radical constructivist network in its current application domains of media sciences, the social sciences, family therapy, architectural design or organizational learning" (Müller 2010, p. 37). Furthermore, mainstream publications must be dramatically increased and RC courses implemented. To have a future in the mainstream, RC must also define open problems and conflicting views, which would make it possible to enter into a scientific debate with mainstream groups.

The future of the third, pluralistic version of radical constructivism is linked with the question of plurality in science. It was Karl Popper who introduced falsificationism in philosophy of science, claiming that in science, testing alternative theories must be possible at any moment. This leads to a methodological pluralism of theories (Popper, 1970). However, according to Popper, pluralism as a method does not imply pluralism as a goal because for the non-constructivist Popper, there is only one truth that can be the superior goal of science. For him, it all boiled down to searching for an all-encompassing theory that explains as many empirical phenomena as possible based on as few theoretical assumptions as possible. Clearly, this cannot be the goal of RC for there is no place for an absolute observer-independent conception of truth. In other words, RC subscribes to Popper's ideal of theory pluralism (and as this paper has shown, there are plenty of radical constructivist approaches to choose from) without buying Popper's ontological monism. However, as pointed out above, the large number of constructivist approaches and the partial incompatibility that comes with this fragmentation could easily lead to a heterogeneous radical constructivist landscape in which scholars lack mutual support and understanding from peers. So, plurality in RC *without* defining it as a paradigm, which unifies theoretical, methodological, empirical, and programmatic aspects, would certainly lead to disagreement and incompatibility among the participating constructivist approaches.[10] Characterizing RC as a mere problem-solving tool would eventually weaken the movement.[11]

CONCLUSION

In order to have a future, radical constructivism must go beyond the problems of philosophical acceptance (cf. Gadenne, 2010), i.e., it must overcome the aversion towards it due to deeply-rooted intuitive convictions. Armin Scholl (2010, p. 54) aptly pointed out that discussions such as whether or not RC denies reality reduces RC "to epistemological questions only and ignores the self-referential logic of second-order cybernetics." Rather, it must aim at replenishing its followers and practitioners by showing its usefulness in various disciplinary contexts and in specific empirical research questions. Educational science is a good case in point as it has developed practical concepts from a constructivist perspective. It is the daily puzzle-solving of normal science that is convincing. While it cannot and must not replace the big epistemological

---

[10] Here, RC clearly parts from postmodernist movements, which like to deconstruct all paradigms because coherent theories are considered as totalizing.

[11] A case in point is Kelly. Most of the published research related to Kelly's PCP was done using his methodology (repertory grid technique), but lacked reference to the theory itself. So separating tools from theoretical principles does nothing to help the model to evolve (Vincent Kenny, personal communication).

debates' painstaking and detailed work in daily research, it is necessary to show that these debates are not an end in themselves. In the case of radical constructivism, these efforts must continue to address traditional areas such as communication science, life sciences, learning environments, organizational studies, media science, social science, family therapy, architectural design, and organizational learning (Müller, 2010). However, new empirical territories need to be added as well:

- Quantum mechanics, where RC provides an alternative to realist-based interpretations of QM that includes Bayesian, Neo-Kantian, phenomenological, anti-realist information theoretical, and quantum cognition approaches showing that quantum structures do not just apply to a mind-independent physical world. A special issue of *Constructivist Foundations* on "Constructivist Interpretations of Quantum Mechanics" is in preparation.
- Cognitive science (Riegler, 2007), artificial intelligence and autonomous robotics (Ziemke, 2001), and computational theory in general, where RC can assess the philosophical and conceptual significance of the computational approach, e.g., whether it is possible to formulate computational models of constructivist processes, and whether computational models can ever create something new. In particular, the specific question of whether computer models are useful heuristics for stimulating an individual's construction of reality needs to be explored. Actual computational models of constructivist concepts and processes and results from conducting experiments with them will significantly contribute to detailing the empirical component of the radical constructivist paradigm—see also the special issue in *Constructivist Foundations* on "Computational Constructivism" (Riegler & Ziemke, 2013).

In all these disciplines, traditional and new, it is important to find exemplars and make predictive promises against which the usefulness of radical constructivism can be measured. Together with the theoretical cores described at the beginning of this article and its reflexive, observer-including methodology, RC will constitute a large paradigm that is ready to conquer current and future problems.

So on the one hand, radical constructivism must demonstrate its usefulness as a "power tool." The goal must be to find wide acceptance in academia (in particular by accounting for counter-intuitive aspects of RC in terms of intuitive premises), which in turn will help to find greater acceptance with more followers who can work on empirical ways to prove its usefulness. However, on the other hand, radical constructivism must also define itself as a *pluralistic paradigm* in order to create a stable, self-sustaining network of researchers and institutions that allows new genera-tions of constructivists to develop and research constructivist concepts and experiments without being exposed to peer pressure to water down their radical constructivist position.

REFERENCES

Cariani P. (2010). Onwards and upwards, radical constructivism. A guest commentary. *Constructivist Foundations, 6*(1), 127–132. Retrieved from http://www.univie.ac.at/constructivism/journal/6/1/127.cariani

Dykstra, D., Jr. (2005). Against realist instruction. *Constructivist Foundations, 1*(1), 49–60. Retrieved from http://www.univie.ac.at/constructivism/journal/1/1/049.dykstra

Gadenne, V. (2010). Why radical constructivism has not become a paradigm. *Constructivist Foundations, 6*(1), 77–83. Retrieved from http://www.univie.ac.at/constructivism/journal/6/1/077.gadenne

Glasersfeld, E. von. (1974). Piaget and the radical constructivist epistemology. In C. D. Smock & E. von Glasersfeld E. (Eds.), *Epistemology and education* (pp. 1–24). Athens, GA: Follow Through Publications. Retrieved from http://www.vonglasersfeld.com/034

Glasersfeld, E. von. (1983). Learning as constructive activity. In J. C. Bergeron & N. Herscovics (Eds.), *Proceedings of the 5th annual meeting of the North American group of psychology in mathematics education, Volume 1* (pp. 41–101). Montreal, Canada: PME-NA. Retrieved from http://www.vongla-sersfeld.com/083

Glasersfeld, E. von. (1991). Knowing without metaphysics: Aspects of the radical constructivist position. In F. Steier (Ed.), *Research and reflexivity. Inquiries into social construction* (pp. 12–29). London: Sage Publications. Retrieved from http://www.vonglasersfeld.com/132

Glasersfeld, E. von. (1995). *Radical constructivism: A way of knowing and learning.* London, England: Falmer Press.

Gross, A. G. (1990). *The rhetoric of science.* Cambridge, MA: Harvard University Press.

Gross, A. G. (2013). Some limits of non-dualism. *Constructivist Foundations, 8*(2), 242–246. Retrieved from http://www.univie.ac.at/constructivism/journal/8/2/242.gross

Kenny V. (2010). Exile on mainstream. Constructivism in psychotherapy and suggestions from a Kellian perspective. *Constructivist Foundations, 6*(1), 65–76. Retrieved from http://www.univie.ac.at/constructivism/journal/6/1/065.kenny

Libet, B. (1985). Unconscious cerebral initiative and the role of conscious will in voluntary action. *Behavioral and Brain Sciences, 8,* 529–566.

Mach, E. (1900). *Prinzipien der Wärmelehre* [Principles of the theory of heat]. Leipzig, Germany: Barth.

Müller, A., & Müller, K. H. (Eds.). (2007). *An unfinished revolution? Heinz von Foerster and the Biological Computer Laboratory BCL 1958–1976.* Vienna, Austria: Edition Echoraum.

Müller, K. H. (2010). The radical constructivist movement and its network formations. *Constructivist Foundations, 6*(1), 31–39. Retrieved from http://www.univie.ac.at/constructivism/journal/6/1/031.mueller

Quale, A. (2008). *Radical constructivism: A relativist epistemic approach to science education.* Rotterdam, The Netherlands: Sense.

Quale, A., & Riegler A. (Eds.). (2010). Can radical constructivism become a mainstream endeavor? *Constructivist Foundations, 6*(1). Retrieved from http://www.univie.ac.at/constructivism/journal/6/1

Popper, K. R. (1970). Normal science and its dangers. In I. Lakatos I. & A. Musgrave A. (Eds.), *Criticism and the growth of knowledge* (pp. 51–58). Cambridge, England: Cambridge University Press.

Riegler, A. (2001). Towards a radical constructivist understanding of science. *Foundations of Science, 6*(1–3): 1–30. Retrieved from http://www.univie.ac.at/constructivism/riegler/20

Riegler, A. (2005). Editorial. The constructivist challenge. *Constructivist Foundations, 1*(1), 1–8. Retrieved from http://www.univie.ac.at/constructivism/journal/1/1/001.riegler

Riegler, A. (2007). The radical constructivist dynamics of cognition. In B. Wallace, (Ed.), *The mind, the body and the world: Psychology after cognitivism?* (pp. 91–115). London, England: Imprint.

Riegler, A., & Scholl A. (2012). Luhmann's relation to and relevance for constructivist approaches. *Constructivist Foundations, 8*(2). Retrieved from http://www.univie.ac.at/constructivism/journal/8/2

Riegler, A., & Ziemke, T. (Eds.) (2013). Computational approaches to constructivism. *Constructivist Foundations, 9*(1). Retrieved from http://www.univie.ac.at/constructivism/journal/9/1

Schmidt, S. J. (Ed.). (1987). *Der dskurs des radikalen konstruktivismus.* Frankfurt on the Main, Germany: Suhrkamp.

Schmidt, S. J. (1993). Zur Ideengeschichte des Radikalen Konstruktivismus. In E. Florey & O. Breidbach (Eds.), *Das Gehirn—Organ der Seele? Zur Ideengeschichte der Neurobiologie* (pp. 327–349). Berlin, Germany: Akademie-Verlag.

Scholl, A. (2010). Radical constructivism in communication science. *Constructivist Foundations, 6*(1), 51–57. Retrieved from http://www.univie.ac.at/constructivism/journal/6/1/051.scholl

Schurz, G. (1998). Koexistenzweisen rivalisierender Paradigmen. Eine begriffserklärende und problemtypologisierende Studie. In G. Schurz & P. Weingartner (Eds.), *Koexistenzweisen rivalisierender Paradigmen. Ein post-Kuhnsche Bestandsaufnahme der Struktur gegenwärtiger Wissenschaft* (pp. 1–52). Wiesbaden, Germany: Wissenschaft, Westdeutscher Verlag.

Tobin, K. (2007). The revolution that was constructivism. In M. Larochelle (Ed.), *Key works in radical constructivism: Ernst von Glasersfeld* (pp. 291–297). Rotterdam, The Netherlands: Sense.

Ziemke, T. (2001). The construction of "reality" in the robot: Constructivist perspectives on situated AI and adaptive robotics. *Foundations of Science, 6*(1), 163–233.

PART II

SOCIAL CONSTRUCTIONISM AND NARRATIVE PSYCHOLOGY

❧ 4 ☙

On Being a Social Constructionist in a More Than Human World

Tom Strong

> *Human and nonhuman agents are associated with one another in networks, and evolve together within those networks.*
>
> (Pickering, 1995, p. 11)

Constructivists increasingly acknowledge a social dimension to how humans construct understandings that help them anticipate and navigate physical and social reality. Social constructionists (part of the constructivist family in this author's view) regard such constructing to also involve negotiating meanings with others. In other words, in relationships humans tend to interact using taken for granted meanings or those they work out and share as acceptably familiar. Taken for granted meanings beg constructive alternatives when they stop working, for both constructivists and constructionists. This contribution adds to a constructivist and social constructionist view by considering how interwoven human meaning has become with aspects of a more than human world. Humans, through their responses to emerging developments within more than human environments, can be seen to co-construct (i.e., through interacting with these developments) meanings and realities in a "posthuman" world.

DECENTERING HUMAN MEANINGS IN A MORE THAN HUMAN WORLD

A centuries' old human conceit has been catching up with us. It took Enlightenment science to help us recognize that the earth was not central in the cosmos. Embedded in Enlightenment science was a conviction that humans could scientifically attain God's omniscience and engineer experience as they wished (Dolnick, 2012). Obscured or perhaps advanced by that conviction was the assumption that we could use basic human constructions—language, for example—to acquire this omniscience. By the mid twentieth century, insights from contextually and linguistically oriented philosophers like Heidegger (1962) and Wittgenstein (1953) were pointing to how human realities were construed and constructed by and through our use of language. In these early years of the twenty-first century, a further humbling insight has become increasingly clear: any human constructing of meaning tends to draw on and play out in our social relationships. However, our constructing efforts now occur in ways and with consequences some deem "posthuman" (e.g., Hekman, 2010). By "posthuman" I refer to a growing literature that aims to decenter humans as actors and meaning-makers, while making evident how humans need to be responsive to emergent features in their environments. Ours is a dynamically changing world that shapes us as much as we shape it, and our constructions not only help us to adapt to this world; they shape that world, in ways to which we need to be constructively responsive.

To write of socially constructed understanding as I have in the past (Lock & Strong, 2010) is to leave the conceit mentioned above unchallenged. It also privileges a view of humans and reality that now seems inadequate to me. So, when Jon Raskin, invited me to contribute to *Studies in Meaning 5* on advances in social constructionist thought and practice, I was in flux with posthuman ideas beyond those which had informed my hybrid (phenomenology, hermeneutics, and communicative interaction) version of social constructionism (Strong, 2014a). These posthuman ideas implicate humans in what Karen Barad (2007) refers to as a "material-discursive" reality and point to how human interactions with features of a more than human world extend constructivist and social constructionist thinking. The conceptual convergence draws from Andrew Pickering's historical studies of "mangles" in science (1995, 2009) and Bruno Latour's (e.g., 2005) actor network theory or what has alternatively come to be known as science and technology studies. It also draws from feminist thinkers concerned with how people reflexively engage with and are affected by material reality, becoming *interactionally* interwoven with it (Barad, 2003, 2007; Hekman, 2010; Manning, 2013). As an example, our interactions with technology, as well as with social and physical reality, are not just constructive, they are reciprocally transformative—we shape and are shaped by these interactions. Finally, and from related ideas, the convergence I highlight draws on practice theory (Nicolini, 2013; Schatzki, 2002, 2010), which contextualizes familiar human understandings and experiences in recurring interactions between human and non-human "actors." Our interactions with each other and with the material world, for practice and posthuman theorists, construct what we experience as recognizably real when these interactions stabilize. Social constructionists are used to what Ken Gergen (2009) has referred to "relational being", a pithy phrase emphasizing that our constructs come from and play out in our relationships. By supplementing this view of social constructionism with posthuman and practice theory ideas I invite consideration of a further dimension to constructivist or constructionist thinking and practice.

The notion of non-human "actors" can be most jarring for readers new to the "posthuman" convergence I will elaborate. Our alternative constructs (for social constructionists, typically forms of language like words or stories) offer ways to enhance our effectiveness in social and physical reality. "Change the name and you change the game" (Efran & Heffner, 1991, p. 50) went a therapeutic version of this notion. But consider how interwoven our lives have become with technology or developments possibly pertaining to the fate of our planet. Inside such "interweaves" are realities we shape and are shaped by, making it increasingly difficult to separate humans from their influential constructions and the material realities into which they are interwoven. Consider our lives without prescription glasses, electricity, laptops, or a 24-hour clock—all transformative constructions that shape human lives and potentials. Considering how such human constructions come to shape our lives can be challenging if one is committed to a view that individual human actors can act and know in fully independent ways. Yet, yes, we can retain aspects of our independence by giving such constructions up.

Where my social constructionist approach intersects with the posthuman views I have been relating is around two challenging notions central to George Kelly's (1963) modern theorizing: anticipation and "constructive alternativism." For Kelly and constructivists after him, what matters are constructions of reality that enable us to effectively anticipate how our understandings and the actions premised on them will play out. In the physical world our anticipations more easily stabilize and become predictable than they do in the social world, though we tend to navigate both spheres of life based on how we sense our understandings and actions will be "received" in either world. Social reality, however, tends to be as much navigated as it is negotiated. People don't just learn to anticipate each other, they negotiate how they will go forward together, based on how they interpret and respond to each other's meaning. This view was at the heart of Bakhtin's (1981) dialogic view that life emerges out of people's responsive and influential interactions with each other. By contrast, monologic relationships are those we can only navigate or seemingly command. By the social constructionist views I am sharing (Gergen, 2009; Lock & Strong, 2010), negotiated or dialogic ways of relating involve more than anticipating how we may be received, they require a critical and generative responsiveness to what *cannot* be anticipated in our interactions with physical and social reality.

Increasingly humans are transforming physical and social reality with their technology, and the effects of population growth. We need to learn to become effectively responsive to (i.e., negotiate with) physical and social realities we are playing a role in transforming, otherwise we are back to the kinds of relations with those realities that Bakhtin referred to as monological. Global warming has made the nearby glaciers that provide my city's (Calgary) water supply a source of concern. This is but one example of how we want our constructs to help us anticipate and address social and physical realities that have become, in effect, moving targets. Whether anticipating familiar circumstances, or constructively responding to unanticipated circumstances, how we construct reality and use our constructions matters. Why "posthuman" ideas may potentially interest constructivists relates to their interests in how human beings not only make sense of their experience, but in how such sense-making helps in constructing, navigating, and negotiating experience.

Herein, I bring together constructivist and social constructionist ideas, along with insights from posthuman and practice theorists, to account for realities that humans responsively negotiate as much as they construct. I situate humans in a dynamic world that as much makes them, as they make it. I focus on negotiated meanings and actions as these develop in and from consequential human interactions with other humans, and with aspects of the more than human world. The more than human (i.e., posthuman) world is the physical, biological and technological world humans interact and become interwoven with. My clinical concern relates to the unintended and unwanted consequences of these interactions, what I will refer to as "capture", and the human-human / human-material world practices that can stabilize us in, or extricate us from, being captured.

CONSTRUCTED MEANING?

"Ours is an *anticipatory* system rather than a *reactive* system," asserted George Kelly (1963, p. 170). Kelly suggests a view of constructed meaning that I share, to a point. We are challenged when our meanings come up short for us, so we learn to find new effective meanings to help us anticipate what reactively catches us off guard. Heidegger (1962) suggested that we are "thrown into" a human world already engaged in meaningful yet largely taken for granted interactions—a world in which we learn to go from reacting to responding in ways Kelly describes as anticipatory. This is neither a world in which we act from fully independent personal meaning systems (as if a discrete system could exist apart from people we could share it with), nor is it a world we could ever fully anticipate with already developed meanings, whether borrowed from others, or from personal constructs alone. Instead it is a world where we pit our best constructions against the challenges life poses, challenging interactions within our social lives included. Sometimes we need to find new meanings or constructions (Kelly's constructive alternativism) when our best constructions need to better help us anticipate experience stop being effective. However, it is in explicating how and where people find these better, or more effective, meanings or constructions that I turn to social constructionist theory (Gergen, 2009; Lock & Strong, 2010).

When most people consider social constructionism they tend to do so in constructivist and cognitive ways that see human understandings as stand-ins for reality. Meaningful constructions or understandings, by this view, are equivalent to maps or schemas of experience, to be evaluated like scientific theories for how well they help humans anticipate experience. Both constructivists and social constructionists forego any sense that constructs, schemas, words, stories, theories, and so on could ever fully and correctly represent experience. Instead human constructions or forms of meaning offer linguistic or symbolic ways we prosthetically (cf.,

Shotter, 1993) navigate a reality we can never fully or correctly know. Constructivists, following Kelly (1963), tend to point to these meaningful prostheses as personally constructed, while social constructionists portray these constructs as social or cultural in origin. For both constructivists and social constructionists, what matters is that we use meanings or constructs that are effective for us, that help us anticipate and navigate the social and physical circumstances in which we find ourselves.

For many social constructionists (e.g., Burr, 2003), when meaning is discussed, linguistic resources (e.g., words or stories) or discourses and how these are used in human interaction, are the focus. Cultural or institutional discourses carve up realms of experience in much the way that Kelly referred to earlier as "anticipatory systems." Each distinctive discourse requires an "insider's" logic or sense of talking and acting in ways appropriate to others sharing the discourse or system of meaning (Paré, 2012). So, for example, speaking of Jung's collective unconscious among a group of rational-emotive therapists might get you a raised eyebrow or an outright dismissal, but those responding to such a notion as "irrational" would be well received. Users of discourse develop and act from particular understandings and actions they deem meaningful, while demarcating and negatively responding to meanings and actions incompatible with the discourse. It is in the latter sense that we can discursively be "out of bounds" or "inappropriate" with the discourse of others. Psychologists often relate such differences to individual attributes, like personality variables or schemas, whereas constructionists identify cultural discourses and discursive interactions (e.g., Edwards & Potter, 1992) when locating such differences in meaning. Discourses, however systematized, are partial meaning systems reflective of human values and circumstances. Kelly's (1963) related notion, that we develop anticipatory systems of meaning, points to a similar inevitability: our meanings for new experiences are bound to be incomplete, and require revising when they fail to help us anticipate and navigate experience.

People are neither determined by discourses (as "cultural dopes" in Garfinkel's, 1967, terms) nor are they unresponsive, like autistic libertarians, to their relational circumstances. They have physical and social worlds to navigate as well as *negotiate*, using the meanings and meaningful behaviors acquired through social and cultural interactions. Much of the navigating occurs in taken-for-granted ways; a blessing provided that things stay acceptably familiar, but a challenge when taken for granted meanings and actions come up short in addressing new challenges, or in getting beyond circumstances that are unacceptably familiar (Strong, 2014b). The kinds of challenges I refer to cannot always be anticipated in either the sense Kelly (1963) has referred to, or with existing discourses. Sometimes new realities need new languages or discourses (or negotiate our use of these with others), according with what Vico (2005/1744) referred to as "poetic wisdom" in facing "linguistic poverty." The other side of poetic wisdom comes when we become constrained in our uses of language, or by other constructions like computers, being on large shared power grids, and driving cars in rush hour traffic.

Constructivists may consider or refer to constructs beyond those which are cognitive. I have become increasingly interested in constructs that posthumanists refer to as material features of a more than human world (Barad, 2003, 2007; Hekman, 2010; Pickering, 1995; Pickering & Guzik, 2009; Sloterdijk, 2013). For example, the Internet influences us, much as we influence its technological developments. Pickering (1995; Pickering & Guzik, 2009) has chronicled what he has referred to as "mangles of practice", circumstances where human actions encounter unexpected forms of natural, institutional, or technical resistance, to which humans find themselves responding in ways that see them depart from their initial actions. Humans, who find themselves in mangles, often need to constructively respond to unintended and unanticipated consequences arising from prior constructive responses.

In relationships of all kinds we face challenges with how our constructs are, or are not, taken up in interactions with others.

Constructivists tend to focus on the cognitive constructs of individuals, and less so on how such individuals coordinate use or reference to their constructs with each other. Our meanings and constructs do not function like shared cartoon character thought bubbles; yet despite considerable differences with other individuals, institutions, and cultures, we negotiate ways to understand and go forward together. Technology added to our abilities to coordinate meanings and lives with others, while creating unanticipated consequences which also now feature in how we negotiate and coordinate our lives. And, this is not just about meaning, it is about meaningful and hopefully agreeable interactions and coordinations of interactions. How our meanings and actions are negotiated, and become part of these bigger coordinations has me curious.

Each human construction may be an intended response to an actual or desired circumstance, but how such a construction plays out in interactions with other humans, nature, or cultural institutions—seems beyond intention. Inventors of the cellphone could likely not have predicted its use for "sexting", for example. Pickering's mangles show how unintended consequences set up new circumstances calling for new, unanticipated responses. The purportedly foolproof algorithms that guided decision-making in financial institutions "too big to fail" encountered unanticipated lending circumstances and crashed (Steiner, 2012), leaving almost everyone with "constructed" realities of major consequence. Such interweaving of human constructs, meaning, action, and our interactive engagement with technology, nature and cultural institutions constructs what others mean by a posthuman world.

By now, it is hopefully clear that the kind of constructionism I am describing refers to more than individuals living by optimal linguistic constructions to anticipate their experience. Navigating and negotiating emerging social, physical, technological and institutional realities occurs in ways people find understandably challenging to disengage from and alternatively navigate and negotiate. Being engaged in navigating and negotiating these realities occurs in ways that have stakes for us, and for others similarly engaged. Sure, we bring our constructed meanings and actions to navigating these realities; but it is the negotiated part of these engagements that in my view goes underemphasized in most constructivist writing.

NEGOTIATING CHANGING REALITIES AND CAPTURES WITH OUR CONSTRUCTIONS?

Negotiating reality sounds odd when contrasted with a more common constructivist view that our job is to anticipate and navigate reality (i.e., as it is) with our best constructions. Reality portrayed as a negotiator seems to anthropomorphize it into having human-like agency (making it, too, a "negotiator"). The term feminist quantum theorist Karen Barad (2003, 2007) has been using is "agential realism", to denote how humans shape and are shaped by their interactions with features of reality. In social reality, we see this all the time as we negotiate our interactions with others. In the immediacies of our relationships, we do transformational things like commit to each other, create what was not possible for one of us alone, and so on. And, political action, taken up culturally and institutionally, can, over time bring about incremental trans- formation, as has been shown in gains made by feminists and civil rights activists. However, the material world has also been changing us, as we change it. For example, how might we better navigate and negotiate technology and Internet-enabled social lives now that our every interaction there can be hacked or be under government surveillance? Our human constructions too often morph, through unanticipated interactions with different "agents", into unintended consequences to which we must constructively respond.

To talk of human constructions, when these play out in ways beyond intended meaning or action is to privilege humans as actors in a more than human world. Our meanings and discourses offer us means to participate in social and cultural interactions, but our meanings and discourses do not determine the outcomes of those interactions. To navigate and negotiate social, physical, technological and institutional realities we face challenges not only in terms of how our meanings and actions fare for us; we also need to resourcefully respond to responses to our meanings and actions that we could not intend or anticipate. We also need to find ways of recognizing and escaping forms of "capture" that result from the mangles to which we contribute.

This notion of "capture" (cf., Massumi, 2011) in webs or mangles to which we humans contribute merits consideration in constructivist practice. The Y2K scare (when many thought that the world's computer programs were improperly calculated without reference to a changing millennium) offered an example of how our linguistic and technological constructs almost captured us—in that case by a calendar and clock, wired into global technology that had not been calibrated for a millennial change. One can point to similar webs or mangles that, while perhaps not fully capturing us, add stress or deficits to our lives: rush hour road rage, depleted fish stocks, or online hacking. These are complex and changing human constructions (or consequences of them) to consider so let's start where constructivist and constructionist practitioners share a focus: on changes to meaning, or Kelly's "constructive alternativism." The shared view is that humans cannot perceive and respond to the world as it is since such perceptions are constructed out of human experience and then are used to help us navigate our world. Our best constructions are those which work so well that we can take their use for granted, though this is precisely where Deleuze (2013) was concerned that our constructions go from being testable propositions to becoming presumed assertions about how things actually are. This is precisely where problems and shortcomings with our constructions can arise, and for several reasons:

1. Our use of the construct/symbol/story (proposition), etc. stops working for us.
2. There may be alternative constructions accessible that can work better for us.

3. We learn we can respond to a circumstance with a number of constructs where formerly we thought only one could work for us (exemplified by either/or binary thinking).

These will seem like fitting ways to consider how we deal with relatively static physical and social realities where our existing constructions are not serving us as well as we need them to. Wittgenstein (1953), saw this as a case of needing to come up with our most perspicuous representations (i.e., constructs, language) for experience—a view consistent with Vico's (2005/1744) "poetic wisdom." Testing out our constructive alternatives in somewhat static physical reality is a different proposition, however, than seeing how they fare in our relationships with each other, or within our developing, technologically-shaped circumstances. We do more than adjust to such realities or circumstances, with the aid of our alternative constructs; we are in dynamic and emerging relationships with these realities and circumstances. Through using our constructs to guide us in these relationships, we often shape what shapes us, though this typically happens in almost imperceptible ways.

In coming to the view of social constructionist practice I previously wrote about (e.g., Lock & Strong, 2010; Strong, 2014a), I became interested in the approaches to meaning and social interaction taken up by ethnomethodologists (e.g., Garfinkel, 1967; Heritage, 1984) and social practice theorists (e.g., Nicolini, 2013; Schatzki, 2002, 2010). The interactional view these theorists take up focus on how people stabilize their interactions with each other, and with their physical/technological circumstances, so as to keep meanings and interactions familiar. John Shotter (personal communication, March 30, 2011) refers to these as "dynamic stabilities", ways we interact so as to create orderly and familiar relationships with social and physical reality. Being able to put a name or meaning so as to make an experience recognizable is only one aspect of constructing dynamic stabilities; our return to such names or meanings with each subsequent encounter with what seems recognizable is another aspect. For Deleuze (1994), this can be where we use our concepts or constructs to impose similarity on experiences that are not exactly the same as those we originally constructed. While we can talk about graduation as a commonly shared construct, invariably aspects of my experience of graduation will not index the same experiences you may have constructed from your experience of graduation. Deleuze was concerned with how our repeated use of such constructs reduced to similarities later developments featuring unique experiences where our prior constructs "capture" them in old, already experienced, meanings.

This detour through Deleuze and practice theorists is important for recognizing the limitations of our constructions. We often straddle a tension between finding constructive ways to keep things familiar, while not over-committing to our constructions in ways that might later capture us or cause problems. Our use of language in physical and social reality is but one example of this tension. Language offers sense-making resources, as "handles" for our experience. When our use of language is shared, it enables us to collectively navigate common experiences and act upon common aims. Constitutions, business agreements, laws, and mission statements are examples of what humans can accomplish by finding shared language to go forward together. However, these social constructions often are negotiated into existence in ways that involve limits to be worked out between the negotiators. How people later interpret and interact based on these common constructions is another matter as politics and interpersonal disagreements highlight.

Constructive uses of language are ways individuals and larger social groups respond to circumstance. Technological innovations are also constructive responses to actual or desired circumstances. How such innovations may get taken up, with intended or unintended consequences, increasingly features in the circumstances humans find themselves constructively responding to. Thus, people find themselves responding to issues with their internet service providers, problems with the new app on their smartphones, and how to use their car's GPS to find a shortcut to a friend's home.

Such innovations—Google glass or high-powered microscopes, for example—are increasingly becoming interwoven with our constructive ways of sense-making. The same can be said for how we construct innovations that might later "capture" us.

Responding to the inadequacies of our language or constructs is a different proposition than escaping from captures akin to Pickering's "mangles." Mangles are those circumstances where meanings and interactions come together, then stabilize, in unintended and recurring ways. Disagreements are one such circumstance where not only can there be a failure to coordinate intended meanings and actions; a new and unintended form of recurring social interaction can emerge between parties over the course of their disagreeing. In other words, the issue moves on to how disagreements over such meanings and actions become performed between people. Such mangles are familiar to systemic or relational therapists who focus on recurring patterns of interaction. In Gregory Bateson's (1980) language, "the pattern's the thing." The constructed meanings and interactions inside these patterns—whether with other people or in our interactions with technology—are our next consideration.

Constructively Modifying Worldviews and Maps?

By a Kantian view of constructivism, our constructs systematize (à la Kelly's anticipatory system) into a relatively stable worldview from which we engage with reality (social and physical reality), though the map needs careful and selective updating. Accordingly, constructive alternativism is needed when constructs within such a worldview need updating or revising. Posthuman and practice theorists (e.g., Hekman, 2010; Pickering, 1995; Pickering & Guzik, 2009; Schatzki, 2002, 2010) view understanding and action in less global and more situated or "local" ways than do most Kantian constructivists. For posthuman and practice theorists, constructed actions and understandings become "bundled up" (Schatzki, 2002) in situated nodes of recurring or patterned interactions between humans, or between humans and responsive aspects of material reality (e.g., humans responding to traffic lights). Inside these nodes particular realities engage humans in particular ways, in under-standings and forms of reason particular to what occurs inside such situated realities. For constructivists, this kind of therapeutic and pedagogical challenge is familiar—but for a more dynamic world than the norm: finding our best constructions to respon-sively adapt to these changing realities that we reflexively shape, and that shape us.

Reflexive is a word that can confuse, particularly given centuries of Cartesian thought and practice that emphasizes a separation between knower and what can be purportedly known. Reflexivity (e.g., Finlay & Gough, 2003) is a term emphasizing how our constructs feature in not only shaping our understandings of reality, but in altering what we try to understand. Objective, "correct" knowledge is the idealized version of what can be known, as knowledge apparently separate from us. Constructivists, since Kelly, embrace a more pragmatic view of knowledge that highlights such things as the fit and effectiveness of our constructions of what we aim to know, or anticipate. While being clear that there are no ways to ultimately evaluate the TRUTH of our constructions, constructivists tend to treat reality as given and separate from our constructions of it. What has primarily mattered to constructivists and social constructionists have been effective constructs for nego-tiating or making our way about reality. Posthuman and practice theorists go a step further, focusing on how realities are reflexively shaped by us, and shaping of us.

Language or mathematics offer two humanly constructed ways we not only represent realities, but enable means by which we alter realities as well. Temperature, a human construction that developed over years of scientific innovation (Chang, 2004)—when adapted to our thermostats, furnaces, and air conditioners—enables a taken-for-grated degree of comfort indoors unavailable to our predecessors. The energy requirements to enable such comfort have reflexively brought other challenges to which we must respond. As much of the workforce adapts to more sedentary activities than was the case in our grandparents' work lives, the bodies of many contemporary workers have become more sizably proportioned, accompanied by related health concerns. With the internet came a new way to conduct the "oldest profession" and with that new means came new kinds of crime requiring new methods of investigation (Kolker, 2013). My point with these examples is to highlight how our technological constructions reflexively shape new realities we must find new ways to constructively respond to. Years ago, in chronicling developments of this kind of emerging "postmodern" era, Walter Truett Anderson (1992) titled a book *Reality Isn't What it Used Uo Be*. The modern view of reality had been that it was ultimately knowable and thus could be placed under human technological control. As reflexive as humans might be in shaping postmodern realities they live by, such realities will not fully submit to human control. Instead, the realities we have been shaping seem to spawn new circumstantial challenges to respond to, with some developing into clinical concerns.

SITUATED AND INSIDER CONSTRUCTIONS?

Somewhat unique to my training as a social constructionist practitioner was an immersion in ethnomethodology (EM; Garfinkel, 1967; Heritage, 1984). One focus of interest in EM is on how situated social (i.e., insider) realities are produced and sustained through members' anticipated interactions; via the kinds of dynamic stabilities described earlier. Such anticipated interactions, in the later writings of Wittgenstein (e.g., 1953) acquire a normative and grammatical (i.e., rule-like) status within broader social interactions he referred to as "language games." The language game of doing greetings in one's extended family is typically different from the language of doing greetings in unfamiliar professional circles, as are the normative grammars which shape one's sense of appropriate action within either language game. Dreyfus (1990), drawing from Heidegger, approaches this sense of doing what is appropriate in established social orders from a different angle. Specifically, his interest was with how such anticipated or expected social behaviors of this kind become tacitly performed, in expected yet taken for granted ways. Practice theorists, such as Schatzki (2002, 2010), take this view of human interaction a step further, embedding human interactions with nonhuman "actors" (technology, features of physical reality) into "practices" that simultaneously engage our thinking, acting, and feeling. Where the ideas above converge is on the arbitrariness of human interactions that come to be anticipated and taken-for-granted. Our lives become organized around how we and the human/nonhuman world interact in situated ways. Family therapy researcher, Ole Dreier (2008), pointed out such situated practices in families outside of therapy.

The arbitrariness of humans interacting and understanding in anticipated and situated ways (cf., Forster, 2005) that can "capture" us, yet are still open to constructive alternatives, is familiar to constructivist practitioners. The stretch for some readers may relate to the dynamic ways such interacting and understanding play out in the responses of the people and nonhuman actors—responses begging possible new forms of understanding and responsiveness from us. Such dynamism, new realities to respond to as we shape them and they shape us, seems akin to the kind of postmodern "hyperrealism" described by Baudrillard (1995). In the last generation, most humans have accepted more technology into their lives, and have altered their physical environments in life-changing ways than has ever been the case. The effects have not been benign and we have done more than just adapt to these changes; our adaptations constructively modify the changing features we thought we were adapting to, changing us in the process. Except when we fail to recognize the need for constructive alternatives and find ourselves captured, not just by our understandings, but the ways of interacting conjoined with them.

For years, John Shotter has been asking readers to look inside our "conversational realities" (1984, 1993), for the particular meanings and ways of interacting we come to share with others. Cultural and institutional discourses offer examples of these socially constructed "realities" because inside them one finds understandings and actions particular to those sharing them. These are larger patterns of interaction than what I had wanted to make my focus here. For theorists like Karen Barad, Susan Hekman, and Andrew Pickering, when we find ourselves interactionally responsive to aspects of material reality, our interactions with those aspects can shape us as much as we shape them. While we might have and use what we think are our individual constructs in our interactions with aspects of physical, technological, and social reality; inside these responsive interactions, new enabling or constraining "realities" emerge particular to those interactions.

Dynamic stabilities develop in and from human interactions with other humans or responsive nonhuman elements, such as technology, or aspects of material reality that respond to our actions in initially unanticipated ways (J. Shotter, personal communication, March 30, 2011). For example, we develop relational habits through how we become predictably responsive to human and nonhuman "agents". Dogs and their owners work such things out in their walks together; over what things dog and owner negotiate as worth sniffing, where and when the dog will pee, and so on. Similarly, we might develop predictable routines around starting up the office computer, or dealing with e-mail. In developing and recurring interactional routines our lives become interwoven with how relevant features of our social and material world respond to us, and how we respond to their responses—in often complex dynamic stabilities. While it is true that humans have exerted considerable dominance over the material world, it is also true that they have had to do so relationally—in ways over which they did not have full dominion (Tuan, 2004).

Posthuman theorists assert that interactions like those described above with aspects of the material world can come to exert a form of agency in human lives. While intent cannot be ascribed to nonhuman "actors", we need to be mindful, to paraphrase Bruno Latour (2005) of how the objects of our interactions with the material and technological world "object" to our interactions. These latter "objections" often seemingly (and agentively) compel responses to unanticipated developments: try being a single character off in entering a computer password, for example. Different kinds of technological agency can also affect us: a Blackberry becomes a "crackberry" to its user, new intimacy problems develop associated with internet romance, and concerns emerge about surveillance into aspects of our formerly private lives. What clinically interests me about these new (posthuman) kinds of problems is less about how they develop (there are always new developments in life to constructively navigate or negotiate) and more about how they stabilize through recurring, responsive, interactions between humans and aspects of their material/technological world.

Looking beyond the individual client and her or his perceptions of these concerns, to larger interactions in which these concerns play out, and sometimes stabilize, offers a different unit of analysis from which to make sense of clinical concerns. Thus, couple and family therapists are interested in problematic patterns of social interaction inside which individual concerns and upsets develop and stabilize in ways that are in effect interactionally anchored. This sense of socially anchored behavior (conversational reality) is often initially counter-intuitive to individually-focused therapists who may separate a parent's nagging about a child's behavior from the child's reaction to the nagging (i.e., focus on the individual constructions, losing sight of how these develop inside what occurs between parent and child). The systemic or relationally focused therapist sees such behaviors as interactionally anchored; the problem requires the patterned ways of interacting (Strong, 2014b). On a more technological front, how else might we explain cursing at our computer screen after accidentally losing or deleting something important? Posthuman clinical thinking offers another assessment and intervention dimension enabling consideration of how "individual" behaviors can become not only interwoven within problematic patterns of responses with other humans; but how problems can stabilize in interactions involving aspects of the material and technological worlds with which clients responsively interact. For therapists, posthuman ideas can add another dimension to their clinical conceptualization and intervention skills. This added dimension is not unlike that which many therapists experience when they expand their considerations of client concerns to include systemic interactions in which these concerns are often embedded.

A CLINICAL EXAMPLE

In my practice as a family therapist I recently consulted in a circumstance in which a 14-year-old daughter of devout Muslim parents had been caught "sexting" (sending naked pictures of herself by cellphone to an older boy). In response, the parents had taken away the daughter's cellphone and discontinued her Internet use then relations broke down between parents and the daughter. The girl was distraught since cell phone use was a key aspect of her social life, as had been her Internet communications. Her parents were shocked, ashamed, and disgusted by their daughter's behavior, and had little sense of the online and cell phone-enabled social life that so engaged a girl they were struggling to accept was becoming a teenager. "Sexting", like online bullying, is a concern that one might associate with forms of pre-internet behavior, but to respond to it as if it was like a pre-internet version (flashing?) would likely fail to address what is different about such a behavior as it was conducted in a very different context and era. The parents' reaction was understandable, while for the daughter, her parents' reaction was tantamount to being banished or jailed, and so she rebelled further.

In the therapy which followed, some improvements to family relations came with better communications and contrition on the daughter's part, and this is as much as I know about any therapeutic outcomes. However, the presenting concern flagged for me how interwoven our human concerns and conflicts can become with aspects of a more-than-human world. No one inventing the cell phone or the camera embedded in the cell phone could likely have predicted "sexting", or perhaps even the degree to which the daughter's social life could become so interwoven with the use of cell phone and internet technology. Sure enough, the daughter and parents were presented with challenges for constructive alternatives that would better serve their relations. The sexting incident had opened up just how different the realities had been living by were from those which were central to their daughter. In reflecting back on this family, I hope that, as jarring as the parents' experience might have been, they may have come to better understand the daughter's technologically-enabled social life and how it had come to so matter to her. Similarly, I would hope that the girl could have been open to learning more from her parents about their distress and the bases for it. When they were initially in therapy their relations had been the casualty—as much from the incident, as from their hurt responses to each other thereafter.

LOOKING INTO A POSTHUMAN FUTURE

Social constructionist thinking (e.g., Gergen, 2009) ushered in new practices that focused on how humans, through their interactions, could construct preferred outcomes. Many constructionists adopted Lyotard's (1984) postmodern credo that it was time to abandon the quest for metanarratives (ultimate truth of any kind) while correspondingly feeling that too great an emphasis had been placed on particular therapeutic methods or models (e.g., Hoffman, 1998). Solution-focused, narrative, and collaborative approaches were premised on social constructionist ideas regarding language and how it is used in human interactions and sense-making matter, but these therapeutic models are now a generation old. The initial excitement associated with solution-focused talk, more preferred stories, and not-knowing dialogue highlighted potentials that might come from therapeutic changes to language and how it was used in preferred ways to navigate social and materials worlds.

Perhaps the greatest innovation associated with the social constructionist therapeutic approaches was the view that therapy itself could be socially constructive (McNamee & Gergen, 1992). Specifically, for social constructionist therapists, therapeutic dialogue is portrayed as intentionally reflexive in dialogic ways focused on negotiating preferred linguistic realities clients can take forward in their lives. In my own writing, I have referred to such therapies as "discursive" for reflexively incorporating the insights of discourse theorists and analysts (e.g., Lock & Strong, 2012; Strong & Pyle, 2009; Strong & Paré, 2004). Incorporating discursive insights occurs through how therapists use questions and their ways of responding to invite further questions about unpreferred discourse (its use is often uncritically taken for granted) while talking more preferred realities into significance and action. Discursive, in this sense, refers to talk as a means to both represent and reflexively intervene into experience, to escape discursive capture and live by preferred or accepted meanings. There is a related notion from early social constructionists, Berger and Luckmann (1967) that I have also found helpful: talk is our primary means of *sustaining* realities, to stabilize such realities through the practices we use to anticipate them. This relates to Anderson and Goolishian's (1988) view that problems organize people in particular forms of conversing and interacting. Similarly, solution-focused therapists differentiate solution-focused conversations from problem-focused conversations (deShazer, 1994). How constructionist therapists join clients necessitates different conversations from those which stabilize clients' understandings and actions in accustomed ways.

These latter points about the organization of talk—about how people interact around problem realities –relate to concerns I have been raising about how nonhuman "actors" (Barad, 2007) feature in client concerns that might have become interwoven with techno-logical and other aspects of material reality. There are many ways humans can be captured by their constructions. Discursive capture (Massumi, 2011) can develop and stabilize according to ways in which language or how we become accustomed to using it come up short for us, constraining other, more effective or helpful, linguistic constructions. One day's constructive solution can become a later day's form of capture. We come to interact partly based on how we anticipate the material (including the technological) world will respond to our interacting with it. Sometimes unintended consequences arise from how we organize such interactions. NASA needed a different way of organizing its institutional interactions after one of its space shuttles exploded after takeoff (i.e., it wasn't just a technological issue). Sometimes our clients need more than a constructive alternative given how any constructive alternative might be responded to in social or material world interactions where clients make use of it.

If this view I have been relating seems plausible a different unit of clinically relevant assessment emerges: not constructs alone, but the interactive practices which engage clients in using the constructs central to clinical concerns they present. What are the component and anticipated interactional features which responsively anchor these concerns and their related constructs? Seen as patterned interactions, by what sequence and grammatical "rules" give the concern's interacting components their dynamic stability? How can clients negotiate new forms of responsiveness to enable changes to practices they previously felt captured by? The units of analysis involved are clearly relational and interactive in their scope and inclusivity, with clients being but one of the actors. This is why negotiating new forms of responsiveness, as opposed to simply navigating one's way forward anew with alternative constructs, is proposed. Clients tell us these sorts of things: if I did "X", "Y" will likely happen; the "Y" typically being a response from someone or something else relevant to the perpetuation of the concerning practice as is. Introducing a new X, in the face of possible Y's clients anticipate (we cannot anticipate or evaluate these for clients) can guide a negotiated process of constructive alternativism, a search for a viable or testable X. More negotia-tions of this kind may be required until a more client-preferred and stable practices can evolve from such negotiations (therapist-client, client/other relevant "actors").

I long ago worked with 11-year old who had developed obsessive fears about germs, and so he washed his hands incessantly, to the point of skin damage. He had learned of this apparent need to be excessively cleanly from experts on television. His parents had done the normal reassuring things to indicate that the boy's hand washing was adequate to kill the germs, but that only galvanized the boy's conviction that the parent didn't understand the severity of these germs. In the course of my negotiating with the family, we worked out a compromise, that sure enough the parents were insufficiently expert on germs, but that there was a toxicologist the family could consult, given the toxicologist's expertise, acknowl-edged by parents and son. The toxicologist consultations occurred twice and then the former interactional pattern ran its therapeutic course. The initial clinical concern developed in response to a science show on TV, got ensnared in a more than human mangle of involving technologically enabled concerns about germs, parents and son. This required a negotiated process of meaning and action, involving a scientist beyond our therapy, who helped new family interactions to emerge.

CONCLUSION

I have offered an update of a social constructionist approach to constructivist practice based on the notion that humans reflex-ively interact with (or respond to) each other, and with aspects of their material environment. Humans engage with material reality in constructive as well as limiting ways, of course. However, when such engagements become of clinical concern, their responsive and emerging circumstances may call for a different kind of constructive alternativism than one targeting somewhat stable circumstances. Typically, the focus in constructivist clinical practice (Neimeyer,

2009) has been on identifying and applying constructive alternatives that enable clients to better navigate their circumstances or
concerns. In social and posthuman circumstances we reflexively
shape and that shape us so more may be required than how we
might alternatively navigate our changing circumstances. We may
need metaphors (Lakoff & Johnson, 1980) to help us consider how
alternative constructed meanings and actions help us reflexively
negotiate (i.e., influence and alter, but not in ways we can unilat-
erally control) these changing circumstances. Negotiating with
the other "actors" in our circumstances requires different relationships from those which follow from seeing ourselves navigate such
actors/circumstances with constructive alternatives that are ours
alone. The relationships conducive to negotiating constructive
alternatives in a more than human world suggest a new kind of
meaningful and responsive frontier.

References

Anderson, H., & Goolishian, H. (1988). Human systems as linguistic systems. *Family Process, 27,* 371–393.

Anderson, W. T. (1992). *Reality isn't what it used to be.* New York, NY: Harperone.

Bakhtin, M. M. (1981). *The dialogic imagination. Four essays.* (M. Holquist, Ed.; C. Emerson & M Holquist, Trans.). Austin, TX: University of Texas Press.

Barad, K. (2003). Posthumanist performativity: Toward an understanding of how matter comes to matter. *Signs: Journal of Women in Culture and Society, 28,* 801–831.

Barad, K. (2007). *Meeting the universe halfway: Quantum physics and the entanglement of matter and meaning.* Durham, NC: Duke University Press.

Bateson, G. (1980). *Mind and nature: a necessary unity.* New York, NY: Bantam New Age.

Baudrillard, J. (1995). *Simulacra and simulation* (S. Glaser, Trans.). Ann Arbor, MI: University of Michigan Press.

Berger, P., & Luckmann, T. (1967). *The social construction of reality: A treatise on the sociology of knowledge.* New York, NY: Anchor Press/Doubleday.

Burr, V. (2003). *Social constructionism* (2nd ed.). London, England: Routledge.

Chang, H. (2004). *Inventing temperature: Measurement and scientific progress.* New York, NY: Oxford.

Deleuze, G. (1994). *Difference and repetition* (P. Patton, Trans.). New York, NY: Columbia University Press.

Deleuze, G. (2013). *Foucault* (S. Hand, Trans.). London, England: Bloomsbury Academic.

deShazer, S. (1994). *Words were originally magic.* New York, NY: Norton.

Dolnick, E. (2012). *The clockwork universe: Isaac Newton, the Royal Society, and the Birth of the Modern World.* New York, NY: Harper Perennial.

Dreyfus, H. (1990). *Being-in-the-world: A commentary on Heidegger's Being and Time, Division I.* Cambridge, MA: MIT Press.

Dreier, O. (2008). *Psychotherapy in everyday life.* New York, NY: Cambridge University Press.

Edwards, D., & Potter, J. (1992). *Discursive psychology.* London, England: Sage.

Efran, J., & Heffner, K. P. (1991). Change the name and you change the game. *Journal of Strategic and Systemic Therapies, 10*(1), 50–65.

Finlay, L., & Gough, B. (Eds.). (2003). *Reflexivity: A practical guide for researchers in health and social sciences.* Oxford, England: Blackwell Publishing.

Forster, M. N. (2005). *Wittgenstein on the arbitrariness of grammar.* Princeton, NJ: Princeton University Press.

Garfinkel, H. (1967). *Studies in ethnomethodology.* New York, NY: Prentice Hall.

Gergen, K. (2009). *Relational being: Beyond self and community.* New York, NY: Oxford.

Heidegger, M. (1962). *Being and Time* (J. MacQuarrie & E. Robinson, Trans.). Oxford, England: Blackwell.

Hekman, S. (2010). *The material of knowledge: Feminist disclosures.* Bloomington, IN: Indiana University Press.

Heritage, J. (1984). *Garfinkel and ethnomethodology.* Cambridge, England: Polity.

Hoffman, L. (1998). Setting aside the model in family therapy. *Journal of Marital and Family Therapy, 24,* 157–163.

Kelly, G. A. (1963). *A theory of personality: The psychology of personal constructs.* New York, NY: W.W. Norton.

Kolker, R. (2013). *Lost girls: An unsolved American mystery.* New York, NY: Harper Collins.

Lakoff, G., & Johnson, M. (1980). *Metaphors we live by.* Chicago, IL: University of Chicago Press.

Latour, B. (2005). *Reassembling the social: An introduction to actor-network theory.* New York, NY: Oxford University Press.

Lock, A. J., & Strong, T. (2010). *Social constructionism: Sources and stirrings in theory and practice.* New York, NY: Cambridge University Press.

Lock, A., & Strong, T. (Eds.) (2012). *Discursive perspectives on therapeutic practice.* New York, NY: Oxford University Press.

Lyotard, J-F. (1984). *The postmodern condition: A report on knowledge* (G. Bennington & B Massumi, Trans.). Minneapolis, MN: University of Minnesota Press.

Manning, E. (2013). *Always more than one: Individuations's dance.* Durham, NC: Duke University Press.

Massumi, B. (2011). *Semblance and event: Activist philosophy and the occurrent arts.* Cambridge, MA: MIT Press.

McNamee, S., & Gergen, K. (Eds.) (1992). *Therapy as social construction.* Newbury Park, CA: Sage.

Neimeyer, R. (2009). *Constructivist psychotherapy: Distinctive features.* New York, NY: Routledge.

Nicolini, D. (2013). *Practice theory, work, and organization: An introduction.* New York, NY: Oxford University Press.

Paré, D. (2012). *The practice of collaborative counseling and psychotherapy: Developing skills in culturally mindful helping.* Los Angeles, CA: Sage.

Pickering, A. (1995). *The mangle of practice: Time, agency, and science.* Chicago, IL: University of Chicago Press.

Pickering, A., & Guzik, K. (Eds.) (2009). *The mangle in practice: Science, society, and becoming.* Durham, NC: Duke University Press.

Schatzki, T. (2002). *The site of the social: A philosophical account of the constitution of social life and change.* Pittsburgh, PA: University of Pennsylvania Press.

Schatzki, T. (2010). *The timespace of human activity: On performance, society, and history as indeterminate teleological events.* Lanham, MD: Rowman & Littlefield.

Shotter, J. (1984). *Social accountability and selfhood.* New York, NY: Cambridge University Press.

Shotter, J. (1993). *Conversational realities.* London, England: Sage.

Sloterdijk, P. (2013). *You must change your life* (W. Hoban, Trans.). Cambridge, England: Polity.

Steiner, C. (2012). *Automate this: How algorithms came to rule our world.* London, England: Penguin.

Strong, T. (2014a). Conceptually downstream: Revisiting old tributaries of thought for "new" constructivist ideas. *Journal of Constructivist Psychology, 27*(2), 77–89.

Strong, T. (2014b). Conceptualizing interactional patterns: Theoretical threads to facilitate recognizing and responding to IPs. In K. Tomm, D. Wulff, S. St. George, & T. Strong (Eds.). *Patterns of interpersonal interactions: Inviting relational understandings for therapeutic change* (pp. 36–56). New York, NY: Routledge.

Strong, T., & Paré, D. (Eds.) (2004). *Furthering talk: Advances in the discursive therapies.* New York, NY: Kluwer/Academic Press.

Strong, T., & Pyle, N. R. (2009). Constructing a conversational 'miracle': Examining the 'miracle question' as it is used in therapeutic dialogue. *Journal of Constructivist Psychology, 22,* 328–353.

Tuan, Y-F. (2004). *Dominance and affection: The making of pets.* New Haven, CT: Yale University Press.

Vico, G. (2005). *New science* (3rd ed.). London, England: Penguin. (Original work published 1744).

Wittgenstein, L. (1953) *Philosophical investigations* (G.E.M. Anscombe, Trans.). New York, NY: MacMillan.

ೞ 5 ೞ

Paradoxes of the Constructed: Narrative Psychology and Beyond

Mark Freeman

When Jerome Bruner agreed to write a blurb for the back cover of my first book, *Rewriting the Self: History, Memory, Narrative* (1993), I was truly thrilled. "A thoughtful and learned book," he wrote, which "deals sensitively with the postmodern problem of how we 'make' the self by construing our lived experience, though constrained by circumstances and history. May it be a harbinger of a new constructivist psychology, freed of positive dogmas and closer to the humanities." Pretty good, except for the fact that a good portion of the book represented an attempt to think beyond the very constructivism being posited. The fact is, I wanted it both ways then, and I still do now. That is, I want to avow (what I would call) the hermeneutical dimension of self-fashioning while moving beyond a full-blown constructivism—if, by constructivism, we are referring in broad terms to the primacy of the *made* over the *found*. That we are always already in the world—including the world of the self—before we come to construe it is surely true. There is no view from nowhere, certainly not when it comes to interpreting and narrating the self. Indeed, there is no view from nowhere when interpreting any "text," any meaningful ensemble of words or actions. When it comes to the text or quasi-text of the self (see Freeman, 1985; Gergen, 1988; Ricoeur, 1981a), this situation is that much more pronounced, for strictly speaking, there *is* no text. Put differently, the very text we seek to interpret is one that, in a very real sense, *we ourselves have constructed.* And this "we" refers not only to the supposedly sovereign "I," doing its solitary work, but to the eminently social we-world in which we live. So, we are talking here about a construction of a construction that's constructed on the basis of the collaborative and coordinative work that we all undertake as social beings, living out our lives with one another, in culture and history. Why, then, try to think beyond constructivism? What can it possibly mean?

The issue is paradoxical, indeed—on many levels, in fact. Following Ricoeur especially, I recognize and avow the "unsurpassability" of the hermeneutical situation. For some, stating this is tantamount to positing the unsurpassability of constructivism as well. If, by "hermeneutics," we are underscoring the constructive dimension of interpretation, whether of self or other, then this near-equivalency is justifiable. Along these lines, some speak of "hermeneutic constructivism" (see Raskin, 2002), the assumption being that interpretation, as an act of *poiesis,* meaning-making, entails rejecting the notion of an "observer-independent reality": "Hermeneutic constructivists do not believe in the existence of an observer-independent reality," Raskin (2002, p. 4) has stated, "They consider knowledge a product of the linguistic activity of a community of observers. Thus, there can be as many knowledge systems as there are groups discursively negotiating them." On Raskin's account, Gergen's social constructionism (e.g., Gergen, 1992) is a variant of this basic position. This may be so. But I don't know whether to call the position a *hermeneutic* one. (I don't think Gadamer, Heidegger, or Ricoeur, arguably the leading proponents of hermeneutic thought, would want to consider themselves "constructivists.") In most forms of constructivism—including those that are more explicitly social in orientation (like Gergen's)—the emphasis remains on the subject side of the subject/object divide. It can remain so subtly and sensitively, mind you; there are surely constructivists who wish to move well beyond subject/object thinking, electing instead to speak in dialogical or relational terms

(Gergen, 2009). But the very notion of construction, especially in its more "severe" forms, remains inescapably tied to the priority of the meaning-giving, value-creating subject, which in turn can serve to diminish the very "otherness" of the world—including that dimension of otherness that is encountered in the project of self-understanding.

Questions abound. Do I construct my own life narrative? Do I construct my "self"? Do I construct my *life*? What about the world, both human and non-human? Do I construct them? The answer is clear: yes and no. With this seemingly paradoxical answer at hand, let me take the opportunity to offer three additional paradoxes tied to narrative understanding, each of which I have considered in earlier work but none of which I have explicated to my own (or, in all likelihood, my readers' own) satisfaction. The first concerns the aforementioned idea of *poiesis*, especially as it relates to poetic creation. "As a general rule," I have suggested,

> the poet is in the business neither of finding meanings, already there in the world, nor of making them, in the sense of fashioning them wholly anew. Rather, the poet is engaged in a process in which meaning is at once found and made—or, to be more explicit still, *meaning is found through being made*. (Freeman, 2010, p. 181)

In considering the meaning-making aspect of narrative *poiesis*, I continued, "the intent is to highlight the constructive, imaginative dimension of the process of articulating and understanding the world, both inner and outer" (p. 181). This dimension is indeed unsurpassable. "But this very dimension," I hastened to add, "is ultimately in the service of disclosing—'unconcealing,' as Heidegger (1971a) might put it, the reality of the past" (Freeman, 2010, p. 181). This perspective may sound untenable to some already. Can one really speak of "the reality of the past"? I have a ready answer to this question too: yes and no. I shall be saying why shortly. For now, I simply wish to offer a thesis (of sorts) that highlights the paradox at hand:

Only through the creative labor of the poet does there exist the possibility of disclosing what is there, in the world. And only through
the creative labor of the narrative imagination does there exist the
possibility of disclosing the meaning and significance of times past.
(Freeman, 2010, p. 181)

The second paradox brings us more fully into the territory of
narrative understanding in particular and historical understanding
more generally. Seen from one angle—and it is a quite prominent
one in the narrative world—narratives cannot help but distort and
even falsify the past. Because self-narratives always issue from
some present perspective, and because this perspective is inevitably
"tainted" with one's interests, wishes, and desires, there is (this
story goes) no getting around this distortive aspect of the process.
(Consider in this context the volume edited by Daniel Schacter
[2005] titled *Memory Distortion: How Minds, Brains, and Societies
Reconstruct the Past*.) Narratives do indeed have to be *constructed*
in some way, told or written; appearances notwithstanding, they
don't tell themselves. I've always loved the way Michael Gazzaniga
puts the matter in his (1998) book *The Mind's Past*: "Autobiography
is hopelessly inventive" (p. 2). How interesting to couple inven-
tiveness with hopelessness! Now it is true, of course, that there
are no "untainted" narratives, and it can also be argued that there
is an irrevocably fictive aspect to the narrative process. "Sure, life
is a fiction," Gazzaniga adds, "but it's our fiction and it feels good
and we are in charge of it" (p. 172). Putting aside the fact that not
everyone feels so good about their particular fictions and that they
may feel quite controlled by them, Gazzaniga is surely on to something here (see also, for instance, Paul John Eakin's [1988] much
more nuanced rendering of these issues in his book *Fictions in
Autobiography: Studies in the Art of Self-Invention*): the process of
narrative understanding, particularly in its autobiographical form,
entails a markedly fictive aspect, thereby appearing to mitigate
the possibility of ever discerning the truth of one's life. But again,
appearances can be deceiving, for it is also the case, I argue, that
narrative understanding, in and through its very fictive nature, is the

requisite condition for discerning the truth of one's life (e.g., Freeman, 1997a, 2002, 2003a, 2012). This perspective is likely to be deemed problematic by some as well, especially those who adhere to what I earlier called a more "severe" brand of constructivism. Can one really speak of "the truth of one's life"? "*the*"? "*truth*"? My answer is unlikely to surprise you: yes and no. I shall say more about this shortly too. For the time being I simply wish to leave you with the possibility that narrative understanding "can be a source not only of error but of insight" and that there may be "a deeper, more capacious way of thinking about truth" (Freeman 2010, p. 182) than the standard view offers.

The third paradox takes these ideas one step farther. Indeed, on some level, it takes us in another direction altogether. In view of what has been said thus far, focused as it has been on the process of narrative understanding, the main reference has been to the self. This stands to reason: narratives issue from individual persons; they are irrevocably *ours*, and there is no story quite like my own. This doesn't mean that these narratives are purely individual products; as Bruner (e.g., 1990) and others have pointed out, they are social and cultural through and through. As Bruner writes, "It is man's participation in culture and the realization of his mental powers *through* culture that make it impossible to construct a human psychology on the basis of the individual alone" (p. 12). When it comes to narrative, this fact becomes even more visible, for the very genres we employ, indeed the very languages we speak, in telling the stories of our lives are given to us by culture and history. Even if the story of my life is mine, it is emphatically not mine alone but is instead part of the tradition in which I live (e.g., Gadamer, 1982; Shils, 1981). As MacIntyre (1981) puts the matter,

> The story of my life is always embedded in those communities from which I derive my identity. . . . What I am, therefore, is a key part of what I inherit, a specific past that is present to some degree in my present. I find myself part of a history and that is generally to say, whether I like it or not, whether I recognize it or not, one of the bearers of a tradition. (pp. 205–206)

So it is that my story moves beyond me, into the very fabric of culture and history.

But there is another way, too, in which my story moves beyond me. For even though "I" may on some very basic level be deemed the source of my story, I am not the only one. On the contrary, to say that my story is "my own" or that it issues from me says nothing whatsoever about its *ultimate* sources—"about the driving forces that propel it forward, giving it meaning and substance" (Freeman, 2014, p. 2). "These forces," I argue, "cannot, and do not, derive from the self but instead derive from the Other" (Freeman, 2010, p. 215; see also Freeman 2007, 2013; also, especially, Levinas, e.g., 1985, 1999). By "Other," I refer not only to other people but also to those non-human others—for instance, nature, art, God—that draw us at once beyond ourselves and to ourselves (Freeman, 2014, p. 3): "Indeed, it might plausibly be said that while the *proximal* source of personal narrative is the self, the *distal* source is the Other." It might also be said—paradoxically (and cautiously)—that "the Other is the distal source of selfhood itself" (Freeman, 2010, p. 215). Even as I construct my life, therefore, I am myself constructed by what is beyond me. I think especially in this context of what Jean-Luc Marion (2008) has referred to as the "saturated phenomenon," the kind of phenomenon that "exceeds the categories and principles of understanding" (p. 34). It could be the birth of a child, or the death of a loved one, or any number of other experiences of the sort that arrest us and remind us of what is most real. "Far from being able to constitute this phenomenon," Marion (2008) writes, "the I experiences itself as constituted by it." This is "because it no longer has at its disposal any dominant point of view over the intuition that overwhelms it" (p. 44). And so, "The constituting subject is succeeded by the constituted witness. As a constituted witness," Marion (2008) adds, "the subject remains the worker of truth, but is no longer its producer" (p. 44).

None of what is being said in this last portion of these introductory comments should be taken to imply that the constructive dimension of narrative self-fashioning is illusory or insignificant.

It's not. But as should already be clear through some of the ideas we have considered thus far, I have come to find myself increasingly interested in moving beyond constructionist thinking—or at least those forms of it that serve to diminish what I earlier referred to as the otherness of the world. In fact, paradoxical though it may seem, given the nature of my own work in narrative psychology over the course of the past three decades or so, I find myself increasingly interested in moving beyond thinking about the *self*, as source, origin, psychological centerpiece. This isn't only, or even mainly, because of the much-discussed problems of narcissism, individualism, and so on; it's because I have become more and more convinced that the Other comes first, as the primary source of "inspiration," we might say, and as the primary source of our ethical and moral energies. More on this in due time.

THE UNSURPASSABILITY OF CONSTRUCTIVE *POIESIS*

Now that I have begun radically to question certain aspects of the constructivist position, broadly conceived, I want to return to the very important task of upholding it, that is, providing some reasons for why it is in fact "unsurpassable." Earlier on, you will recall, I briefly discussed the poet and the process of *poiesis*. I did this mainly to introduce the first paradox, which had to do with the notion that "meaning is found through being made." Let us look more closely at this (seemingly) paradoxical state of affairs and see whether we can gain some ground in thinking about both the possibilities and the limits of constructivism.

I said before that Heidegger, well known as a spokesperson for hermeneutics, would more than likely not be comfortable being labeled a constructivist. Why? If in fact "language is the house of Being," as Heidegger (1947/1993; see also 1959/1971b) has put it, and language is something we use to build a world, why wouldn't he consider himself a constructivist? The reason is that in thinking Being comes to language. Language is the house of Being [because] in its home man dwells. Those who think and those who create are the guardians of this home. Their guardianship accomplishes the manifestation of Being insofar as they bring the manifestation to language and maintain it in language through their speech. (Heidegger, 1947/1993, p. 217)

As Heidegger adds shortly after, "man is not only a living creature who possesses language along with other capacities. Rather, language is the house of Being in which man ek-sists by dwelling, in that he belongs to the truth of Being, guarding it" (p. 237). Admittedly, it is no easy task to make sense of this proclamation of Heidegger's. At a most basic level, however, what I take it to mean is that we live and think within language, and that language is precisely what makes our existence a *human* one. In keeping with the constructivist position, there is neither world nor self without language. So far, so good. But what about Being?

Let us turn for a few moments to poetry to try to answer this difficult question. Poet and critic Yves Bonnefoy, on the occasion of presenting his inaugural address to the College de France (December, 1981), recollected his initial attraction with the "excess in words" highlighted in surrealist writing in a quite beautiful passage:

> What a call, as if from an unknown heaven, in these clusters of lawless tropes! What energy, it seemed, in this unpredictable bubbling up from the depths of language! But once the initial fascination was over, I took no joy in these words which I was told were free. I had before my eyes another kind of evidence, nourished by other poets, the evidence of running water, of a fire burning peacefully in our daily existence, and of time and chance of which these realities are made, and it seemed to me fairly soon that the transgressions of automatic writing were less the desired surreality, existing beyond the too superficial realisms of controlled thought whose signifieds remain fixed, than a reluctance to raise the question of the self, whose richest potentiality is perhaps in the life that one takes on day after day, without illusions, in the midst of what is simple. What are all the subtleties of language, after all, even turned upside down in a thousand different ways, next to the perception one can have, directly,

mysteriously, of the movement of the leaves against the sky, or of the noise fruit makes when it falls into the grass? And always throughout this whole time I kept in mind, as an encouragement and even as a proof, the moment when the young reader opens passionately a great book and finds words, of course, but also things and people, and the horizon, and the sky: in short, a whole world given all at once to his thirst. (Bonnefoy, 1989, p. 162)

Bonnefoy (1989, p. 162) is emphatically not talking about a world apart from language: "Words are there for him, of course; he can feel the vibrations of the signifiers which lead him toward other words in the labyrinths of the signifiers." At the same time,

he knows that there is a signified amongst them, a signified which depends on no one of them in particular and on all of them at once, which is intensity as such. The reader of poetry does not analyze— he pledges to the author, his brother, that he too will remain in intensity. And soon he closes up his book, anxious to go and live out the promise. He has rediscovered a hope. And this is what gives us the right to think that one should not give up hope in poetry. (1989, p. 162)

What is this hope about which Bonnefoy is speaking? On my reading, it is nothing less than to gain access to the world, to behold it for what it palpably is. With this idea, we come back to the poet, trying as best as he or she can, to find words that will somehow do justice to the world, let it open. What is curious, Bonnefoy (1989) goes on to say, is that "this world which cuts itself off from the world seems to the person who creates it not only more satisfying than the first but also more real" (p. 162). He also speaks of the "impression of a reality at last fully incarnate, which comes to us, paradoxically, through words which have turned away from incarnation" (p. 164) and of the opportunity "to bear witness to an existence beyond, to a being, to a plenitude they don't even know how to name" (p. 167). As Heidegger (1971a) puts it, "The work holds open the open of the world" (p. 45).

Words are needed to get there, to be sure. So is the imagination. Constructive *poiesis* is indeed unsurpassable—and not only

127

in poetry but in narrative as well. Earlier on, I suggested, with Heidegger's help, that this constructive dimension of narrative is ultimately in the service of disclosing, or "unconcealing," what I audaciously called "the reality of the past." I am not speaking here of that reality which we associate with the past-present—the fleshy reality of the former moment, would that we could return to it. Rather, I am talking about the reality of the past *qua* past. "This past," Merleau-Ponty (1962) notes, "exists only when a subjectivity is there to disrupt the plenitude of being in itself, to adumbrate a perspective" (p. 421). It was not "there" before, in other words; the past *qua* past comes into existence when there is a narrator of some sort, someone who steps out of the flow of momentary being and, looking backward, brings it to mind. In view of this, how, one might again ask, can one possibly speak of the reality of the past? The challenge is twofold. First, it is imperative to think of "reality" differently than it's often thought about. Oftentimes, it is associated with the fleshy immediacy of the present moment, the *now*. And if that's the case, narratives, less fleshy as they are compared to such moments, are bound to come off either as less real or as distortions, falsifications of the past "as it was." This is a mistake, and a crudely positivistic one at that. For while it is certainly the case that narratives can and sometimes do distort and falsify reality, they can also "unconceal" it, perhaps even in such a way that the resultant story may give one the conviction of having witnessed "a reality at last fully incarnate," as Bonnefoy had put it. Given that this so, it behooves us to think "reality" anew, in a more fully hermeneutical way, recognizing that the very condition of possibility for its disclosure is that sort of constructive *poiesis* we have been considering.

The second challenge is different. In fact, it is a challenge for which the language of construction seems impertinent. As Patricia Hampl (1999) has noted, "Intimacy with a piece of writing, as with a person, comes from paying attention to the revelations it is capable of giving, not by imposing my own notions and agenda, no matter how well intentioned they might be" (p. 28). Simone

Weil (1952/1997) says something similar of her encounter with the larger world: "When I am in any place, I disturb the silence of heaven and earth by my breathing and the beating of my heart" (p. 37). She therefore has a wish: "May I disappear in order that those things that I see may become perfect in their beauty from the very fact that they are no longer things I see" (p. 37). Weil's paradoxical aim: "To see a landscape as it is when I am not there" (p. 37). Needless to say, this is impossible; as we noted earlier, there is no view from nowhere. Nor is there a view from no one. Any and all views are always and inevitably partial, their meaning always and inevitably a function of what we bring to them. True enough. But this in no way obviates the profound challenge, voiced by Weil and others—poets, especially—to see the world for what it is and to find words to help others see the same. "At its best," Jay Parini (2008) has written, "poetry is a language adequate to our experience" (p. 9). So too is narrative, and it requires not only imagining and constructing but seeing and listening.

NARRATIVE RECONSTRUCTION AS THE CONDITION OF TRUTH

Thus far, I have considered the idea of narrative in only the broadest of terms. Now, it is time to home in further and identify its most distinctive characteristics. I shall begin by addressing some larger issues in historiography and the philosophy of history, drawing especially on the work of Hans-Georg Gadamer. In an essay titled "The Problem of Historical Consciousness," Gadamer (1963/1979, p. 145) sought to provide a "sketch of the foundations of a hermeneutic." First things first: "Historical knowledge cannot be described according to the model of an objectivist knowledge because it is itself a process with all the characteristics of an historical event. . . . Objectivism is an illusion" (p. 145). No surprises there. Shortly after, he goes on to describe the familiar hermeneutical circle, that is, "the circular relation between the whole and its parts: the anticipated meaning of a whole is understood through its parts, but it is in light of the whole that the parts take on their illuminating function" (p. 146). Nowhere is this more evident, I have noted (1997b), than in narrative understanding, where the relation between episodes and plot serves as an instantiation of the more general movement between part and whole emblematic of the hermeneutical circle.

As Heidegger (1927/1962, p. 153) has emphasized, the hermeneutic circle "is not to be reduced to the level of a vicious circle or even a circle which is merely tolerated." On the contrary, "In the circle is hidden a positive possibility of the most primordial kind of knowing" and

> we take hold of this possibility only when, in our interpretation, we have understood that our first, last, and constant task is never to allow our fore-having, fore-sight, and fore-conceptions to be presented to us by fancies and popular conceptions, but rather to make the scientific theme secure by working out these fore-structures in terms of the things themselves. (p. 153)

This is what makes Heidegger's hermeneutics a phenomenological hermeneutics—or, if it is preferred, a hermeneutic phenomenology: the "things themselves" remain central. But what exactly is meant by "scientific" in this statement? And how exactly is one to think about this idea of the things themselves?

Gadamer (1979), referring to Heidegger's passage, notes that "for the very first time the *positive ontological meaning* of the circle that understanding implies is explicitly affirmed," the main idea being that "every authentic interpretation must provide itself against the happenstance arbitration of baroque ideas and against the limitations caused by unconscious habits of thought" (pp. 148-149). He adds: "It is evident that in order to be authentic the inquiring gaze must be focused on the 'thing itself,' and in such manner that it be grasped, as it were, 'in person'" (p. 149). Consider the case of textual interpretation:

> As soon as he discovers some initially understandable elements, the interpreter sketches out the meaning of the whole text. But these first meaningful elements only come to the fore provided that he sets

about reading with a more or less definite interest. Understanding the "thing" which arises there, before him, is nothing less than elaborating a preliminary project which will be progressively corrected in the course of the interpretative reading. (p. 149)

The process is a challenging one, indeed: "One who follows this course always risks falling under the suggestion of his own rough drafts" (p. 149). In other words,

he runs the risk that the anticipations which he has prepared may not conform to what the thing is. Therefore, the constant task of understanding lies in the elaboration of projects that are authentic and more proportionate to its object. What we can term here as objectivity . . . cannot be anything other than the confirmation of an anticipation which results even in the very course of its elaboration. (pp. 149–150)

On the face of it, some of what Gadamer has to say may sound surprisingly objectifying, even objectivistic. He is aware of this:

But do not make me say what I have not in fact said; and I have not said that when we listen to someone or when we read we ought to forget about our own opinions or shield ourselves against forming an anticipatory idea about the content of the communication. In reality, to be open to "other people's opinions," to a text, and so forth, implies right off that they are *situated* in my system of opinions, or better, that I situate myself in relation to them. (p. 151)

Now, "it is of course true . . . that other people's opinions"—as well as texts and what I earlier referred to as the "quasi-texts" of people's lives—"can have 'in themselves' an indefinite manifold of different meanings . . . ;*in concreto*, however, when we listen to someone or read a text we discriminate, from our own standpoint, among the different possible meanings—namely, what we consider possible—and we reject the remainder which seem to us 'unquestionably absurd'" (p. 151). And so,

The authentic intention of understanding . . . is this: in reading a text, in wishing to understand it, what we always expect is that it will *inform* us of something. A consciousness formed by the authentic hermeneutical attitude will be receptive to the origins and entirely foreign features of that which comes to it from outside its own horizons. Yet this receptivity was not acquired with an objectivist "neutrality"; it is neither possible, necessary, nor desirable that we put ourselves within brackets. The hermeneutical attitude supposes only that we self-consciously designate our opinions and prejudices and qualify them as such, and in so doing strip them of their extreme character. In keeping to this attitude we grant the text the opportunity to appear as an authentically different being and to manifest its own truth, over and against our preconceived notions. (p. 152)

What a wonderfully clear rendition of the hermeneutical attitude. Is this constructivism? I would say no; it is not. And the reason it is not is because, in the end, the emphasis is not on the meaning-making process of the interpreter, but on the otherness of the text, its existence as an "authentically different being." As for why this otherness is important, it is because insofar as we can truly *listen* to what it has to say, we can become enlarged by it, both *dis*placed and *re*placed by its meaning.

Now that we have followed, via Gadamer, Heidegger's path of affirming the "positive ontological meaning" of the hermeneutical circle, it is but a short step to the more specific domain of historical understanding, as it relates to both life-historical narrative and historical narrative more generally. Gadamer (1979) touches on this very issue when he begins to consider the idea of "temporal distance." "Contrary to what we often imagine," he tells us, "time is not a chasm which we could bridge over in order to recover the past; in reality it is the ground which supports the arrival of the past and where the present takes its roots." Therefore, "'temporal distance,' is not a distance in the sense of a distance to be bridged or overcome. This was the naïve prejudice of historicism," which imagined "it could reach the solid terrain of historical objectivity by striving to place itself within the vantage point of a past age and think with the concepts and representations particular to that epoch" (pp. 155–156). No such return is possible. Nor is it possible in the context of my own history. For to return to the concepts and representations particular to my own previous historical epochs would require the wholesale effacement of my own interpretive position, indeed of *me*; and that, of course, is patently impossible. More to the point, however, is the fact that it is also undesirable. To return to the past—or, again, past-present—as it was would be to return to it in all of its openness and indeterminacy. And in order to move from this to a more comprehensive *understanding*, some measure of distance is involved. Along the lines being drawn, temporal distance is to be considered "a fundament of positive and productive possibilities for understanding" (Gadamer, 1979, p. 156).

Let me try to unpack this important idea; in my view, it is at the very heart of narrative understanding. In *Truth and Method*, Gadamer (1982) explores the challenge of interpreting works of art.

> Everyone knows that curious impotence of our judgment where the distance in time has not given us sure criteria. Thus the judgment of contemporary works of art is desperately uncertain for the scientific consciousness. Obviously we approach such creations with the prejudices we are not in control of, presuppositions that have too great an influence over us for us to know about them; these can give to contemporary creations an extra resonance that does not correspond to their true content and their true significance. Only when all their relations to the present time have faded away can their real nature appear, so that the understanding of what is said in them can claim to be authoritative and universal. (p. 265)

Whether one should speak in this context of what is "authoritative and universal" is questionable. In any case:

> It is this experience that has led to the idea in historical studies that objective knowledge can be arrived at only when there has been a certain historical distance. . . . what a thing has to say, its intrinsic content, first appears only after it is divorced from the fleeting circumstances of its actuality. (Gadamer, 1982, p. 265)

In this sense, temporal distance "lets the true meaning of the object emerge fully" (p. 265). Gadamer (1982) goes on to acknowledge that

> the discovery of the true meaning of a text or a work of art is never finished; it is in fact an infinite process. Not only are fresh sources of

error constantly excluded, so that the true meaning has filtered out of it all kinds of things that obscure it, but there emerge continually new sources of understanding, which reveal unsuspected elements of understanding. The temporal distance that performs the filtering process is not a closed dimension, but is itself undergoing constant movement and extension. And with the negative side of the filtering process brought about by temporal distance there is also the positive side, namely the value it has for understanding. It not only lets those prejudices that are of a particular and limited nature die away, but causes those that bring about genuine understanding to emerge clearly as such. (pp. 265–266)

Gadamer's main focus in conceptualizing temporal distance is the idea of (hermeneutical) prejudice. "It is only this temporal distance that can solve the really critical question of hermeneutics, namely of distinguishing the true prejudices, by which we understand, from the false ones by which we misunderstand. Hence the historically trained mind will also include historical consciousness" and "will make conscious the prejudices governing our own understanding, so that the text, as another's meaning, can be isolated and valued on its own" (p. 266). With this idea, we return once more to the importance of recognizing and indeed *respecting* the text's otherness.

Ricoeur takes this set of ideas a significant step farther by recognizing not only "the positive and productive function of distanciation at the heart of the historicity of human experience" (1981a, pp. 131–132), but the positive and productive function of narrative itself. As Ricoeur was to show in a variety of works throughout the 1980s and 1990s (e.g., 1981b, 1988, 1991), a further rationale for considering the productive dimension of narrative understanding concerns the idea that the meaning and significance of events and experiences frequently becomes transformed as a function of what comes after. There is thus a kind of dual temporality in narrative. Following the idea of history as a repository of what is irrevocably past, what comes before leads to what comes later. From this temporal perspective, then, we are following the well-known arrow of time, tracing the trajectory of events. This is the *episodic* dimension of narrative. It is also the case, however, that what comes later refigures the meaning and significance of what comes before—hence Ricoeur's reference to "the narrative we construct." This is the *configurational* dimensions of narrative, and it involves the poetic process by which the relevant episodes are synthesized into a whole. Taken together, these two dimensions, the episodic and the configurational, do well to illustrate the particularity of narrative understanding. The configurational dimension, especially, also does well to highlight what I earlier referred to as the fictive nature of narrative understanding. But in what sense might it be said—in what sense *should* it be said, if at all—that narrative understanding, in and through this fictive nature, is the requisite condition for discerning the truth of one's life?

"'Truth,'" Nietzsche (1888/1968) has suggested, is not to be regarded as simply "there," in the manner of a thing, but is instead "something that must be created and that gives a name to a process, or rather to a will to overcome that has in itself no end—introducing truth as a *processus in infinitum*, an active determining—not a becoming conscious of something that is in itself firm and determined" (p. 552). This is surely so of the kind of truth we find in narrative; it is a function of "active authorial work on the agent's part" (Flanagan, 1996, p. 66), and thus can never be circumscribed in the "firm and determined" way Nietzsche refers to. Moreover, and again, there is surely no definitive end to this process, no way to seal the truth of a life, shut it tight. And yet, it is clearly the case that, looking backward, we can sometimes discern what has gone on in a way we couldn't earlier on. We can correct our view of things, and in such correction, such reconstruction, we can move on to a better way, one that is more adequate to the life we have lived.

This is not a matter of "correspondence." Narrative is not about re-producing the past (i.e., the past-present)—as it was; it is about fashioning an interpretive context within which the events of our lives find a ready home. "What matters to us," Ian Hacking (1995) has written, "may not have been quite so definite as it now seems. When we remember what we did, or what other people did, we may also rethink, redescribe, and refeel the past. These redescriptions," Hacking continues, "may be perfectly true of the past. That is, they are truths that we now assert about the past. And yet, paradoxically, they may not have been true in the past" (p. 249). The idea of temporal distance is key in this context: by being "at a remove" from what has gone on, we may be in the position to see things more clearly. But that is not all, because, as we have just observed, what temporal distance also does, or at least can do, is allow us to see the events and experiences of the past as parts of some larger whole—that is, episodes in an evolving narrative. This seeing is constructive; it is an effort after meaning, an effort to integrate the tortuous march of events into some semblance of a pattern, an interconnected ensemble of meaning:

> Between the parts we see a connection which neither is, nor is intended to be the simple likeness of a life of so many years, but which, because understanding is involved, expresses what the individual knows about the continuity of his life. (Dilthey, 1910/1976)

The constructive dimension, again, is paramount. (The piece from which this quotation was extracted is titled "The construction of the historical world in the human studies.") But it is not to be mistaken for an "imposition" of meaning onto the past. As Ricoeur (1991) puts the matter,

> Our life, when then embraced in a single glance, appears to us as the field of a constructive activity, borrowed from narrative under-standing, by which we attempt to discover and not simply to impose from outside the narrative identity which constitutes us. I am stressing the expression "narrative identity" for what we call subjectivity is neither an incoherent series of events nor an immutable substanti-ality, impervious to evolution. This is precisely the sort of identity which narrative composition alone can create through its dynamism. (p. 32)

Well said—and, it would seem, a useful variant of the idea that meaning is found through being made. Actually, though, this may not be quite right: by continuing to use the language of the found and the made, I may be perpetuating one of those nasty binaries that many wish to move beyond. But now that I've done so, let me proceed with one more.

FROM THE PRIORITY OF THE SELF TO THE PRIORITY OF THE OTHER

As I have suggested in some recent (e.g., Freeman, 2012) work, there are at least three fundamental reasons for taking the "narrative turn" in psychology. The first of these is hermeneutic, and has to do with the opacity of consciousness and the consequent need to establish a "roundabout" method for gaining self-understanding. Following Ricoeur, who is himself following Freud in broad outline, we are mysteries to ourselves, unable to gain the self-understanding we seek through sovereign acts of self-reflection. "Reflection," Ricoeur (1970) writes, "must become interpretation because I cannot grasp the act of existing except in signs scattered in the world" (p. 46). And this interpretation must be retrospective in nature, a looking-backward, over the terrain of the past. So it is that psychoanalysis becomes a narrative psychology, which finds in the interpretation of life history a vitally important inroad into discerning the truth of one's life.

The second reason for taking the narrative turn picks up on this idea. As we have observed, what occurs in the moment is in flux. There is an event or experience, and it may have some meaning at the time of its occurrence, but this meaning has yet to be potentiated, drawn forward. Consequently, there is the need to await further events—which will in turn retroactively transfigure what has come before. In line with the Freudian view just discussed, it may be that there are things I can't see or won't see; I might therefore look back at what has gone on with a measure of humility or embarrassment or horror. How, I might ask, could I have said that or done that? What was I thinking? But this isn't the only reason for reconstructing the meaning of the personal past, for it is also frequently the case that as new events come along, the meaning and significance of earlier ones may change.

The third reason for taking the narrative turn is the one I want most to concentrate on in this section, and it has to do with what I have come to call "moral lateness" (e.g., Freeman, 2003b, 2010). And by this, I am referring to the fact that, in the moral realm especially, we human beings have a marked tendency to act first and think later. For the sake of making this idea a bit more concrete, let me take the opportunity to return to a case that illustrates the idea of moral lateness—as well as the idea of the priority of the Other—all too well. In a chapter entitled "Shame" from his book *The Drowned and the Saved* (1989), Primo Levi notes that there is a tendency to think of the moment of liberation from the concentration camps as one of relief, even joy. Unfortunately, however, he insists, this story is largely false. Far from there being relief, for many there was instead newfound suffering, for it would suddenly become clear that they had been living "at an animal level," their "days [having] been encumbered from dawn to dusk by hunger, fatigue, cold, and fear," such that "any space for reflection, reasoning, experiencing emotions was wiped out" (p. 75). What had also become clear, Levi adds, is that "We had not only forgotten our country and our culture, but also our family, our past, the future we had imagined for ourselves, because like animals, we were confined to the present moment" (p. 75).

Notice here that the issue of temporality and the issue of otherness are intimately intertwined: being confined to the present moment also meant being confined to the ego, hungry and exhausted. So too with the process of "liberation": being released from the present moment meant moving beyond the ego and reacquiring some cognizance of, and connection to, the Other. Narrative becomes a double-edged sword in this context. On the one hand, following Gadamer's notion of temporal distance, it presents a positive possibility, an opportunity to move beyond the animal-like confines of the present moment: with distance from the events he had lived through, Levi is able to see, all too clearly, the full measure of his own diminishment, and it was precisely this seeing, from afar, that had caused so much pain. There were numerous reasons for this tragic outcome. Foremost among them was the conviction that they hadn't done enough against the "system" at hand. Levi and his fellow camp inmates would occasionally witness the strength of resistors, some of whom were hanged publicly. "This is a thought that then barely grazed us," Levi writes, "but that returned 'afterward': you too could have, you certainly should have" (pp. 77–78). There could also be the shame of having failed their fellow prisoners and having lost any sense of community. "Few survivors feel guilty about having deliberately damaged, robbed, or beaten a companion," Levi notes. "By contrast, however, almost everybody feels guilty of having omitted to offer help" (p. 78). There were, of course, good reasons for their behaving the way they did at the time; they did what they could to survive. But this did little to ease their guilt and shame.

Narrative, so often portrayed as a source of solace, comfort, and positive self-regard, a balm to soothe the wounds of one's life, can generate wounds of its own. Looking backward, one can sometimes see certain features of the past for the very first time; and while the result can be great joy and gratitude, it can also be the deepest pain and regret. The tragic irony of Levi's situation is that in this very narrative seeing he had returned to his moral self, his human self. To see the moral depravity and animality of his own behavior, and to suffer from it as much as he did, is itself a sign of virtue, even a kind of transcendence. A fully human being, he recognized, surpasses the condition of animality. One notable way of doing so is precisely though narrative—that is, by moving beyond the confines of the present, with its more imme-diate impulses, wishes, and needs, and gathering a broader view of things. Herein lies the irony: Only through Levi's deep and abiding humanity could he become witness to his own in-humanity. How awful that he failed to receive any consolation from this.

What Levi had experienced during the period of his imprisonment in the camps was a painful reduction in the realm of temporality. Confined largely to the present moment, he had been essentially stripped of past and future alike; there was no remembering or imagining, only acting, in the service of dear life. This was concomitant with a kind of existential autism, such that any and all dimensions of otherness—his relation to the other people, to the world, and to what Martin Buber has referred to as "the mystery of being" (e.g., 1965, 1970)—were virtually obliterated. Horrifying though his imprisonment had been, there is a very real sense in which, for Levi and his comrades, "Liberation" had been even more so. For upon being released from the confines of the present moment, the world had surged back, flooding them with guilt and shame over what they had—and hadn't—done. They could now remember what it meant to be a human being, who could pause and reflect, who was responsible and who cared for the fate of others, perhaps even before themselves. This remembering proved to be extremely painful—so painful, for the likes of Levi, that he could not imagine a future that would be any different from the shame-soaked condition that had befallen him.

There is some evidence indicating that Levi eventually committed suicide. Whether he did or not, what he reveals through his story is a profound—and in some ways laudable—image of the human being. It is not untarnished. As Levi himself well knew, human beings—perpetrators and victims alike—could be weak and selfish and hurtful, particularly when placed in extreme circumstances. But they, we, could also be thoughtful and caring and could recognize and uphold the priority of the Other, including the priority of those moral and ethical demands without which one would remain a mere animal. These demands, transcendent in nature, would appear to be part and parcel of the human condition. Moreover, as is radiantly and tragically clear in the present case, they very much affect the shape and substance of one's life narrative. Why "transcendent"? Levi, it appears, had asked a related question in the aftermath of his experience in the camps. "Are you ashamed," he asked, "because you are alive in place of another? And in particular, of a man more generous, more sensitive, more useful, wiser, worthier of living than you? You cannot block out such feelings (1989, p. 81) . . . I felt innocent, yes, but enrolled among the saved and therefore in permanent search of a justification in my own eyes and those of others" (p. 82). It is entirely possible, of course, that Levi's feelings are a function of widely held societal expectations; in this sense, his anguish may reflect little more than a loss of self-esteem, tied to his having fallen short of the social mark. This kind of account seems patently inadequate, however. His perceived failure cuts deep, and the kinds of images he has of who might have been "worthier of living" than he was seem to go beyond—that is, *transcend*—social norms or ideals. There thus appears to exist what I have referred to elsewhere (Freeman, 2010) as "the *transcendent horizon* of the life story," which, not unlike Plato's form of the Good (2003), may be understood an "horizon of ultimate meaning and value" (p. 94) that conditions the judgments we make not only about right and wrong, good and bad, but about the very substance and worth of our lives.

If Charles Taylor (1989) is right, "we are only selves insofar as we move within a certain space of questions, as we seek and find an orientation to the good" (p. 34), and this orientation "has to be woven into my life as an unfolding story" (p. 48). But again, why posit this good in transcendent terms? We should also ask, with Iris Murdoch (1970), among others: "Is there . . . any true transcendence, or is this idea always a consoling dream projected by human need onto an empty sky?" (p. 57). Her very cautious response to this question is affirmative. Yes, it is quite real: For "are we not certain that there is a 'true direction' towards better conduct, that goodness 'really matters,' and does not that certainty about a standard suggest an idea of permanence which cannot be reduced to psychological or any other set of empirical terms?" (p. 59). The term "goodness," Murdoch (1970) continues, "refers us to a perfection which is perhaps never exemplified in the world we know . . . and which carries with it the ideas of hierarchy and transcendence" (p. 93). In the course of everyday life, "We see differences, we sense directions, and we know that the Good is still somewhere beyond" (p. 93). At one and the same time, it becomes clear that "the self, the place where we live, is a place of illusion. Therefore, "goodness is connected with the attempt to see the unself, to see and respond to the real world in the light of a virtuous consciousness" (p. 93). One might also speak of the soul in this context. What it all comes down to for Murdoch, in any case, is that

> There is . . . something in the serious attempt to look compassionately at human things which automatically suggests that "there is more than this." The "there is more than this," if it is not to be corrupted by some sort of quasi-theological finality, must remain a very tiny spark of insight. . . . But it seems to me that the spark is real. (p. 73)

In speaking of the transcendent horizon of the life story, I am essentially referring to this "tiny spark" Murdoch is considering. It is this spark that suggests that the stories of our lives sometimes make contact with standards and ideals that "cannot be reduced to psychological or any other set of empirical terms," as Murdoch (1970, p. 59) had put the matter. Not unlike Murdoch, I posit this not out of faith but out of my reading of stories like Primo Levi's and others who, on looking backward over the course of their lives, find that the evaluative stakes are very high—higher, in fact, than reason might lead one to believe. What is the potential import of this alleged transcendent horizon of the life story? To my mind, it leads to a somewhat different conception of the person, one that lives not only in a constructed world, a world of our own making, but in one that has its own presence and power and that serves to constrain the constructions we might fashion. My aim in moving in this direction is in no way to minimize the very clear significance of constructivist thinking, in narrative inquiry and beyond. Rather, it is to encourage us to consider what might exist beyond the constructed world and beyond the perimeter of the meaning-making self. As noted earlier, I have come to frame this project in terms of the priority of the Other, and my foremost hope is that it will open up new possibilities thinking about the human condition.

CODA: MEANING, CONSTRUCTIVISM, AND THE CHALLENGE OF NARRATIVE PSYCHOLOGY

In this final section of the chapter, I want to share a few additional words about some challenges narrative psychology might pose to constructivist thinking. I have already identified several of them: the importance of clearing an appropriate space for thorny ideas like "reality" and "truth"; the importance of seeing and listening to what is *there,* in a given text, including the quasi-text of the self; and, most recently, the importance of thinking "Otherwise" about the human condition. For present purposes, I want to home in on one more issue that might serve to cast some of these challenges into fuller relief, and it has to do with whether we can plausibly speak of "better" and "worse" constructions of our lives. I believe we can indeed do so. I also believe that doing so entails more than positing their pragmatic efficacy in constructing and reconstructing our life stories and, in turn, our selves.

In keeping with what was said earlier regarding the importance of seeing and listening, I want to suggest, first, that a requisite condition for differentiating between better and worse constructions of our lives is a kind of "hermeneutical mindfulness" (Freeman, 2012) that involves both a willingness and a capacity to see oneself as Other (see Ricoeur, 1992). It is difficult, for to do so requires what Murdoch (1970) calls "unselfing," divesting oneself of ego-driven preoccupations, anxieties, and defenses such that the Other—whatever it may be—can be encountered in its otherness. Not unlike what was said earlier regarding Simone Weil's wish to see the world as if she weren't there, this task, strictly speaking, is impossible. It is "unhermeneutical," we might say, and presents the possibility that we can somehow extricate ourselves from our very history and being. That, of course, we cannot do. And when the particular Other being encountered is ourselves, the task at hand becomes that much more unrealizable. And yet, we do at times come to see things more clearly than we had before: we identify some of our prejudices, heretofore working behind the scenes; we suddenly see what we could not or would not see earlier; something new is learned, even discovered, about who and what we are. It can be humbling, indeed. But this process of learning and discovering is one of the great legacies of narrative psychology. Without in any way denying or minimizing the constructive nature of the process, it holds out the possibility we can grow, move forward in our own self-understanding, arrive at a sense of ourselves that is better—more inclusive, more adequate, more truthful—than the one we had before.

I do not mean to suggest that it always works this way—or, for that matter, that it usually does. Frequently, our new self-understandings are as fraught as the previous ones—though of course we can't see this until later on. Moreover, it could be argued that the only reason to proclaim any one interpretation to be better than any other is that it "works" better, is more effective for conducting one's life. There is something to be said for this perspective: better to have a narrative that functions well than one that does not. But the question of pragmatic efficacy and the question of truth are two quite different matters.

Freud's (1937/1964) essay "Constructions in Analysis" may be helpful here. "What we are in search of," he writes, "is a picture of the patient's forgotten years that shall be alike trustworthy and in all essential respects complete" (p. 258). The analyst's task is therefore "to make out what has been forgotten from the traces which it has left behind or, more correctly, to construct it" (p. 258). On Freud's account, the analyst's

> work of construction, or, if it is preferred, of reconstruction, resembles to a great extent an archaeologist's excavation of some dwelling-place that has been destroyed and buried or of some ancient edifice. The two processes are in fact identical, except that the analyst works under better conditions and has more material at his command to

144

assist him, since what he is dealing with is not something destroyed
but something that is still alive. (p. 259)

Freud's way of framing this constructive process is problematic at
times. In his view, "All of the essentials are preserved; even things
that seem completely forgotten are present somehow and somewhere, and have merely been buried and made inaccessible to the
subject" (p. 260). It therefore seems as if the process at hand was
merely one of locating these buried pieces of the past and reassembling them, into the more or less "complete" account being
sought. At the same time, he also is well aware of the constructive
dimension. For one, not all these buried pieces of the past can be
found. Consequently, a good deal of interpretive interpolation is
necessary: "it is a 'construction' when one lays before the subject
of the analysis a piece of his early history that he has forgotten"
(Freud, 1937/1964, p. 261). But the broader interpretations of
the patient's life are constructions too: far from merely being
re-presentations of what happened when, they are constellations
of meaning, *narrative meaning*, that seek to make sense of some
aspect of the past.

But what if the constructions the analyst lays before the
patient are false? Freud's answer is an interesting one, paradoxical
in its own right, for the challenge is precisely to differentiate true
constructions from false ones. According to Freud,

> no damage is done if . . . we make a mistake and offer the patient a
> wrong construction as the probable historical truth. A waste of time
> is, of course, involved, and anyone who does nothing but present
> the patient with false combinations will neither create a very good
> impression on him nor carry the treatment very far; but a single
> mistake of the sort can do no harm. (Freud, 1937/1964, p. 261)

As for the oft-mentioned possibility that suggestion is at work,
Freud's (1937/1964) response is swift and to the point: "The danger
of our leading a patient astray by suggestion, by persuading him to
accept things which we ourselves believe but which he ought not
to, has certainly been enormously exaggerated" (p. 261). Again, "If

the construction is wrong, there is no change in the patient; but if it is right or gives an approximation to the truth, he reacts to it with an unmistakable aggravation of his symptoms and of his general condition" (p. 265). And so, "Only only the further course of the analysis enables us to decide whether our constructions are correct or unserviceable" (p. 265). Now here, one might argue that the idea of a "wrong" or a "correct" construction is oxymoronic, that the constructive nature of the process at hand all but obviates the very idea of truth. What's more, and again, the notion of a construction being "serviceable" or "unserviceable" implies that, in the end, all that we are considering are more or less useful fictions for living one's life. There is surely no denying this pragmatic dimension of Freud's perspective on life narratives. But it is also the case that, for Freud, there is no separating out the serviceability of these narratives from their truth value.

Should we follow his lead? Or was he so thoroughly ensnared in his own scientistic conception of things that he just couldn't shake the idea of truth? Does it really make sense to speak of better and worse constructions of reality except in a purely pragmatic way? In the end, this argument might continue, there can only be *different* constructions, some of which function better than others in a given context. There is no question but that Freud sometimes succumbed to crudely scientistic renditions of how constructions in analysis actually worked. He also seemed at times to be operating with a crude conception of the idea of truth, picturing it as something that could simply be found, in the manner of a thing, inert and unchangeable. But much of his work moves well beyond these crudenesses, giving us a picture of life narratives that is thoroughly constructivist in orientation and, at the same time, firmly committed to the possibility of these narratives speaking something akin to the truth. How is this possible? And how might narrative psychology be of service in carrying forward our understanding of the challenge before us?

In closing, let me try to answer these questions by beginning with what I take to be a simple fact—namely, that we human-folk sometimes construct narratives about our lives that are quite clearly false: illusory, self-deceived, defensive, and more. Others may see this in radiantly clear fashion, and wonder how it is that we could be so blind, or needy, or what have you. I add to this seemingly simple fact another one: in the very process of identifying our misconstruals and illusions for what they are, we have begun to move beyond them. We may only have taken a baby step, of course; to identify and name one's illusions is not quite the same as discerning the truth. But there is no way to speak about the process being described without there being some reference to the truth—which is to say, to a mode of self-understanding that is less illusory or ill-conceived or problematically "prejudiced" than what had existed before. The truth about which I am speaking is not the (putatively) pristine, unvarnished truth that is so much the lore of objectivist thinking. Rather, it is the truth that sometimes emerges by our being "receptive to the origins and entirely foreign features of that which comes to [us] from outside its own horizons," as Gadamer (1979, pp. 151–152) put it. This receptivity is the "hermeneutical attitude," and "in keeping to this attitude," Gadamer (1979) added, "we grant the text the opportunity to appear as an authentically different being and to manifest its own truth, over and against our preconceived notions" (p. 152).

The resultant interpretation is not to be construed as the revelation of some sort of bounded, encapsulated meaning. On the contrary, the "betterness" of this interpretation is a function of the interpretation it has displaced. As I put the matter some time ago (Freeman, 1991, p. 97), we know what is better "precisely by the juxtaposition of our newly fashioned interpretive context against our old one, which becomes inadequate in the very process of its supersession." The idea of "better," therefore, "derives not from a comparison of two readings of experience held apart from one another in putatively objective fashion, but rather from their relationship, from the transformation of the one into the other" (p. 97). As Charles Taylor (1989, p. 72) put it, the process being considered is one of "reasoning in transitions. . . . [and] aims to establish, not that some position is correct but rather that some position is superior to some other." Why "superior"? Taylor (1989) explains:

> We are convinced that a certain view is superior because we have lived a transition which we understand as error-reducing and hence as epistemic gain. I see that I was confused about the relation of resentment and love, or I see that there is a depth to love conferred by time, which I was quite insensitive to before. (p. 72)

Positing such a superior view is thus a matter neither of mere preference nor of practical utility, alone, but is instead a matter of our being able to correct our previous view and to move in the direction of one that is demonstrably more adequate, capacious, and/or ethically sound than the one it has superseded.

In speaking about truth in this context, one might consider it a kind of "region" (Freeman, 2002, 2010). One can enter this region only by degrees; meanings are always provisional and revisable. Narrative psychology underscores this fact by calling attention to the myriad ways in which meanings are reconstructed and the personal past "rewritten." As we have observed, sometimes these processes serve to distort the past. As we have also observed, however, they sometimes serve to reveal it, leading us toward the kind of truth that can be disclosed only through that particular form of constructive *poiesis* we find narrative. The challenge is large, indeed, and requires that we "unself" ourselves enough that we can at least begin to see what's really there—that is, what might exist beyond our constructions. At this juncture, the paradoxical nature of the situation reaches a fever pitch. Strictly speaking, there is no getting beyond these constructions; they are part and parcel of our world, our languaged home. And yet, this is precisely what we must do in order to make our way into the region of truth. Narrative psychology, I believe, provides a way for us not only to think this paradoxical thought but to live it in a way that is, at once, appropriately critical of our own constructions as well as radically open to our own otherness and what it might disclose about the innermost realities of our lives.

REFERENCES

Bonnefoy, Y. (1989). *The act and place of poetry.* Chicago, IL: University of Chicago Press.

Bruner, J. (1990). *Acts of meaning.* Cambridge, MA: Harvard University Press.

Buber, M. (1965). *Between man and man.* New York, NY: Macmillan Publishing Company.

Buber, M. (1970). *I and thou.* New York, NY: Charles Scribner's Sons.

Dilthey, W. (1976). The construction of the historical world in the human studies. In H. P Rickman (Ed.), *Dilthey: Selected writings* (pp. 168–245). Cambridge, England: Cambridge University Press. (Original work published 1910)

Eakin, P. J. (1988). *Fictions in autiobiography: Studies in the art of self-invention.* Princeton, NJ: Princeton University Press.

Flanagan, O. (1996). *Self expressions: Mind, morals, and the meaning of life.* New York, NY: Oxford University Press.

Freeman, M. (1985). Paul Ricoeur on interpretation: The model of the text and the idea of development. *Human Development, 28,* 295–312.

Freeman, M. (1991). Rewriting the self: Development as moral practice. In M. B. Tappan & M. J. Packer (Eds.), Narrative approaches to moral development. *New Directions for Child Development, 54,* 83–101.

Freeman, M. (1993). *Rewriting the self: History, memory, narrative.* London, England: Routledge.

Freeman, M. (1997a). Death, narrative integrity, and the radical challenge of self-understanding: A reading of Tolstoy's *Death of Ivan Ilych. Ageing and Society, 17,* 373–398.

Freeman, M. (1997b). Why narrative? Hermeneutics, historical understanding, and the significance of stories. *Journal of Narrative and Life History, 71,* 169–176.

Freeman, M. (2002). The burden of truth: Psychoanalytic *poiesis* and narrative understanding. In W. Patterson (Ed.), *Strategic narrative: New perspectives on the power of personal and cultural stories* (pp. 9–27). Lanham, MD: Lexington Books.

Freeman, M. (2003a). Rethinking the fictive, reclaiming the real: Autobiography, narrative time, and the burden of truth. In G. Fireman, T. McVay, & O. Flanagan (Eds.), *Narrative and consciousness: Literature, psychology, and the brain* (pp. 115–128). New York, NY: Oxford University Press.

Freeman, M. (2003b). Too late: The temporality of memory and the challenge of moral life. *Journal für Psychologie, 11,* 54–74.

Freeman, M. (2007). Narrative and relation: The place of the Other in the story of the self. In R. Josselson, A. Lieblich, & D. McAdams (Eds.), *The meaning of others: Narrative studies of relationships* (pp. 11–19). Washington, DC: APA Books.

Freeman, M. (2010). *Hindsight: The promise and peril of looking backward.* New York, NY: Oxford University Press.

Freeman, M. (2012). Self-observation theory in the narrative tradition: Rescuing the possibility of self-understanding. In J. Clegg (Ed.), *Self-observation in the social sciences* (pp. 239–257). Piscataway, NJ: Transaction.

Freeman, M. (2013). Storied persons: The "double triad" of narrative identity. In J. Martin & M. H. Bickhard (Eds.), *Contemporary perspectives in the psychology of personhood: Philosophical, historical, psychological, and narrative* (pp. 223–241). Cambridge, England: Cambridge University Press.

Freeman, M. (2014). *The priority of the Other: Thinking and living beyond the self.* New York, NY: Oxford University Press.

Freud, S. (1964). Constructions in analysis. *Standard Edition XXIII* (pp. 257–269). London, England: Hogarth. (Original work published 1937)

Gadamer, H.-G. (1979). The problem of historical consciousness. In P. Rabinow & W. M. Sullivan (Eds.), *Interpretive social science: A reader* (pp. 103–160). Berkeley, CA: University of California Press.

Gadamer, H.-G. (1982). *Truth and method.* New York, NY: Crossroad.

Gazzaniga, M. (1998). *The mind's past.* Berkeley, CA: University of California Press.

Gergen, K. (1988). If persons are texts. In S. B. Messer, L. A. Sass, & R. L. Woolfolk (Eds.), *Hermeneutics and psychological theory* (pp. 28–51). New Brunswick, NJ: Rutgers University Press.

Gergen, K. J. (1992). *The saturated self: Dilemmas of identity in contemporary life.* New York, NY: Basic Books

Gergen, K. J. (2009). *Relational being: Beyond self and community.* New York, NY: Oxford University Press.

Hacking, I. (1995). *Rewriting the soul: Multiple personality and the sciences of memory.* Princeton, NJ: Princeton University Press.

Hampl, P. (1999). *I could tell you stories: Sojourns in the land of memory.* New York, NY: Norton.

Heidegger, M. (1962). *Being and time.* New York, NY: Harper and Row.

Heidegger, M. (1971a). *On the way to language.* New York, NY: Harper & Row. (Original work published 1959)

Heidegger, M. (1971b). *Poetry, language, thought.* New York, NY: Harper Colophon.

Heidegger, M. (1993). Letter on humanism. In D. F. Krell (Ed.), *Martin Heidegger: Basic writings* (pp. 213–266). New York, NY: Harper Collins. (Original work published 1947)

Levi, P. (1989). *The drowned and the saved.* New York, NY: Vintage.

Levinas, E. (1985). *Ethics and infinity.* Pittsburgh, PA: Duquesne University Press.

Levinas, E. (1999). *Alterity and transcendence.* New York, NY: Columbia University Press.

MacIntyre, A. (1981). *After virtue: A study in moral theory.* Notre Dame, IN: University of Notre Dame Press.

Marion, J.-L. (2008). *The visible and the revealed.* New York, NY: Fordham University Press.

Merleau-Ponty, M. (1962). *The phenomenology of perception.* Pittsburgh, PA: Duquesne University Press.

Murdoch, I. (1970). *The sovereignty of good.* London, England: Routledge.

Nietzsche, F.W. (1968). *The will to power.* New York, NY: Vintage. (Original work published 1888)

Parini, J. (2008). *Why poetry matters.* New Haven, CT: Yale University Press.

Plato. (2003). *The Republic.* New York, NY: Penguin.

Raskin, J. D. (2002). Constructivism in psychology: Personal construct psychology, radical constructivism, and social constructionism. *American Communication Journal, 5,* 1–24.

Ricoeur, P. (1970). *Freud and philosophy: An essay on interpretation.* New Haven, CT: Yale University Press.

Ricoeur, P. (1981a). *Hermeneutics and the human sciences.* Cambridge, England: Cambridge University Press.

Ricoeur, P. (1981b). Narrative time. In W. J. T. Mitchell (Ed.), *On narrative* (pp. 165-186). Chicago, IL: University of Chicago Press.

Ricoeur, P. (1988). *Time and narrative* (Vol. 3). Chicago, IL: University of Chicago Press.

Ricoeur, P. (1991). Life in quest of narrative. In D. Wood (Ed.), *On Paul Ricoeur: Narrative and interpretation* (pp. 20–33). London, England: Routledge.

Ricoeur, P. (1992). *Oneself as another.* Chicago, IL: University of Chicago Press.

Schacter, D. L. (Ed.) (2005). *Memory distortion: How minds, brains, and societies reconstruct the past.* Cambridge, MA: Harvard University Press.

Shils, E. A. (1981). *Tradition.* Chicago, IL: University of Chicago Press.

Taylor, C. (1989). *Sources of the self: The making of the modern identity.* Cambridge, MA: Harvard University Press.

Weil, S. (1997). *Gravity and grace.* London, England: Routledge. (Originally work published 1952)

PART III

CONSTRUCTIVIST PSYCHOTHERAPY

☙ 6 ❧

Where's the Gimmick? Future Prospects for Constructivist Psychotherapy[1]

Jay S. Efran and Jonah N. Cohen

There is a scene in *Gypsy*—the Styne-Sondheim-Laurents musical about stripper Gypsy Rose Lee—in which three jaded burlesque queens give the young Louise advice about how to succeed in show business. It's not really about talent, they explain, it's about finding the right gimmick: "You can bump in a dump till you're dead," but "you gotta get a gimmick if you wanna get ahead." Anyone paying careful attention to the shifting trends in the field of psychotherapy might come to a similar conclusion. Over the years, clinicians have been attracted to a long succession of enticing methods, including Rogers' (1951) nondirective reflection, Wolpe's (1958) systematic desensitization, Frankl's (1963) paradoxical intention, Stampfl's (1970) implosive therapy, Janov's (1970) primal scream, Perls' (1973) empty chair technique, Selvini Palazzoli's (1986) invariant prescription, de Shazer's (1988) miracle question, Shapiro's (1995) eye-movement desensitization (EMDR), and— our latest obsessions—anything with attachment (e.g., Johnson & Whiffen, 2003) or mindfulness (e.g., Germer, Siegel, & Fulton, 2005) in the title.

Historically, practitioners have been more attracted to the techniques themselves than the theories on which they are based. For example, many clinicians using Perls' empty chair exercise

---

[1] The authors thank Elsa R. Efran for her editorial assistance.

know nothing about his writings on Gestalt theory. Similarly, of the dozens of therapists who have adopted Steven Hayes' Chinese finger trap demonstration, only a handful have read the relational frame theory that justifies it (Hayes, Strosahl, & Wilson, 2012). Given such facts, it seems clear that the popularity of many schools of therapy is more attributable to the novelty of their methods than the elegance of their theories or the superiority of their results. In fact, once investigator allegiances are taken into account, differences in therapy outcomes are hard to come by (Wampold, 2001)— the equivalence of treatments turns out to be one of the most robust findings in the entire psychological literature (Hubble, Duncan, & Miller, 2009).

We mention all this as a prelude to addressing the editors' two main questions: First, why hasn't personal construct therapy (or its derivatives) become more popular and, second, are there aspects of these approaches that still deserve our time and attention?

PERSISTENT MISINTERPRETATIONS

To begin at the beginning, we should note that shortly after his mammoth two volumes on personal construct theory (PCT) appeared in print, Kelly (1955) began grumbling that his ideas were falling on deaf ears, being misinterpreted, or both. Of course, this was to have been expected—given that, at the time, academic psychology was in the midst of a love affair with learning theory, and psychoanalysis ruled the roost in mental health. Kelly's theory was out of step with both of those traditions. It was also at odds with the only other model gaining momentum at the time—the "third force" humanism of Rogers, Maslow, and Perls.

Further, Kelly upset some readers by throwing the notion of learning overboard altogether and dispensing with most other familiar concepts, such as ego, emotion, motivation, reinforcement, drive, and the unconscious. This set the stage for some highly original psychological theorizing but made his views harder to digest. To make matters worse, he declined to bolster his arguments with empirical evidence or provide detailed references.

His reluctance to situate his ideas in a larger theoretical context bothered the two psychologists who first penned reviews of Kelly's volumes—Carl Rogers (1956) and Jerome Bruner (1956). While expressing admiration for his originality, they both struggled over how to locate his ideas in existing psychological space. Bruner, for example, wrote that "one misses reference to such works as Piaget's *The Child's Construction of Reality*, the early work of Werner, and the writings of Harry Stack Sullivan, Lewin, and Allport" (p. 357). He wondered why Kelly would not have availed himself of these potentially "good allies." Rogers, too, commended Kelly's willingness to "launch out on his own" (p. 358) but criticized his dogged reliance on his own experience.

These first two reviews also contained harbingers of the misinterpretations that have plagued PCT ever since. Rogers, for example, critiqued Kelly's therapy as being overly intellectual, lacking in depth, and leaving little room for developing "an emotional relationship with a client" (1956, p. 358). Ironically, he also faulted Kelly (the inventor of personal constructs) for not having greater faith in his clients' personal constructions.

Bruner, too, found Kelly's approach ultra-cognitive, accusing him of "failing to [deal] convincingly with the human passions" (p. 357). He wrote that "If Freud's clinical world [was] a grotesque of *fin de sicle* Vienna, Kelly's [was] a gloss on the post-adolescent peer group of Columbus, Ohio." Because so many considered Kelly's approach too cerebral, he once quipped that he was going to have to write a second book to clarify that he "wanted no part of cognitive theory" (1969, p. 216). He was also forced to battle those who insisted on labeling him an existentialist, a dialectical materialist, a psychoanalyst, a Zen Buddhist, and—much to his amusement—a learning theorist. Even authors of personality texts who wanted to include a chapter on PCT were often puzzled about which section to put it in.

A MORE POSITIVE RECEPTION

Kelly took comfort in the fact that his writings received a better reception overseas than in America. European psychologists—less caught up in the logical positivism that was sweeping the States—seemed receptive to his "softer," more philosophical approach. To this day, PCT has had more impact in Europe and Australia than in the States.

Perhaps it was this compatibility between Continental psychology and Kelly's thinking that prompted him to spend his 1960 sabbatical year meeting with groups of psychologists in 37 countries, including England, Denmark, Germany, Russia, Finland, Iceland, and Sweden.[2] When he returned, he complained that Ohio State doctoral students were far too parochial. Therefore, he initiated a project to send all Ohio State clinical students abroad for a second internship year. First, they would do a regular internship stateside, absorbing a full "dose" of this country's mental health practices. Then, they would spend an additional year in Europe, immersed in the psychology of another culture. Although the project never got off the ground, it illustrates the value Kelly placed on having individuals—even lowly psychology trainees—expand their construct systems.

An exception to the generally cool American response occurred during a successful visit to Harvard. When he returned to Ohio State, a beaming Kelly made sure to tease his advisees for being "slow" to grasp the full implications of his approach. Cambridge types, he boasted, were far quicker on the uptake!

TOO MANY DETAILS

In addition to those who considered Kelly's approach overly intellective, some complained about what might be called an

---

[2] The reader might want to consult the intriguing account of this sojourn that he presented at the 1962 Nebraska Symposium on Motivation (Kelly, 1962).

embarrassment of riches. They were put off by the prospect of studying Kelly's "ten types of weeping," "nine techniques for reducing anxiety," "twelve techniques" for prompting movement, and "fifteen criteria" for establishing client readiness (Rogers, 1956, p. 358). By the same token, they had difficulty figuring out how to integrate his eclectic list of techniques. At a minimum, these included assigning behavioral activities, offering interpretations, exploiting the transference, reflecting feelings, analyzing dreams, playing back session tapes, and helping clients tighten and loosen their constructs. Whereas Rogers' one-size-fits-all approach seemed excessively narrow, Kelly's catalog of possibilities was utterly overwhelming.

For comparison, consider the relatively succinct narrative approach of White and Epston (1990). They devised two "signature" procedures, each with several secondary elaborations. First, they suggested externalizing the client's problems, sometimes using cute personifications. For instance, they labeled a child's enuretic struggles "sneaky wee" (p. 194). Second, they recommended writing formal letters to clients, summarizing what had happened in the previous session and proposing a plan for going forward. Both of these methods were easy to grasp, novel, intuitively appealing, and widely applicable. Without such "gimmicks" it is unlikely that the White and Epston brand would have gained as much traction.

Similarly, Albert Ellis' (1993) bombastic style and arsenal of catch phrases (e.g., "must-urbation" and "awfulizing") helped catapult rational-emotive behavioral therapy (REBT) to the top of the therapy hit parade (Simon, 2007). Although many thoughtful clinicians dismissed his approach as too dogmatic and rationalistic, it attracted many novices because they could pick up the basics at an evening seminar or a weekend workshop. Unfortunately, PCT has no such crowd-pleasing "hooks." Therefore, it tends to be ignored.

THE FIXED-ROLE GIMMICK

Despite their misgivings about other aspects of Kellyian therapy, both Rogers and Bruner applauded the fixed-role procedure as a genuinely creative therapeutic departure. It is as close as PCT comes to having a bona fide gimmick.[3] Briefly, fixed-role therapy invites clients to participate in a time-limited experiment in which they role play somebody else. Although clients continue answering to their real name (to avoid confusing family and friends), they act and react as if they are this other person. The role they play is designed by a team of psychologists with extensive knowledge of the case. It usually includes subtle reframings of the client's self perceptions. For instance, clients who considered themselves "shy" might be asked to play someone who is "thoughtful." Thus, they might still be reserved, but their low participation level is now construed in terms of speaking when you have something to contribute, rather than remaining quiet because you fear rejection.

While immersed in the fixed-role experience, clients meet regularly with their therapist to work out any ambiguities in the role description. At the end of the agreed-upon time—usually about a month—the individual "returns from vacation" and has a chance to reflect on how life appeared when seen through this alternative set of lenses. Kelly was emphatic that the purpose of the fixed-role exercise was not to replace a defective personality with a healthier persona, but to help individuals experience new aspects of themselves and the world.

---

[3] PCT does contain a gimmick that we have not yet discussed—the Role Construct Repertory Test. This has been a boon to researchers and, like fixed-role therapy, is an element of the theory that has enjoyed independent, sustained success. In the clinic, it has proven valuable for a multitude of diagnostic and assessment tasks and has become even more useful now that computer programs have simplified the analysis of grid data. However, because this chapter focuses on therapy rather than assessment or research, we will not say more about this measurement technology, except to note that, once again, it shows how a concrete tool can enhance the popularity of a theory.

Unfortunately, the fixed role method is not suitable for routine use. First, doing it "by the book" requires a committee of professionals who can craft adroit role descriptions. Second, the client has to be willing and able to attempt this rather odd and demanding experiment. Therefore, at least in terms of gimmicks, PCT and its derivatives remain at a competitive disadvantage.

SEEKING PRACTICAL GUIDELINES

Many of us had high hopes that Michael J. Mahoney's (2003) book, *Constructive Psychotherapy: A Practical Guide* would rectify the situation. The title promised the kind of "how-to" guide for which many of us had been waiting. Unfortunately, the book was a dud. If anything, it reinforced the view that constructivist therapy is an amorphous conglomerate of ill-defined procedures. He advised, for instance, that constructive practitioners "draw on the full spectrum of therapeutic and teaching techniques," adding that this "creativity and spirit cannot be formalized in a particular procedure" (p. 58). In other words, no gimmicks!

Mahoney does describe lots of interventions, from stream of consciousness techniques to having clients study their mirror images. However, these seem to be an eclectic hodgepodge of procedures rather than a disciplined methodology. For instance, in one bizarre incident, he reports instructing a distraught workshop volunteer to place his finger on his own forehead, then on his abdomen, and then back on his forehead. After Mahoney and the volunteer repeat these gestures three times, slowly and in synchrony, Mahoney says "I don't know if this will be helpful or not, but I would encourage you to practice [this] whenever you begin to feel distressed" (2003, p. 186). That evening, the chairperson of the conference asked Mahoney how he knew to do this and where workshop attendees might read more about the technique. Mahoney replied that he had never done anything like it before, adding: "I don't know why I did it, or what it means." Such spur of the moment impulses, devoid of either empirical support

161

or theoretical justification, are bound to leave potential converts adrift in a sea of ambiguity.

Even some of us who studied directly with George Kelly felt the need for a set of simple, concrete guidelines. Thus, before embracing PCT, the first author experimented with using Wolpe's (1958) systematic desensitization (SD). It was a brand-new methodology that was getting a lot of attention. However, a research project in which the author was involved demonstrated that SD's underlying theory was flawed. The same outcomes could be achieved just as easily using a pseudo-conditioning procedure that had been designed to purposely violate the laws of learning on which SD was presumably based (Marcia, Rubin, & Efran, 1969; Woy & Efran, 1972). Thus, the successes of SD seemed mainly due to the fact that clients had an opportunity to reevaluate their beliefs. This idea—that therapy is a place for clients to test their perceptions accords with Kelly's notion, unique at the time, that therapy is basically a "protected laboratory where hypotheses [can] be formulated, test-tube sized experiments [can] be performed, field trials [can be] planned, and outcomes [can be] evaluated" (1969, p. 229). In this case, clients were given a chance to learn more about the snakes and spiders they had previously avoided.

At the time, however, defining therapists as "research consultants" wasn't very popular. It clashed with the field's strong commitment to the medical model and the disease-entity approach. Mental health workers classified psychotherapy as a "treatment," thereby committing what philosopher Gilbert Ryle (1949) called a "category mistake" (p. 16)—that is, placing something in the wrong conceptual envelope. Category mistakes vastly complicate our attempts to understand what we do because they invoke a set of concepts ill-suited to the task at hand. Although it is true that the term "psycho-therapy" literally means "mind treatment," Thomas Szasz (1988) reminded us long ago that therapy is basically rhetoric—not medicine. Therapists do not apply ointments, prescribe medications, or perform surgery. They do not cure any diseases, even if these have been relabeled "disorders" to make the venture seem more plausible.

Therapists listen to and tell stories, pose questions, propose options, and encourage inquiry. Furthermore, because therapy is dialogue, improvisational elements must always be a part of the process. Unlike pharmaceuticals, therapeutic discourse cannot be dispensed in tidy, standardized doses. Each client-therapist interaction is a unique collaboration with partially unpredictable results. Ironically, although research studies keep reaffirming that therapeutic outcomes are largely attributable to client and therapist characteristics and the alliance they establish, the medical model compels us to keep writing cookbook-like manuals and devising new and glitzier gimmicks (Hubble et al., 2009).

THERAPY AS RESEARCH

Although the idea of the therapist as a research consultant never caught on, we consider it an aspect of constructivist therapy that is well worth preserving and perhaps promoting more loudly. Kelly's model of small-scale, client-centered investigation incorporates the virtues of the scientific method without lapsing into a rigid and inappropriate scientism. In addition, this therapy-as-research model has a surprisingly contemporary flavor, fitting nicely with today's renewed interest in idiographic studies and single case designs (e.g., Barlow & Nock, 2009; Barlow, Nock, & Hersen, 2009).

Lately, even CBT practitioners have tried to lay claim to the research mantle, arguing that the homework they assign provides clients with opportunities to test their beliefs. However, because it is grounded in metaphysical realism, CBT assignments are mainly designed to show clients that their thinking is irrational. Thus, the outcomes are more or less preordained. By contrast, Kelly eschewed such fake investigations—he wanted clients to know that he was a "fellow experimenter, not an unctuous priest" (1969, p. 53). He favored genuine research, knowing full well that it involved the risk of blind alleys and unpredictable outcomes. Furthermore, because Kelly understood that many alternative life pathways are legitimate, he refrained from prejudging his client's thoughts or thought processes.

Like any good investigator, Kelly knew that good research requires a good research question. Trivial, academic, or poorly framed questions can stymie the process. He also understood that clients do not necessarily need better answers to their announced questions. Often, they simply need better questions. In our own work, we test that proposition by asking clients what they would tell a friend who had a similar problem. We find that in response to that task, most clients voice the kinds of advice that some therapists would have otherwise wasted time dispensing. For example, clients who ask about how to lose weight, stop smoking, or avoid procrastinating frequently know more than the therapist about the latest diets, nicotine patches, and study strategies. Similarly, couples who begin by saying that they need to learn to "communicate" soon prove that they are experts at predicting each other's responses. Thus, their problem cannot be communication, per se. They know exactly what their partner is thinking—they just don't like it. So, before going down these investigatory paths, it is important to check whether the question at hand is a substantive issue.

We submit that Kelly's notion of therapy as research, skillfully done, is a workable framework for the constructivist therapy of the future. It is the first of our suggestions for modernizing practice. The second concerns the need to strengthen the focus on social context.

BRINGING BACK CONTEXT

Both the medical model and the pharmaceutical juggernaut have perpetuated a decontextualized view of individuals. There was a brief period when many clinicians were persuaded that mental health problems had systemic roots and that family and communal influences needed to be taken into account (e.g., Bowen, 1978; Minuchin & Fishman, 2004; Nichols & Schwartz, 1995). However, now that the heyday of family and systems therapy is over—the *Family Therapy Networker* had to be renamed *The Psychotherapy Networker*—we have reverted to a near-exclusive emphasis on the individual (Efran, Lukens, & Greene, 2007). This has been a persistent weakness of PCT. Kelly's supporters correctly note that he never entirely ignored the social milieu. On the other hand, perhaps because he wrote during the era of individual treatment models, he never fully transcended the "personal" aspect of personal constructs.

Overlooking context is a major detriment. Over a century ago, philosopher Wilhelm Dilthey (cited in Prus, 2000) recognized that meaningful human behavior is contingent on communal interaction and cannot be understood as a series of individual, decontextualized elements. Yet, that is exactly what many therapists are still trying to do. For example, CBT therapists treat "maladaptive thoughts" as if they were freestanding entities that could just be plucked out of the person's psyche and replaced, one-by-one, with healthier cognitions. This overlooks the all-important communal narrative from which such thoughts emanate (Burns, 2012).

Interpersonal conflicts largely arise because people are members of overlapping "clubs," each with its own membership requirements. As essayist Mignon McLaughlin (1960) explains, "It's impossible to be loyal to your family, your friends, your country, and your principles, all at the same time" (p. 58). Although the conversations that define our lives seem to take place in our heads, they actually constitute a kind of social dance that takes place in communal space (Efran & Fauber, 1995). Thoughts and images are not just private possessions—they are the tools of social negotiation. When the choreography is going well, it is a smooth waltz and we are barely aware of the linguistic machinations we use to sustain our relationships with others. However, if things go awry, we become self conscious, lose the beat, and begin stepping on toes. If things get really awkward, people seek therapy! This is

why Szasz described symptoms as "declarations of [social] independence and dependence" (1973, p. 88–89) made by individuals
experiencing the strain of conflicting group loyalties.

As we have implied, earlier forms of PCT short-changed these
contextual issues. By contrast, we explicitly define therapy as a
place to investigate contradictory role demands and determine
which club affiliations clients might want to preserve and which
they should modify or abandon. To do this research, it helps
if clients understand that all of their beliefs are man-made—not
decrees from on high or direct reflections of reality. Constructivist
therapists are ideally positioned to communicate that message.
They recognize that anything said by a human being is said from a
tradition (Varela, 1979) and that all such assertions reflect the "real
or imagined demands of [constituencies] that exist in the person's
experience" (Efran & Fauber, 1995, p. 283). In helping clients make
this shift from realism to constructivism, we often quote Kelly's
dictum that "whatever exists can be reconstrued" (1969, p. 227).
Like the Zen notion of "detachment," Kelly's mantra helps clients
recognize that their "certainties" are just strongly held beliefs.

Because we are dealing with club affiliations, a factor that
affects the success of the therapeutic collaboration is the degree of
similarity between the backgrounds of client and therapist. In this
connection, we like Szasz's (1973) depiction of the psychotherapist
as a kind of court jester. Jesters had to be familiar enough with the
mores of the court to be able to understand the king's plight but
cosmopolitan enough to envision fresh solutions. If the jester was
too mired in the court culture, he would not have the perspective
he needed to do his job. Also, by playing the fool, the jester could
be granted enough leeway from court etiquette to challenge the
king's most cherished beliefs (without losing his head). Therapists,
too, need sufficient detachment to broach touchy subjects without
permanently damaging the therapeutic alliance.

After all, effective therapy research requires that everything
be open to question. There can be no sacred cows. Clients have
to be able to freely voice thoughts that might constitute heresy

elsewhere. Too much club overlap can inhibit that process. Thus, we have to be wary whenever client and therapist are of the same gender, religion, ethnic group, social class, profession, sexual orientation, political persuasion, and so on. From our perspective, pastoral counseling is not always the best option for a religious individual and feminist therapy can inadvertently constrain a female client. By the same token, we reject the conventional wisdom that addicts should always be seen by recovering addicts and gay clients must be seen by gay therapists. Again, the ideal arrangement is for the therapist to comprehend the club traditions but not be wedded to them.

At a conference years ago, we were amused to hear a gay client report that he had consulted three different therapists—one gay, one straight, and one bisexual. Each urged him to be what they were—gay, straight, or bi. Presumably, the field has progressed since those days, but we still need to be on the alert to the danger of overlapping backgrounds hindering exploration.

Because individualism is such a strong bias in our culture, contextual factors are easily overlooked. Consider, for a moment, the successes of CBT. These are typically attributed to cognitive and behavioral retraining. Yet, they are probably due to contextual factors—particularly unnoticed shifts in communal rhetoric. Psychotherapy critic Robert Fancher (1995) points out that CBT inducts clients into a particular subculture that peddles a series of healing fictions as scientific truths. "By becoming a member of this [therapeutic] culture, one gets to believe an overly simple, inaccurate, optimistic notion of how minds work and what simple methods of empirical logic can accomplish" (p. 214). However, the CBT message—as American as apple pie—is enormously appealing to clients. Therefore, even though the method rests on scientific hokum, it often succeeds in boosting client morale and encouraging proactive behavior.

Kelly, too, realized that "preposterous interpretations" (1969, p. 54) are sometimes effective. To work, they must "account for the crucial facts as the client [sees] them" and "[carry] implications for approaching the future in a different way." Note that these are the very same ingredients that make White and Epston's (1990) letters to clients effective. It makes one wonder if all therapies succeed because they create a novel "club" in which the participants agree on an explanation for the client's plight and a plan for moving forward (Frank, 1973).

To reiterate, our proposed revision of constructivist therapy uses Kelly's therapy-as-research model as the framework and focuses on the exigencies of social context as the content. We next propose borrowing several concepts from Maturana's theory of structure determinism (Maturana & Varela, 1987) to modernize our understanding of therapeutic change.

RATIONAL SUPREMACY AND THEORIES OF CHANGE

Humberto Maturana is a renowned biologist and cyberneticist whose ideas are fully compatible with the constructivist stance. His concepts of orthogonal and instructive interaction are useful additions to our traditional views, streamlining our understanding of therapeutic change.

Most people—including many therapists—subscribe to what constructivist Mahoney (1991) called the "doctrine of rational supremacy" (p. 446). This is the belief that "reason and rationality can and should control everything 'below' them in the human organism." Fancher (1995) considers this "one of the grand myths of western culture" (p. 244). Of course, if it was really true, dieting would be a snap, Alcoholics Anonymous could close up shop, and the $11 billion self-help market would dry up overnight. Counseling would be a breeze. Therapists would merely review the facts with their clients, and they would then venture forth and live happily ever after. Obviously, it doesn't work that way. Smart people do incredibly stupid things, and even those who pride themselves on their "willpower" stumble badly on the road to self improvement. It is not that such folks have secret motives for staying ill or derive some perverse pleasure from thwarting helpers. Few of them wake up each morning thinking up new ways to mess up their lives. Contrary to public opinion, all of us come by our problems honestly and do our best to solve them (Gregson & Efran, 2002).

The problem is that the doctrine of rational supremacy seduces us into accepting a flawed theory of change. As Maturana (1988) explains, change is not about having a superior intellect or great self discipline. It is about *orthogonal interaction*. In a nutshell, it occurs when a system component bumps into a non-system component and is modified by that interaction. Consider an auto mechanic who adjusts the gap of a spark plug. When the adjusted plug is reinserted in the engine, the car runs more smoothly. In this example, the spark plug is a component of the engine and the mechanic is the non-system component with which it temporarily interacts. Their exchange is orthogonal—literally, at right angles— to what normally happens to spark plugs when they are seated in the engine (Efran, Lukens, & Lukens, 1990).

A fictional example may help clarify the issue. In *A Christmas Carol* (Dickens, 1843/1991), Ebenezer Scrooge is visited by the spirits of Christmas past, present, and future. These three spirits engage him in interaction that is thoroughly orthogonal to his everyday experiences. Therefore, when dawn arrives, he emerges as a transformed individual who then automatically interacts differently with everyone he meets. Because most individuals have no access to Dickensian apparitions, they have to make do with a therapist. Nevertheless, orthogonal interaction is the principle at work in both settings.

Years ago, the first author treated a young man who was trying to come to grips with his homosexuality. During one of their sessions, the author suggested that he go to see Harvey Fierstein's *Torch Song Trilogy* (which was playing on Broadway at the time). As the reader may know, Fierstein's trilogy depicts various aspects of the gay lifestyle in touching, humorous, and insightful ways. The client agreed that seeing the show might be a good idea, but he complained that he could neither afford the price of the ticket nor the train fare to New York. The author replied, "That's why I intend to pay for both!" Although a bit flabbergasted at first, the client accepted the offer. The trip turned out to be a turning point in both his therapy and his life. He had grown up in a small town and had a very limited and very negative perception of what it meant to be gay. The show was an eye-opening experience. However, it was the audience's enthusiastic response that made the biggest impression on him. He had not imagined that theatregoers of different sexual orientations would respond so positively to gay themes.

This vignette illustrates orthogonality at many levels. The therapist's monetary offer illustrated that rules are meant to be broken and that life does not always need to follow the same predictable pattern. It also demonstrated that even mental health professionals can be flexible, inventive, and determined to achieve their goals. In case the reader is wondering, paying for this client's trip ultimately proved cost effective because of the large number of referrals this client provided.

Of course, Kelly didn't use the concept of "orthogonal interaction," but he certainly argued that clinicians were too rule-bound, especially given how little we know about which interventions might work. Why do sessions have to be scheduled at weekly intervals? Why do they have to last 45 or 50 minutes, even if the client and therapist have little to talk about? Neither surgeons nor shoe salesmen would agree to such ridiculous constraints. In our own work, the pace of the project determines when we schedule meetings—not the clock or the calendar. Thus, we have had sessions as short as fifteen minutes and as long as four hours. We have seen clients as often as two days in a row and as infrequently as once every several months.

Again, orthogonal interaction takes many forms, both in and out of the consulting room. As Kelly surmised, living in a foreign culture can be a life-altering experience for many. We recall an individual whose life plan changed dramatically following a near-fatal rowboat accident. Another person left his wife of twenty years after a chance encounter with his former high-school sweetheart. These sorts of orthogonality generate change, but the myth of instructive interaction virtually guarantees that the change produced will not turn out exactly as planned (Efran & Lukens, 1985). In fact, predicting the exact effect of any particular orthogonal event is next to impossible. The problem is that the nervous system operates only on internal correlations. Therefore, although it can be "triggered" by an environmental event, it cannot be "instructed" by external forces. In other words, you can turn out the bedroom light but cannot force yourself to fall asleep. Parents can punish their children for leaving toys around, but this will not necessarily instill a passion for neatness.

Cyberneticist Gregory Bateson used to challenge his learning-theory colleagues with a tale about a mother who rewarded her daughter with ice cream whenever she ate her spinach. He then asked these psychologists what they needed to know to be able to predict whether the daughter would grow up (a) loving spinach, (b) hating ice cream, or (c) hating her mother. Of course, it would only be possible to make an accurate prediction if instructive inter-action really existed.

If it did, teachers would not need to bother with classroom tests. They could simply provide students with the relevant infor-mation and be confident that everyone "got it." As Maturana points out, the only place where true instructive interaction exists is in the fable of King Midas. Because he did a favor for the god Dionysus, King Midas was granted his wish that whatever he touched would turn to gold. He soon discovered that this wasn't such a great idea. For instance, anything he wanted to eat turned to gold before he could ingest it. One day he made the mistake of touching his daughter, and she turned to gold. Maturana comments wryly that the tragedy of King Midas is that he could never become an analytic chemist! Chemistry, of course, depends on substances reacting in their own characteristic ways to the chemist's probe. If they all reacted similarly, the science of chemistry would grind to a halt. Although electricity "triggers" both toasters and coffee-makers, their responses to that trigger are different—toasters toast and coffeemakers brew (Efran & Lukens, 1985).

Because instructive interaction is mythical, the best any therapist can do is make educated guesses about the kinds of orthogonal interventions that might generate a desired effect. Such guesses are often correct because they are based on our past experience with ourselves and other people (including clients). However, nothing is surefire. Even experienced therapists have their surprises, which is what makes being a therapist continually challenging and infinitely interesting.

A client the first author saw early in his career returned years later to thank him for what they had accomplished. This individual said that during one of their sessions, the author had said something truly inspirational. He wrote it down on a piece of paper and has carried it with him ever since. Hearing about this, the author was breathless with anticipation to see what this "gem" of therapeutic legerdemain might be. Perhaps it could work similar miracles with other clients. At this point, the ex-client proudly took a tattered slip of paper out of his wallet, carefully unfolded it, and showed it to the author. It said, "Every cloud has a silver lining." Huh? That was the earth shattering nugget of therapeutic wisdom the client had been carrying around all these years? What about the hard-won therapeutic insights discovered during our sessions? To tell the truth, the author was chagrined to think that he had ever uttered such a lame cliché, and still more dumbfounded to learn that this was the moment the client remembered. Yet, we could multiply such surprising incidents ten-fold.

For instance, a socially anxious elementary school student, being treated as part of a Temple University research project, was asked which aspects of her therapy had been the most important. She immediately cited the time her therapist tripped over a wastebasket that had been left in the hallway. Why was this so important? She noticed that when the therapist stumbled, several people came to her assistance and none of them laughed or made fun of her for being clumsy. That incident—more than any of the manualized exercises they did together—convinced the girl that people are allowed to make mistakes!

What works magically with one client may have no effect on the next, and—as we have said—there is no guaranteed way of knowing in advance which bit of orthogonality might do the trick. Thus, Adlerian Harold Mosak tells his trainees that "if one tactic, response, or interpretation does not work," move right on to the next (Mosak & Maniacci, 1998, p. 3). He also teaches that even though a trainee may not always know what to do, he or she can be sure that there is always something that can be done. Orthogonality is always a possibility.

On the other hand, because change requires novelty, merely listening empathically to the client's story, week after week, is not apt to produce dramatic results. In fact, research shows that short-term or time-limited approaches are more effective than long term therapy, and initial sessions are more impactful than later meetings (e.g., Sharma, 1986). We propose that this is because as clients and therapists accommodate to each other, it becomes more difficult to generate orthogonal input. Woody Allen, who has been in analysis for over thirty years, was fond of saying that he could not imagine being out of treatment. Of course, he added quickly, he could not imagine changing either!

Because therapists tend to lose leverage over time, we begin intervening right away, postponing any detailed history-taking for later. We start by inquiring about the client's "upset"—the event that prompted him or her to pick up the phone and make an appointment. There may be other background problems, but therapies that do not deal effectively with the initial upset are not likely to be successful. Like Szasz' court jester, our goal is to demonstrate that we grasp the problem and have some idea about how to go about "fixing" it. Similar to the content of the White and Epston letters, we make an educated guess about the current circumstances and offer a tentative investigative plan. If we are successful, the client should leave that first session (a) feeling understood, (b) experiencing some symptom relief, (c) agreeing to an initial therapeutic contract, and (d) eagerly anticipating what comes next.

We have described how Maturana's concepts can help constructivists understand the dynamics of change. To have an impact, client therapist collaborations must generate orthogonal interaction. One of the simplest ways to do this is through the creative use of language.

WORD PLAY

Aldous Huxley (1940/1962) wrote that "words have the power to mold men's thinking, to canalize their feeling, [and] to direct their willing and acting" (p. 2). Fresh metaphors and novel distinctions galvanize attention and invigorate conversation. For instance, in first sessions with couples, we frequently accuse them of engaging in a "conversation of recrimination, accusation, and characterization" (Efran, Lukens, & Lukens, 1990, p. 185). Never having heard that expression before, they are all ears. This gives us an opportunity to emphasize the differences between the blame game and a problem-solving dialogue. We explain that these are two separate conversational domains with entirely different purposes. They cannot take place simultaneously. The couple soon becomes proficient at hearing when they shift from one domain to the other, and they begin to self monitor their nonproductive discourse. Of course, we could have just said, "The two of you are arguing again," but that phrasing would not have had the same punch.

A youngster once told well known child therapist Haim Ginott that he did not want to go to school. Ginott replied, "Is that your *considered* opinion?" The boy was thrilled to discover that he not only had an opinion, but that it was a considered opinion! By the time they got back to talking about his school fears, they were no longer positioned as adversaries. Ginott's phrasing was orthogonal to what the boy was expecting to hear from an adult, and that made all the difference.

In our clinical work, we have gotten great mileage out of distinguishing between the "mind" and the "self." Because we have described this linguistic maneuver elsewhere (Efran & Soler-

Baillo, 2008), we will only touch upon it lightly here. Following Smothermon (1979), we define "mind" as the totality of the person's survival mechanisms and defensive postures. By definition, it is fear-driven and risk-averse. When people operate from mind, they are focused on winning, dominating, and being right. The self, on the other hand, represents our connection to others and to the larger community. A person operating from self is more interested in contributing than dominating; more interested in *living* than *surviving*.

Everyone has both a mind and a self. The trick is to keep them in balance. The mind is always worried about what it perceives as dire consequences. Therefore, whenever it grabs the microphone, it overreacts and drowns out the voice of the self. Metaphorically, we can say that successful therapy consists of lowering the mind's volume control. When we discuss the mind and the self with clients, we also invoke a series of subsidiary distinctions that empower them to untangle their relationship quandaries. For instance, we discuss the differences between mastery and avoidance, and we distinguish between living "at cause" (as the responsible party) and living "at effect" (as the victim). Again, it helps that many of these phrasings are a bit offbeat.

Constructivists should be receptive to this emphasis on linguistic subtlety, recognizing that it is in language that problems are created and resolved. Note that even seemingly unbearable circumstances do not become "problems" until someone—using words and symbols—says so and someone else agrees. In other words, to have a problem, you have to make something of something! Similarly, it is the client who says when a problem ceases to exist—when his or her questions have been answered.

CONCLUSION

The prospects of constructivist therapy are, of course, tied to the overall state of the therapy market. And, given the current economic downturn and the increased influence of the pharmaceutical industry, the news is not good. Recently, a piece in the *New York Times* (Gottlieb, 2012) suggested that the only therapists prospering are those who have carved out trendy specialties for themselves. The article suggests that therapists hire branding consultants. Who knew there were such things?

If constructivists had such a consultant, he or she would probably suggest immediately ditching the constructivist moniker as a label that has lost its cachet. These days, few are startled to learn that reality is as much invented as discovered (Watzlawick, 1984). Furthermore, the distinctiveness of the constructivist brand has been eroded by its shameless appropriation by therapists of other persuasions. Consider the following quote from cognitivist Donald Meichenbaum (1993): "It is not as if there is one reality and clients distort that reality . . . rather, there are multiple realities, and the task for the therapist is to help clients become aware of how they create these realities and of the consequences of such constructions" (p. 203). Even Ellis (1993), toward the end of his career, discreetly climbed aboard the constructivist bandwagon.

An attendee at last year's *Psychotherapy Networker Symposium* summed it up nicely. He noted that soon none of our therapy school affiliations will matter because CBT will have gobbled up all of the competition, having "oozed" over the mental health landscape like a giant amoeba. Indeed, we already have a Mindfulness-based CBT and an Emotion focused CBT (Suveg, Kendall, Comer, & Robin, 2006). Despite the incompatibility in world views, this leaves little doubt that there will soon be an "official" Constructivist CBT.

In fact, very few therapy brands retain their identities, their purity, or their popularity. Consider Eric Berne's (1972) transactional analysis (TA). It was once a hot topic on the talk-show circuit, and the TA organization had established an international network of training centers. Now, it is practiced in its original form only by a shrinking band of devoted followers. Similarly, we rarely hear much about William Glasser's (1965) reality therapy or Yalom's (1980) existential approach. The integrationist movement (Stricker & Gold, 1993), introduced in the '70s, continues to limp along, neither capturing market share nor being completely overlooked. Even psychoanalysis, once the King of the Hill, has been reduced to a mere shadow of its former self, remaining viable mainly in large metropolitan areas. Against this backdrop, the current status of constructivist approaches hardly seems surprising.

As we have argued, PCT has always been a tough sell. With the possible exception of the fixed-role procedure and Kelly's grid technology, it lacks the pat formulas and nifty gimmicks that have boosted the popularity of other modalities. Kelly's thousand pages may contain clinical jewels, but mining these is not a task for the faint at heart. Then, too, PCT came along at a time when behavior therapy, psychoanalysis, and the humanistic approaches were battling it out for the upper hand—and PCT got lost in the shuffle. Before it could get a secure foothold, it was dismissed as a limited, cognitive approach that failed to adequately address clients' emotional lives.

Kelly himself predicted that even if PCT was wildly successful, it would—like any good theory—sow the seeds of its own destruction. He felt that it would be quite an achievement if it lasted one or two decades before being replaced by something more elegant. He modestly talked about it as a "theoretical vessel" (1969, p. 95), designed to launch a voyage of discovery. He was clear from the outset that those aboard were free to turn back at any time or to search for something more seaworthy. Personally, we are not yet ready to jump ship. Instead, in this chapter, we have recommended several updates to the ship's aging navigational equipment.

In brief, our four recommendations are (a) to highlight the notion of therapy as a research enterprise, (b) to focus squarely on issues of interpersonal context, (c) to adopt Maturana's theory of change, and (d) to use novel linguistic distinctions to generate orthogonality. These proposals are probably not catchy enough to qualify as therapy gimmicks, and it is doubtful that any such suggestions will propel constructivism into the mainstream of contemporary practice. However, these revisions are necessary

correctives that will improve how constructivist therapy is practiced and enable it to keep up with changing times.

References

Barlow, D. H., & Nock, M. K. (2009). Why can't we be more idiographic in our research? *Perspectives on Psychological Science, 4,* 19–21.
Barlow, D. H., Nock, M. K., & Hersen, M. (2009). *Single case experimental designs: Strategies for studying behavior change* (3rd ed.). Boston, MA: Allyn & Bacon.
Berne, E. (1972). *What do you say after you say hello?* New York, NY: Grove Press.
Bowen, M. (1978). *Family therapy in clinical practice.* Northvale, NJ: Jason Aronson.
Bruner, J. S. (1956). A cognitive theory of personality. [Review of the book *The psychology of personal constructs*]. *Contemporary Psychology: A Journal of Reviews, 1,* 355–357. doi: 10.1037/005215
Burns, D. (2013). Living with the devil we know. *Psychotherapy Networker, 37*(1), 29–35, 56.
de Shazer, S. (1988). *Clues: Investigating solutions in brief therapy.* New York, NY: Norton.
Dickens, C. (1991). *A Christmas carol.* Mineola, New York: Dover Publications. (Reprinted from *A Christmas carol,* 1843, London, England: Chapman & Hall)
Efran, J. S., & Fauber, R. L. (1995). Radical constructivism: Questions and answers. In R. A. Neimeyer & M. J. Mahoney (Eds.). *Constructivism in psychotherapy* (pp. 275–304). Washington, DC: American Psychological Association.
Efran, J. S., & Lukens, M. D. (1985). The world according to Humberto Maturana. *The Family Therapy Networker 9*(3): 23–25, 27–28, 72–75.
Efran, J., Lukens, M., & Greene, M. (2007). Defining psychotherapy. *Psychotherapy Networker, 31*(2), 40–44, 47, 52–55, 66.
Efran, J. S., Lukens, M. D., & Lukens, R. J. (1990). *Language, structure, and change: Frameworks of meaning in psychotherapy.* New York, NY: Norton.
Efran, J. S., & Soler-Baillo, J. (2008). The mind and self in context-centered therapy. In J. D. Raskin & S. K. Bridges (Eds.), *Studies in meaning 3: Constructivist therapy in the real world* (pp. 85–105). New York, NY: Pace University Press.
Ellis, A. (1993). Reflections on rational-emotive therapy. *Journal of Consulting and Clinical Psychology, 61,* 199–201.
Fancher, R. T. (1995). *Cultures of healing: Correcting the image of American mental health care.* New York, NY: W. H. Freeman.
Frank, J. D. (1973). *Persuasion and healing: A comparative study of psychotherapy* (rev. ed.). Baltimore, MD: Johns Hopkins University Press.

Frankl, V. (1963). *Man's search for meaning.* New York, NY: Washington Square Press.

Germer, C. K., Siegel, R. D., & Fulton, P. R. (Eds.). (2005). *Mindfulness and psychotherapy.* New York, NY: Guilford Press.

Glasser, W. (1965). *Reality therapy: A new approach to psychiatry.* New York, NY: Harper & Row.

Gottlieb, L. (2012, November 25). *The branding cure.* New York Times, p. MM36.

Gregson, D., & Efran, J. S. (2002). *The tao of sobriety: Helping you recover from alcohol and drug addiction.* New York, NY: St. Martin's Press.

Hayes, S. C., Strosahl, K. D., & Wilson, K. G. (2012). *Acceptance and commitment therapy: The process and practice of mindful change* (2nd ed.). New York, NY: Guilford Press.

Hubble, M. A., Duncan, B. L., & Miller, S. D. (Eds.). (2009). *The heart and soul of change: What works in therapy* (2nd ed.). Washington, DC: American Psychological Association.

Huxley, A. L. (1962). Words and their meanings. In M. Black (Ed.) *The importance of language* (pp. 1–13). Englewood Cliffs, NJ: Prentice-Hall. (Reprinted from *Words and their meanings*, 1940, Los Angeles, CA: Ward Ritchie Press)

Janov, A. (1970). *The primal scream.* New York, NY: Dell.

Johnson, S. M., & Whiffen, E. (Eds.) (2003). *Attachment processes in couple and family therapy.* New York, NY: Guilford Press.

Kelly, G. A. (1955). *The psychology of personal constructs* (Vols. 1 & 2). New York, NY: Norton.

Kelly, G. A. (1962). Europe's matrix of decision. In M. R. Jones (Ed.), *Nebraska Symposium on Motivation 1962* (pp. 83–125). Lincoln, NE: University of Nebraska Press.

Kelly, G. A. (1969). *Clinical psychology and personality: The selected papers of George Kelly* (B. Maher, Ed.). New York, NY: John Wiley & Sons.

Mahoney, M. J. (1991). *Human change processes: The scientific foundations of psychotherapy.* New York, NY: Basic Books.

Mahoney, M. J. (2003). *Constructive psychotherapy: A practical guide.* New York, NY: Guilford Press.

Marcia, J. E., Rubin, B. M., & Efran, J. S. (1969). Systematic desensitization: Expectancy change or counter conditioning? *Journal of Abnormal Psychology, 74,* 382–387.

Maturana, H. R., & Varela, F. J. (1987). *The tree of knowledge: The biological roots of human understanding.* Boston, MA: Shambhala Publications.

McLaughlin, M. (1960). *The neurotics' notebook.* Indianapolis, IN: Bobbs-Merrill.

Meichenbaum, D. (1993). Changing conceptions of cognitive behavior modification: Retrospect and prospect. *Journal of Consulting and Clinical Psychology, 61,* 202–204.

Minuchin, S. & Fishman, H. C. (2004). *Family therapy techniques*. Boston, MA: Harvard University Press.

Mosak, H. H., & Maniacci, M. P. (1998). *Tactics in counseling and psychotherapy*. Itasca, IL: F. E. Peacock Publishers

Nichols, M. P., & Schwartz, R. C. (1995). *Family therapy: Concepts and methods* (3rd ed.). Needham Heights, MA: Allyn & Bacon.

Perls, F. (1973). *The gestalt approach & eye witness to therapy*. Ben Lomond, CA: Science and Behavior Books.

Prus, R. (2000). Human lived experience and the persistent failings of psychology [Review of the book *Lilies of the field: Marginal people who live for the moment* by S. Day, E. Papataxiarchis, & M. Stewart (Eds.)] *Contemporary Psychology, A Journal of Reviews, 45*, 264–265.

Rogers, C. (1951). *Client-centered therapy: Its current practice, implications and theory*. London, England: Constable.

Rogers, C. R. (1956). Intellectualized psychotherapy. [Review of the book *The psychology of personal constructs* by G. A. Kelly]. *Contemporary Psychology: A Journal of Reviews, 1*, 357–358. doi: 10.1037/005216

Ryle, G. (1949). *The concept of mind*. New York, NY: Barnes & Noble.

Selvini Palazzoli, M. (1986). Towards a general model of psychotic family games. *Journal of Marital and Family Therapy, 12*, 339–349.

Shapiro, F. (1995). *Eye movement desensitization and reprocessing: Basic principles, protocols, and procedures*. New York, NY: Guilford Press.

Sharma, S. L. (1986). *The therapeutic dialogue: A theoretical and practical guide to psychotherapy*. Albuquerque, NM: University of New Mexico Press.

Simon, R. (2007). The top 10: The most influential therapists of the past quarter-century. *Psychotherapy Networker, 31*(2), pp. 24–37, 68.

Smothermon, R. (1979). *Winning through enlightenment*. San Francisco, CA: Context Publications.

Stampfl, T. G. (1970). Implosive therapy: An emphasis on covert stimulation. In D. J. Levis (Ed.) *Learning approaches to therapeutic behavior change* (pp. 182–204). Chicago, IL: Aldine.

Stricker, G., & Gold, J. R. (Eds.). (1993). *Comprehensive handbook of psychotherapy integration*. New York, NY: Plenum Press.

Suveg, C., Kendall, P. C., Comer, J. S., & Robin, J. (2006). Emotion-focused cognitive-behavioral therapy for anxious youth: A multiple-baseline evaluation. *Journal of Contemporary Psychotherapy, 36*(2), 77–85.

Szasz, T. (1973). *The second sin*. New York, NY: Anchor Press/Doubleday.

Szasz, T. S. (1988). *The myth of psychotherapy: Mental healing as religion, repression, and rhetoric*. Syracuse, NY: Syracuse University Press.

Varela, F. J. (1979). *Principles of biological autonomy*. New York, NY: Elsevier-North Holland.

Wampold, B. E. (2001). *The great psychotherapy debate: Models, methods, and findings* (2nd ed.). New York, NY: Routledge.

Watzlawick, P. (Ed.). (1984). *The invented reality: How do we know what we believe we know?: Contributions to constructivism.* New York, NY: Norton.

White, M., & Epston, D. (1990). *Narrative means to therapeutic ends.* New York, NY: Norton.

Wolpe, J. (1958). *Psychotherapy by reciprocal inhibition.* Stanford, CA: Stanford University Press.

Woy, J. R., & Efran, J. S. (1972). Systematic desensitization and expectancy in the treatment of speaking anxiety. *Behaviour Research and Therapy, 10,* 43–49.

Yalom, I. (1980). *Existential psychotherapy.* New York, NY: Basic Books.

∝ 7 ⟡

Developing a Dialogue: Constructivist Convergence in Psychotherapy and Beyond

Robert A. Neimeyer, Donald Meichenbaum, and
Caroline M. Stanley

To explore the converging perspectives of two clinical psychologists who have long been active in constructivist theory, research and practice, a "next generation" colleague conducted a joint interview with them exploring themes of narrative, meaning making and social engagement as reflected in their evolving careers, while also adding her own perspectives. What follows faithfully captures the conversation that resulted, with only slight "narrative smoothing" and the addition of some implied references.

Caroline: Maybe I could start us off with a question. This is just a thought that came from me personally. I have to say that I am patently aware of the fact that I am conversing with two prominent figures in the field of psychology; figures whose names are in the textbooks, figures who have had a real influence on the field of psychology and its evolution. For me, I would be interested in hearing about each of your own perspectives regarding the evolution of the field in the last 30 or 40 years and how you construe your own role in it. Likewise, I would be interested in hearing each of your perspectives regarding the contributions of the other. For example, Bob, how has Don's work been meaningful for you? What do you view as

Don's major contributions to the field? And Don, the same questions go for you about Bob.

Don: I like that, Caroline. The notion that we've been around for 40 years is a bit troublesome but other than that, I think . . .

Bob: [laughing] I have to say that I was doing the math myself to see if I could measure up to that but, sadly, I think that I came out with an affirmative answer, Don!

Don: [laughing] I think you're aging us!

Caroline: [laughing] Aging us? How about you reconstrue that . . . into another narrative that's more meaningful and coherent?

Don: Why don't you start us off, Bob?

Bob: Well, I suppose in some ways we enter this dialogue as an insider and an outsider who moved inside to constructivism, or at least this is my construction of our respective paths. For my part, really from my earliest immersion in psychology as an undergraduate, I initially grafted onto a personal construct framework, in a George Kelly mode. That really became my native home base and although I've wandered far afield from it in many ways, I've always come back to it. I've continued to teach personal construct theory as a graduate seminar, one that you took some years ago, Caroline. So I suppose I could say that I feel natively constructivist, and I could talk a little about how I felt primed by life experiences for that a little later in our conversation.

           To answer the other part of your question, Caroline, one of the reasons I was very eager to have Don in this dialogue is that he was one of the first and few "cognitive-behavioral" people who made any sense to me, in part because he never seemed, in my history of acquaintance with him, to overvalue rationality or empiricism to the exclusion of an emotional and relational dimension. This became very clear in his writing as he made a shift towards an attention to metaphor and storytelling and deeply incorporated a narrative perspective. But it was clear to me, even before that, in his vividly experiential style with clients. I found the theatrical quality of some of his interventions—his willingness to not simply talk about relationships with clients, but rather to enact and perform them, to be an authentic representative of the social world—all of that seemed much more alive to me. By engaging clients emotionally, vividly, he enabled them to reflect on the way in which they were constructing and maintaining relationships and patterns of symptomatology and distress, but not in a way that simply registered it in a triple column technique on paper or that rationally disputed certain cognitive distortions. Instead, he made therapy a living encounter between a therapist who was very much in the room and a client who was drawn deeper into the room. So, for me, that was my early and consistent impression of Don, and the reason I regard him as a fellow traveler.

Don: That's very gracious of you, Bob. It's fascinating that you start with George Kelly. I was an undergraduate at City College in New York City from 1958–1962. City College was a hotbed of Freudian psychodynamic psychotherapists. They had a visiting professor one year who would come and lecture. I became fascinated with this fellow and I sat at his knee listening. It turns out that his name was George Kelly!

Bob: I had no idea!

Don: I became enamored with his notion of a constructivist, story perspective and that not everything was drive reduction—that there was something else driving folks. I left there and went to the University of Illinois, which was a hotbed of behavioral psychology. At that point, just think about where we were: this was the onset of behavior therapy with Wolpe, Lazarus, Skinner, and so forth. In fact, as a kind of footnote to this, at that time, you could not submit an article to *JABA* (*Journal of Applied Behavioral Analysis*) that used the word cognition. All of cognitions apropos to Skinner were sort of mands, operants and coverants and, supposedly, thinking and accompanying emotions were subject to the same laws of learning as overt behavior. Now we've come to understand that the laws of learning don't even apply to overt behavior, let alone covert behavior. In the midst of all of that, they had a visiting professor who came and lectured—his name was Viktor Frankl. So I sat at his feet and absorbed his explanatory system of resiliency and storytelling, meaning-making and logotherapy. And at that time, the view of cognition shifted from a learning framework into an information-processing framework— that is, we were sort of like mini-computers. We were coding and decoding, we had schemas, and all of that. That became the language. In fact, I've written up this history and it's been published (Meichenbaum, 1977, 1992).

          One of the things that emerged that was interesting was that I became steeped in clinical work, especially with people who had traumatic experiences and were diagnosed with PTSD. It turns out that PTSD is essentially a disorder of autobiographical memory. That is, something bad has to have had happened to you in the past (what *DSM* [*Diagnostic and Statistical Manual of Mental Disorders*] calls a Criterion A event) and not only that, but you have to remember that detail and tell a story either to yourself or to others about that event and its lingering impact and implications. So I became an exquisite listener to the stories people tell themselves and others—and I've written about the personal background that led me to this perspective (Meichenbaum, 1977). That immediately embeds you into this constructive narrative perspective. And you cannot embrace that perspective without reaching in and reading Bob's writings about the role that storytelling plays. For many of the clients that I was dealing with, it was complicated grief, because there were all kinds of losses accompanying that trauma. So I was enamored and learned a great deal from Bob's writing and his creative interventions on how to help people become unstuck from the hotspots and to transform their stories.

Historically, if we take your mandate of 40 years, Caroline, we can track the evolutionary perspective, and I think that the field of psychotherapy is stuck because it is atheoretical. It's about evidence-based concerns, but we don't know the mechanisms that lead to change. And I am very hopeful that a constructivist narrative perspective can really become the explanatory model of behavior change. I'll conclude by saying that we are each not only *homo sapiens*, but *homo narrans*. That means that we are all storytellers. I'll argue that the nature of the stories that people tell themselves and others is really critical. This is what I've highlighted in my recent book, *Roadmaps to Resilience* (Meichenbaum, 2013), and I've even given an algorithm of what you need to do to have chronic PTSD. But that's the evolution—you can start to see the telltale people, like Kelly and Frankl. I also spent some time with Jerome Bruner and crossed paths with

Aaron Beck, Albert Ellis, and other people who were highlighting the cognitive perspective, though my take on cognitive behavior was always slightly different from theirs.

Bob: I appreciate the scope and depth of that substantial introduction, Don. I appreciate the generosity of it as well, with respect to your openness to learning from many people. And at least some of them are still alive, I'm happy to report! It's a delight, in that way, to extend the conversation.

PERSONAL ACCOUNTS THAT ILLUSTRATE A CONSTRUCTIVE NARRATIVE PERSPECTIVE

Bob: So let me also shift to a personal level. It strikes me that, although I didn't realize it at the time, or for many years subsequently, I really represented a kind of case study of that trauma-based disruption of narrative that you allude to as having been centrally important in the way you think about narrative. Certainly I found myself attempting to put together a story that accommodated some autobiographical episodes that were incoherent or didn't easily fit within the plot or thematic structure of my life story. So if I were to trace back to what was happening for me about the time you were encountering Kelly and Frankl, what I was encountering was a father who died by suicide during a period of deep depression just before my 12th birthday. One cold January morning in Ohio, my brother and I woke up to our mother's panicked entry to our bedroom saying, "Boys, boys, I can't wake your father!" As we got out of bed in our footed pajamas and nervously went to the threshold of their bedroom and peered in around the door jamb, I saw her reach down and try to awaken my dad under this turquoise bedspread that covered him, his face turned away from us. And he just kind of flopped onto his back as she tugged at his shoulder. At that point, she let out a scream that basically ended childhood for us and launched us into a very different place. The ways that we were able, each of the three of us children—me being the oldest, my brother Greg (there beside me), and our little sister (still sleeping in her room)—we were all launched into an effort to somehow make sense of an utterly senseless event that fractured the foundation of the world we lived in.

Looking back, I managed in the ways I could as a teenager, focusing on work and school as a more stable alternative to a family context in crisis. But ultimately, as I moved into college and encountered my first substantial immersion in psychology in a class taught by Seth Krieger (a student of Franz Epting, himself a student of Kelly's), I began to find in George Kelly's work a frame that could help me begin to hold some of the terror, complexity, and strangeness of the world to which Dad's drug overdose had introduced us. I was especially drawn to what Kelly called "dimensions of transition": concepts like *anxiety* understood as confronting a world that you simply couldn't scaffold, anticipate, place meanings upon; the idea of *threat*, of finding yourself now in a world in which you were nothing like you thought you ought to be or would be. These concepts made a visceral kind of sense to me. So my own attempts at meaning making really benefited from having a Kellian vocabulary to wrap around them. I found myself then working in suicide intervention centers and beginning to do research from a personal construct standpoint on people's attitudes towards death (Neimeyer, 2000). Eventually, that moved into a focus upon trauma and bereavement (Neimeyer, 2009). In this way, I suppose you could say that, across the course of a career, I came home to myself, but always with an investment in the practice of therapy, the study of its processes, and the role of meaning-making in the development and breakdown of life narratives.

Don: That's quite a story, and the way in which you've been able to transform your life given that developmental tragedy is indeed impressive. I spend a lot of time now working with returning soldiers from Iraq and Afghanistan and deal a lot with the aftermath of natural and other disasters. For example, tomorrow I am going to Biloxi, Mississippi, to consult with the VA [U.S. Department of Veterans Affairs]. The following Wednesday, I am going to Atlantic City to talk to the mental health community dealing with victims of Hurricane Sandy. I sort of go from disaster to disaster. When you hear stories such as your own, Bob, or of the returning soldiers, or the victims of natural disasters, the one thing to keep in mind, which is really impressive, is if you look at the work of George Bonanno, Anne Masten or other people I've written about on the Melissa Institute Website (see www.melissainstitute.org), 75% in the aftermath of these kinds of tragedies evidence an impact but then go on to evidence resilience, if not posttraumatic growth (Meichenbaum, 2013). And 25% of people show some kind of persistent PTSD. So what I find interesting is that the people who are in the 75% group—and I put you there, Bob—find a framework to do meaning making. And that which was credible for you was the Kellian framework. But, for instance, in the aftermath of trauma—like the Newtown school shooting or in the aftermath Hurricane Katrina, or others—in all of these instances, the major way that people cope with trauma is by using some form of spirituality (See Meichenbaum, n.d.). So one of the things that becomes interesting from my perspective as a constructivist isn't that there was anything special about the Kellian framework or anything special about the spiritual framework that you have, but that you have some therapeutic benefit to hang this event on and to find meaning in it. So, as a constructivist, I am really fascinated with the way people fabricate meaning in order to bolster their resilience. For you, Bob, given that you were saturated in psychology and saw that as a professional direction, a Kellian perspective may be appropriate. But when I present workshops on PTSD, I show a video called "Where was God on 9/11?" for people who lost loved ones there. And you can see the way in which they reach out to some kind of spiritual meaning or some sense of tradition. And that becomes the coping mechanism. So, I'm interested in what are the communalities of the psychological mechanisms that put people in the 75% group versus the 25% group.

What was it about the Kellian framework that you found particularly therapeutic? So, Bob, imagine that you are my client for a moment.

Bob: Oh, I love the idea! Why didn't you think of this years ago?

Don: How did finding that meaning system in any way help you with that remarkably distressing event that happened?

Bob: The answer would begin with recognizing that we do not search for what we haven't lost. Had my existing spiritual framework of Roman Catholicism held in the wake of that tsunami of distress, I probably would never have been a constructivist. I might be a priest today instead! But, in fact, my spiritual framework ultimately collapsed under the weight of dad's death. My immersion in the Latin mass, the recent conversion to English—none of that had gelled into a mature spirituality for this 12-year-old kid. And so I relinquished that. I spent a couple of years exploring a more fundamental Christian perspective and then abandoned that as too concrete, too historically situated to have specific relevance to my family's psychosocial struggles in the second half of the 20th century. And after a period of reading Camus, Sartre and other existentialists, I was pretty thoroughly secular by the time I encountered Kelly. What Kelly offered, then, was something on the other side of nothingness. There was a "somethingness" about his theory. There were concepts that held mirrors to my soul, in a secular, psychological way, and helped me understand some of what I and others had experienced and suffered, in the sense of Frankl's statement that those who have a meaning for suffering—a "why" for what has happened—can survive nearly any "how." I began to construct that meaning in Kellian terms. Kelly offered language that had to do with sense-making while also accommodating emotions as intrinsically meaningful signals of the state of our efforts to negotiate reality, to anticipate and interact with it, especially the reality of the social world. That made a native sense to me and it provided me with an initial scaffold on which, ultimately, a larger constructivist edifice began to rise.

Don: One of the things I train clinicians to do is to be exquisite listeners to their client's language. Let's reflect on what you've just said. What it is about the Kelly framework that you found particularly valuable? You have bathed your social discourse . . . I was taking notes as you spoke—you can't take the clinician out of me . . .

Bob: [laughing] I wouldn't want to try!

191

Don: You use words like "accommodate," "meaning-making," that you "anticipate." You bathed your storytelling in what was comforting. There are a lot of what I call "metacognitive-active-transitive" verbs. In your story now, you have a lot of hopeful, "change-talk" words. You gave up one thing and have now found another. So you gave up your Catholicism, and the evangelical kind of perspective, and you were on a search. And your poetry comes out. You have a "mirror on your soul." That's poetry! If I were the clinician, I would be interested to pluck that metaphor. So I'd go, "Bob, mirror on your soul? Is that mirror still there now?" . . . You know, that kind of conversation.

So I think that we could develop a metric—a type of coding system—an analysis of what are the key elements of peoples' speech that you have to include in order to not get stuck. As a teenager, you had the potential of going the other route, of being in that 25% group . . . So, as you tell your story, you just naturally embed within it these metacognitive-active-transitive verbs. Not only that, but you embed, also, "re" verbs—you know, like "I re-gain composure," "I re-connected," etc. So I think that the next step for a constructivist narrative perspective is to develop a methodology—where you could actually do content analysis—and see how people change stories. I could have done this interview with someone who was a born again Christian and he or she would have said how they found their faith, then re-arranged their priorities, they found meaning in the divine, sense-making . . . Bob, does this make sense to you?

Bob: It makes compelling sense to me. One thing I love about it is that, as a coding system, it focuses on the verbs rather than the nouns. It looks not at categories of meaning made, something we've actually done in our own research (Gillies, Neimeyer, & Milman, 2014), but it instead looks at how those meanings are transformed. I think that verbs get too little look in psychotherapy generally. The field in general tends to have a classificatory approach to diagnosis, looking at boxing people in, but you're really opening the boxes with your attention how they introduce change—the language they use to structure that, or the absence of such language— language of foreclosure, language of certainty, language of closing down.

Don: I was just using you as a case study, an N of 1, here . . .

Bob: Please, feel free.

Don: You have the courage to poignantly not only share it here, but in writing as well, about this particular loss. If you read Tom Joiner's (2005) book, he starts off in the same way. I do a workshop on suicidality. In fact, if you go to the Melissa Institute (see www.melissainstitute.org) I have a handout there, where I wrote out what it is that you have to tell yourself in order to die by suicide. What were the thinking processes that your Dad, or whoever engages in this type of behavior, must engage in to get to that point, such as the power of the word "only," or the degree to which you engage in black or white thinking. I think the literature gives you a pretty good script of exactly what you need to do to get to that focal point (Meichenbaum, 2006a, 2006b, 2013; Meichenbaum & Fong, 1993). Similarly, I could do a script on what you need to do to get PTSD. If there is any merit to these scripts, it would have a lot of implications. How do you get people unstuck from that script? It would be interesting to take a variety of conditions—PTSD, suicidality, and more—and write out what the constructive narrative perspective proposes as a sequence of things that you have to engage in as a sort of mood induction.

Bob: Caroline, why don't we invite your reactions before I jump right back in. I'm eager to do so, but want to make room for you.

Caroline: I've actually been quite intrigued by this whole process. We've just had a conversation in which Bob talked about a profound and painful experience—about a trauma that profoundly impacted the course of his life. And we connected that experience to Don's work on resilience and, interestingly, Bob's path to resiliency is this very narrative, constructivist, meaning-making approach that now guides his approach to psychology and psychotherapy. I wonder, Bob, whether you're the first person to give credit to constructivism for doing that—for creating a path to resiliency that bolstered both you and the theory itself. I'm just sort of struck by the beauty of what has unfolded here in our discussion. There is something reflexive about what just transpired: constructivism was used to transform Bob and, in the process—because of Bob's subsequent accomplishments in the field—constructivism, too, was transformed.

Don: [to Caroline] When we analyze this transcript, focus on how Bob described this incident. If you analyzed that segment, then you could see how I was able to pluck out and attend to specific things that make that story a resilient story. How his mother's scream ended his childhood. Or how he then searched for meaning and came to George Kelly. If you type out that 3 minute thing that he said—that is the story of resilience, how he gets himself into the 75% group.

Bob: I want to underscore the 75%, because we're not talking about an exception to the rule, in my case; we're talking about the rule. And it's the commonplace audacity of people in all walks of life, drawing on all kinds of life narratives to somehow surmount tragedy. We do it frequently, not merely once in a lifetime but often multiple times. Ultimately, we recognize that every person, every place, every project, every possession we love, we will one day lose. Our lives are marinated in loss. Most of the time, we manage to swim through the soup of that pretty well and come up on the other side, as our research also documents (Currier, Holland, & Neimeyer, 2012; Neimeyer & Sands, 2011). I think that Don's genius in recognizing that I'm just part of the majority is very compatible with Kelly's view of reflexivity—that we need to construct a psychology that is adequate to who we are as psychologists, as theorists, as human beings who are attempting to make sense of our own behavior and that of other people. This is one of the draws, magnetically, for me, to constructivist work. That is, the constructivist mirror of our souls, to go back to that image, is one that I think is well-polished—it lets us see ourselves with some level of clarity. We don't feel shrunk or distorted by the reflection; if anything, it ennobles us—even in our most despairing times—to recognize that we're still passionately pursuing a way of being that makes sense, that has coherence, that connects with others, and with a purposeful future . . . even in our anguish.

Don: One of the things to keep in mind is that you can be both resilient and still have post trauma stress. The sense of loss and mourning—the loss of your childhood and all the other things—can coexist with your being a major contributor and using your own personal experience to help others. It isn't as if it's an "either or" kind of process.

My major concern in all of this is: How do you get those who are embracing a constructivist perspective to have an impact on the rest of the field, so that we don't become the Fox News of psychology, only talking to each other, people who believe in the same things. From my perspective—especially if I were starting my career like Caroline and wanted to have an impact—it would be really interesting to develop some line of research that demonstrates that the constructivist perspective has major implications. That it has predictive power to tell—in the aftermath of Newtown or Hurricane Sandy—who is going to fall in the 75% versus the 25%. And that you would get story telling from these people over the course of the recovery process. And they would be able to count the number of verbs, the number of "re" verbs, the ability to find meaning, the degree to which you can nurture social supports. When I lecture on trauma/spirituality/recovery, one thing I say is that believing in a higher power is like outsourcing social support. You have this higher power you can read into. If you ask people what it is about spirituality that is particularly helpful from a narrative perspective, you can see that the way in which you embrace Kelly, they embrace these others. The metaphors they use aren't that much different from the ones that you use. You get a figure of speech in your head and it triggers another, and you stay with that metaphor. Every one of these has one thing in common: that it is a *journey*. They don't know where it's going to lead but from that landmark event—when your mother screamed—that put you on a different trajectory than the one you were on beforehand. And you are negotiating that trajectory. There's an implicit sense of movement to the storytelling. There is not only the content of the verbs and the number of "re" verbs, but the degree to which an independent judge could read this and see the commitment to a journey that is hopeful. The other thematic thing is meaning-making. You, Bob, have been able to transform this into a personal journey of a career. You translated this tragedy into being able to become the go-to man in grief therapy.

When obtaining multiple stories of people who have been victimized, such as in the recent Boston marathon bombing—how are they going to recover? The key question is: If you had the opportunity to just be an observer of their storytelling, what would that look like? I've often characterized myself as a cognitive ethologist. As an observer, imagine that you're a cognitive ethologist studying how peoples' narrative changes over the course of time. If we could develop a metric that people could use, then constructivists would have a real impact on the rest of the field.

Bob: We've done a fair amount of research on some of these processes, at a certain level, and yet there's a gap, Don, that I think you can help fill. What we've established through studies of bereaved young persons, people who experienced the violent death of a loved one (homicide survivors), those who are bereaved in later life (loss of a spouse), parents who have lost children, a whole range of losses, is that those who are unable to construct a meaning of the experience tend to suffer much greater risk of complicated grief outcomes; prolonged, intense yearning; destruction of their lives—often across a period of many years (Neimeyer, 2011). We also know, from some of our longitudinal studies that those who are able to find meaning in the event—to be able to make sense of it, very often, as you say, in spiritual terms—tend to do better in the long run (Coleman & Neimeyer, 2010; Holland, Currier, Coleman, & Neimeyer, 2010). As much as four full years later, they experience a heightened state of well-being, confidence, hopefulness, joy, and so on, than those who do not achieve that kind of meaning-making in the earlier aftermath of loss.

With respect to spirituality specifically, we do find evidence that people who are able somehow to wrap their hearts and minds around the loss in spiritual terms—to see it as God's will, to have hope for reunion—are comforted by this and suffer less complication and anguish in their grieving, and more psychological growth (Burke & Neimeyer, 2011; Currier, Malott, Martinez, Sandy, & Neimeyer, 2012). But they sometimes find that their religiosity becomes more a source of complication than comfort. We have found that about 25% of spiritually-leaning bereaved people faced with more severe crises, like the murder of a loved one, tend to experience not merely complicated grief, but also what we are referring to as *complicated spiritual grief* (Burke, Neimeyer, McDevitt-Murphy, Ippolito, & Roberts, 2011). When we look at the data longitudinally, these survivors' earlier experience of complicated grief—this intense, separation-distress with reference to their lost loved one—begins to generalize into a kind of separation-distress in relation to God. They begin to feel that God either was not on duty, didn't care, was powerless to avert the tragedy, or—in a more sinister way—is inflicting the death of the loved one on them as a kind of punishment for their own lack of faith or wrongdoing (Burke et al., 2011; Burke et al., 2014 b; Neimeyer & Burke, 2011).

Interestingly, what happens is that these religiously-inclined people almost never doubt the existence of God, but rather they re-narrate their relationship with God as a neglectful or abusive parent. They may also experience a second level of disruption, in addition to this vertical dimension with God, as the horizontal dimension of their relationship with their faith community also may erode. So we've developed some measures to look at things like the integration of stressful life experiences, the attribution of meaning to them, sense-making, finding a new, practical footing in the world (Holland et al., 2010). We've also developed a measure to look at complicated spiritual grief in the terms we're speaking of here—the erosion of a secure relationship with God, as well as disruption of religious practice and community (Burke et al., 2014a). All of that converges with what we're speaking about, but it leaves the critical clinical processes, which could be revealed under this lens of cognitive ethology, a mystery. That is, we still need that close analysis of language; we still need to listen with a clinician's ear to the evolving story of our clients in session, which we may inflect in one direction or another to render more hopefulness in the account. That's what we lack, and that's what I think you're pointing us to: the next step in our research and our clinical horizons.

Don: That's definitely quite fascinating. In my *Roadmaps to Resilience* book, I highlight a lot of the work of Ken Pargament and his colleagues because they've highlighted both the positive and negative aspects of spiritual involvement in fostering resilience or not. Insofar as the individual who has had the losses that you describe believes that God has abandoned them or punished them, their anger interferes with the healing process. You could actually look at those individuals who still turn to a higher power for some meaning making, but come to an interpretation that would exacerbate their stress. In fact, one of the things that becomes evident is that after a certain point in time, it is mostly likely therapeutic to no longer continue to search for meaning. There comes a point when whatever happened with your dad, or other kinds of losses, does not have an explanation. Therefore, how do you come to terms with this? For instance, an anecdote that I cited in the *Roadmaps to Resilience* book comes from Elie Wiesel. What he reports is that in the concentration camps the Jewish inmates held a trial. They wanted to know if God was guilty—in the sense that He could have prevented this or He could have done things along the way. So they hold this trial and the jury decides that God is guilty. He's just guilty. And after the trial they all go back and pray. So the fact that they found Him guilty in no way precludes that He would still be a beneficial belief system for them to have. So there are these beautiful incompatibilities that occur.

With regard to cognitive ethology, you could go to the literature on religious coping and spirituality and see who falls into the 25% group. The thing that is interesting is that people can be resilient interpersonally, or in other kinds of activities, but strictly have that compartment of when they give up their faith. You did not find Catholicism as being supportive in your key personal transition and you gave up others along the way. It's like the *Life of Pi*, but here it's the *Life of Robert*. Have you seen that movie?

Bob: Yes, I've seen at least some good portions of it.

Don: It's a story of searching for meaning.

Bob: In pointing to the casualties to religious faith that can accumulate on this journey, it's also useful to remember that it's those very fracture points in the foundation of our belief that often permit new growth to occur, or reorganization to happen. That's how beliefs of any kind tend to be tried and tested and, when found wanting, are more commonly reconstructed than they are relinquished. I think that's in some way the source of spiritual maturation or development . . . or one might say developing more philosophical *gravitas*. I don't want to refer only to spirituality, especially in that kind of Judeo-Christian frame that we have been implicitly assuming. There are many other forms of spiritually, in a Buddhist, Hindu, Taoist or Islamic frame, a New Age kind of relationship to the divine, or, of a secular sort of philosophy that can equally be tested and grown in response to these loses.

Don: Think about this at the level of the therapist. The fundamental question of therapy, from my perspective, is, "How do you get the client to re-narrate? How do you get them to re-story? How do you get them to re-author their lives?" It's not that they're going to develop a better story that's delusional in some sense, but they actually develop the accompanying coping skills that lead to corrective experiences. They take data from those experiences to confirm this belief. It's kind of an evolving journey perspective. You sort of get disconfirmations or confirmations—and that's where I thought George Kelly fit in really well. In his personal construct model, you can think of the polar opposites. In his fixed-role therapy, he would get people to act as if they were different, which would lead to corrective experiences. Then Kelly would play this Colombo-like character and with puzzlement say, "What are you telling me? Are you saying that you are not this nerd, nebbish, withdrawn person?" That kind of evidential model . . . in some sense, you're turning the client into becoming their own detective, their own therapist.

        One of my favorite questions to ask a client is: "Let me ask you something a bit different or unusual. Bob, do you ever find yourself, in your day-to-day experiences, asking yourself the kind of questions that we ask each other right here in this dialogue? Do you ever ask yourself, I wonder how many verbs I just used in telling my story? Do you ever start to reflect on the number of 're' verbs you re-narrate?" And your verbs are terrific! They "mirror" the soul; they "swim" in things. You're a walking poet!

That is what constructive narrative is all about. And there are dozens of other strategies that therapists can use to get clients to re-narrate, re-author, re-story, re-gain, re-connect. . . .

Bob: I love that. That's the font of clinical creativity—when you move to that level of interactive exactness in being able to offer a strategic view in which people see themselves differently.

We often think of narrative in a representational way—it's a story *about* something, a description, an explanation. But in connecting the idea, as you have, with Kelly's fixed-role therapy—where he is having clients go out and do the world differently, to try on a different set of constructs and observe their relational and identity implications—what we're reminded of is that narratives are essentially *scripts*. They tell us *how* to be, *who* to be, who to be *with* and how. One of the tragedies of a more thinly-textured cognitive-behavioral view is that it privatizes experience; it makes it something that is almost purely internal and largely intellectual, with a few arrows going back and forth to another box that contains vaguely-described affects or symptomatology (usually conveyed in psychiatric terms). What we need to do is to *externalize* constructs, to see them as ways of being with others. And our narratives both capture and inform how we engage the social world.

That step that you, Don, were inviting me to take—to start paying attention to the verbs I use in real social context, in a real world—is exactly where we need to be going. It's bringing the world to bear on our psychotherapeutic experience.

Don: It has wide implications. I'll give you two examples. I was invited to write material for individuals who do peace negations in the Middle East and other settings. I wrote a chapter of what the world would be like if political leaders actually had a constructive narrative perspective as part of their vocabulary (Meichenbaum, 2011). Just imagine if the two of us, Bob, were there when Bush and Cheney were deciding to invade Iraq. Imagine how we would do the therapy to get them to look at their decision-making. I wrote up the twelve, "dirty dozen" errors that lead political leaders, from the narrative perspective, to make war-engendering decisions. I included a session with the president. As the therapist, I say "Mr. President, I notice something and I wondered if you notice it, too?"

Not only at the level of clinicians, but if you think about it in much broader terms, how do people make decisions to blow up other people? What are the steps of making a terrorist? Of going to war? They are all these kinds of narratives—to be a member of a political party or religious group who evidences little or no compassion for the suffering of others and who treats them as "objects." I think that the constructive narrative perspective is much broader than just the clinical domain. All of these decisions are based on stories, fallible stories, as in Chamberlin's narrative of Hitler's intentions . . . they use metaphors from the past. You may find the chapter interesting because it goes through all of these historical accounts where politicians made the wrong decision. The Bay of Pigs, the invasion of Iraq, the escalation, the

Surge—all of these were fallible people making incorrect decisions based on the stories they were telling themselves and others.

So in my 40 years as a therapist, Caroline, I've now come to the point of becoming grandiose to think that this has a much broader perspective than just the field of psychotherapy.

STEPS TO A CONSTRUCTIVIST PSYCHOLOGY

Caroline: Well, Don, what you just said—about constructivism potentially being a much broader perspective beyond the field of psychotherapy—inspires me quite profoundly, and it segues very nicely to a question that I have been eager to ask: Could there be a meaning-making revolution in psychology? With regard to my constructivist/narrative inclinations, a colleague recently referred to me as a member of the "unsung minority." Is there any chance that we might become a more dominant voice someday? I'm not sure whether my own answer would be optimistic or pessimistic. I'm not sure whether I believe that such a paradigm shift will unfold in psychology.

When looking at the Melissa Institute website I was—probably for the first time in a long while—a little bit more inspired. I was inspired because, Don, it seems that you are using the constructivist approach in research that is now being used to advocate for social change and public policy. If I were to think of an avenue towards such a revolution, that would be one pathway.

Don: One quick comment, Caroline: Get rid of the word "revolution."

Caroline: Why?

Don: There are no revolutions in psychology or in science. It's "evolution." There are many people: back from Wundt to Breuer to Freud to Korzybski to Kelly to McAdams. I did the history of the constructive narrative perspective (Meichenbaum, 2003) and Wilhelm Wundt was a constructivist, so we're catching up with the past. It's cycles. That's the way paradigm shifts occur. You know, you get these guys—like Hayes and others who are into acceptance theory—and it's the "third revolution." There are no revolutions! But I think your point is well taken.

Caroline: Okay, so if we were to see a meaning-making *evolution*, what would we need to be doing well in order to see such an evolution transpire?

Bob: I think that Don's point that there is a kind of persuasive rhetoric in the social sciences, founded on an empiricist model . . . and we, no less than others, can play that game well, and, indeed, be informed by it—sometimes even to the point of being surprised by our own results! So there is a research paradigm that is implied in what Don is talking about. It's only partially realized in current constructivist research and it could be greatly deepened by moving to that speaking-turn-by-speaking-turn analysis that he is talking about. Essentially, a kind of pragmatic discourse analysis is being advocated and is entirely feasible to pursue.

            However, just to speak on the other side of this for a moment, I think all of us could also look at the current state of the world and the field, and we might admit that the field is not very propitious for the kind of evolution that we're talking about. We have indebted ourselves to a psychiatric system of classificatory diagnoses; reduced our imaginings to something far less than a grand narrative theory: to looking at clusters of symptomatology or the biological basis that presumably underpins them. All of that tilts the field away from this human, relational, discursive, rhetorical shift that we're endorsing and exploring. And ironically, it may be that these clinical insights will in some way be best cultivated outside the clinical arena. It may be in the analysis of politics, maybe in leadership development in the business world, maybe in coaching people in various forms of not only non-violent communication [laughing], but also in non-violent *cognition*. Maybe we need to get outside of the psychotherapy field in order to realize this possibility.

Don: I'll take the other side of the coin. There are two major things happening in the field of psychopathology and psychotherapy that speak well for a constructive perspective. First, there is increasing data that the so-called evidence-based therapies—the actual, specific treatments—count for a very small proportion of the variance of outcome. It has to do all with therapeutic alliance, and the characteristics of the personality of the therapist and how he or she behaves therein. If that kind of argument is upheld, then, once again, they're now looking for what it is that characterizes these therapists in terms of the core skills. Once you enumerate that, it becomes apparent that expert therapists are really good storytellers, are really good at getting people to alter their stories, to engage in corrective experiences. When we start to look at the content analysis—as Miller, Duncan, Lambert and those guys are doing—you're going to find that they're going to eventually embrace a constructive narrative perspective. That's the one side of this.

The other side is that the NIMH [U.S. National Institute of Mental Health] is now questioning the *DSM-5*. That's going to open up a whole new search for what I call transdiagnostic communalities across psychopathology, and a whole new classification system. If you look at people across a whole variety of disorders—whether it's psychotic, bipolar, schizophrenia, anxiety, depression, and so forth—I think the communality that is going to emerge is also a constructive narrative perspective. I'm really quite hopeful for both of those efforts. For people who have committed their lives to evidence-based therapies, and people are shouting at them to reconsider how important the specific interventions contribute to change versus the role of the therapeutic alliance . . . well, it's quite a challenge!

Next Saturday, I am going to have dinner with Aaron Beck. I have the highest regard for him, just as a human being. He has developed cognitive therapy and deserves every credit. There is now a review in the clinical psych literature that shows that cognitive therapy for depression is no better than bona fide comparisons (Baardseth et al., 2013). I don't know how to break the news to him. I'm going to tell him that I'm in a quandary because I train clinicians. The key question is, do I advocate for one specific way? I just came back from San Antonio where I was training people who do Internet therapy with soldiers from all over the world. The key question is what was I going to advocate? Do I go for the exposure-based cognitive processing that the VA embraced? Or do I highlight that there are multiple other models, other kinds of interventions? So I think that as the field is coming to recognize these limitations, it opens it up to a new paradigm. That is, you needed some questioning of the already-existing paradigms, and when they don't work, when you find out that the laws of learning don't apply to overt behavior let alone covert behavior, when you find out that information-processing is a metaphor that has limitations, that people use metaphors and other kinds of things that guide their scripts, then it opens it up.

So I'm much more optimistic. I wish I was as young as you, Caroline, so I could see what the next 40 years would look like and where the constructive narrative will fit in.

CAN CONSTRUCTIVISM EVOLVE BEYOND PSYCHOLOGY?

Bob: Maybe that's a good question to turn to. It's certainly one that you and I can engage, but maybe Caroline also has a perspective on that from her own generational standpoint, as to what this field is evolving toward.

Caroline: Well, to be honest, I vacillate between two feelings. Sometimes I experience optimism regarding all the prospects we've just discussed—that psychology may evolve to new ways of thinking about therapy, diagnosis, and psychopathology and that constructivism may play a strong role in leading us there. Sometimes I feel pessimistic when thinking about all the obstacles that we face as a group or as a non-dominant voice.

Just to think of another direction for constructivism, an area to which I would like to personally contribute: How can I make use of the constructivist and narrative approaches as an instructor? As an educator? How do I bring that into my life and the work that I do? For me, I can answer that question by bringing more of it into the teaching of psychology. I recently conducted a study that adapted Kelly's fixed-role enactment into a class assignment. I should say that this was actually inspired by your work, Bob. I remember that while I was in graduate school you were doing that study, the fishbowl

. . .

Bob: Yes, "Fixed-Role in a Fishbowl," I think we called it (Neimeyer et al., 2003).

Caroline: I remember you doing that with graduate students to teach them about Kelly's fixed-role enactment and how to employ that in a clinical setting. I wanted to introduce something to undergraduates rooted in Kelly. In doing so, I was hoping to assist students in conceptualizing personality more broadly, to consider personality as a process that can evolve over time. I wanted them to use role enactment to entertain new possibilities and—borrowing from Don's language—I wanted them to experience "re"-verbs . . . to see how we have the power and the freedom to re-evaluate ourselves, to re-construct our lives and our views of ourselves. This study suggested that students find this enactment to be profoundly meaningful (Stanley, Glendening, Hatfield, & Boldoser, 2012).

         So I would like to see continued growth in using these techniques in the classrooms—using constructivism to promote profoundly meaningful experiences for students regarding personal change. So I hope that answers the question a bit, about another area in which I would like to see growth.

Bob: The whole area of pedagogy is a fascinating domain of application and one in which we have been long engaged. As recently as three weeks ago I was doing that same exercise, having a group of 10 graduate students in counseling and clinical psychology collaborate to analyze the character sketch written by one person of himself and then, basically, to deconstruct it and reconstruct it along very different lines. We put together a noble character whose name was Samson Knight. I think the first line of the enactment sketch was something like, "Like the rest of us, Samson carries a lot of baggage, but he carries it better than most of us." We went on to construct a two-page identity to inhabit for a two-week period. It was a life-changing experience for him and a great experience for the collaborative witnesses to the change.

What I started doing, in keeping with these ideas of narratives as scripts—whether in that traditional Kellian sense transposed into the classroom or going out into the broader world analyzing struggles in the way that Don is doing—is that I've started partnering with a theatrical group called *Playback Memphis*. This is a group of professional and amateur improvisational actors who perform stories spontaneously told by members of communities. It's community-wide in the city of Memphis where people—Black, White, Hispanic, Asian, of all ethnicities and social stations—convene in a theater to tell stories about their lives that may be suggestive, whimsical, and brief, or deep, tragic, or extended, and to have these then performed in the moment spontaneously by actors who step forward and dramatize the affect, dramatize the internal sense of conflict, uncertainty, ambiguity, division. Typically they play out the more challenging narratives in a way that is hopeful or redemptive. For example, we've done this when an entire auditorium was filled with homicide survivors, and the stories being performed—prompted by stories told from the floor, in the theater, by survivors of the loved one's murder—are then performed immediately, with no rehearsal or script by the actors, in a way that captures, validates, honors the story of love—not the story of the traumatic loss, but the enduring story of love that goes beyond the loss (Murphy & Neimeyer, 2014). The amount of transformation that happens within and between people is palpable. So one of the ways in which I'd like to see us carry forward the work with narrative is in this very experiential way.

In Spanish we'd use the word *vivencial*—that is, a much more embodied, active, relational, public way of working. For example, we have a grant-supported research study entitled *Performing the Peace* we're now launching that looks at the impact of this kind of community performance of narratives as a transformative process in improving relations with police in violence-saturated communities. Many other expressive arts approaches—visual, musical, dance and movement oriented as well as involving creative writing—can greatly expand the range of our meaning making practices in therapy (Neimeyer, 2012; Thompson & Neimeyer, 2014).

Don: What you are describing is what Mandela and others did in South Africa. It's what happened when they took victims and perpetrators and, rather than seek revenge, they found the mode of storytelling. I've written about a variety of interventions that they use (Meichenbaum, 2009). For example, in the work of Agger and Jensen and so forth, they're working with victims of trauma from South America and they use what is called the *testimony procedure*, which is basically storytelling. In fact, I consulted to a mental health community who work with 400,000 torture victims who live in the United States. And it turns out that that kind of narrative approach really works well with people from South America and others. But when dealing with victims of South East Asia (the Cambodians, and so forth) then that narrative backfires and their focus is much more on problem solving. So, you have to do this in a culturally sensitive way. I've worked with native populations where storytelling is really critical. It would be very interesting to get multiple examples of how storytelling has been used as part of the healing process. To document—from torture victims, to homicide survivors—their narratives. There are many examples along those lines.

One quick thing to Caroline—because I listened to your language very carefully: Instead of seeing constructivism as facing "obstacles," you want to see them as "challenges." If only you see these as challenges you are less likely to become depressed. In your language you have "obstacles," you view people as "unaccepting" . . .

Caroline: I see. So seeing it as "challenges" will elicit my optimism, but seeing it as "obstacles" will bring out my pessimism.

Don: What you need to have is a delusional system. This is what makes an effective researcher: Think that you have discovered a "truth" and it is your job to come up with persuasive evidence. So these are not obstacles. These are opportunities for you to enlighten other people.

Caroline: I like it!

Don: You can't talk to me without some aspect of your language being analyzed. So, Caroline, you have some things that you can take away from our discussion: You're not going to use the word *revolution*, you're going to use the word *evolution*, and . . .

Caroline: . . . yes, I'll say *challenges* and *opportunities*, rather than *obstacles*. Very good, practical advice!

Don: Well, just keep that it mind . . .

Bob: . . . especially as you launch a new phase of your career! Don, in closing let me just also observe that earlier you talked about the importance of master therapists being good storytellers, but I'd like to add—with you as a prime example—that a master therapist is also an excellent editor!

SUMMARY AND CONCLUSIONS:
THE FUTURE OF CONSTRUCTIVISM

The foregoing transcript depicts an unscripted conversation among two prominent figures in the field of constructivist psychology and me (Caroline), a "next generation" constructivist psychologist. Emerging first in our dialogue was a discussion regarding the evolution of the constructivist perspective. In the process, these leaders reflected on their personal trajectories within constructivist psychology and the thinkers who influenced their work. What followed—as Bob shared the details of a personal life tragedy and as Don elaborated upon it—was an analysis of resilience using a constructive narrative perspective. After experiencing this first-hand account of the practical applications of constructivism, our dialogue focused on the future of the field. Specifically, we considered how a constructivist perspective could further the evolution of psychology and whether constructivism had implications beyond psychotherapy.

As a "next generation-er," this interview inspired a sense of optimism regarding the future of constructivism. This optimism may be explained, in part, by a compelling realization that constructivism is strongly rooted in psychology. Constructivist ideas are not new; constructivist thinking is apparent in early psychological theories (i.e., Wundt) and such thinking has persisted over time in the work of influential figures (i.e., Frankl, Kelly). In this sense, constructivism has a longstanding presence or a unique "narrative" within the history of psychology. Likewise, as exemplified by Bob's inclusion of Gorge Kelly's work into the field of grief, constructivist ideas have expanded and evolved over time. Further, as illustrated in Don's constructive narrative approach—a perspective that draws from cognitive, behavioral, and meaning-making frameworks—constructivist theories can and do evolve in ways that are not incompatible with traditional psychology. In essence, the next generation of constructivists may be well-equipped to advance constructivist ideas in quite the same way as before: through integration with other psychological theories and frameworks.

It must be noted, however, that the potential for constructivism is much broader than psychology. Also addressed in this interview were the practical applications of constructivism to the domains of public policy, education, community relations, and to the analysis of politics. In many respects, constructivism can be strengthened by its application beyond psychology.

If we were to be "exquisite listeners" to the language of these two leaders, several additional themes emerge regarding the future of constructivism. The first pertains to research methodology. Some striking excerpts in this transcript include: "we still need that close analysis of language;" and "[we need] a methodology...[to] see how people change stories." Don and Bob's language reflects a yearning for some sort of "coding system," "content analysis," "metric," "pragmatic discourse analysis," or "line of research" to better analyze the key elements of storytelling. In essence, a great need for constructivism is the systematic application of a methodology that would allow us to better assess and analyze how meaning systems evolve and transform over time. In doing so, we may be better able to demonstrate—to those both within and outside the constructivist arena—the predictive power of storytelling. In short, to *have a greater impact on the field, we must generate stronger methodology.*

However, what also emerges from our interview may be considered hopeful, "change-talk" expressions regarding constructivism and its future. The use of pragmatic research methods is described as "entirely feasible to pursue" and as "a game" that we can "play well." Likewise, psychology is portrayed as having gaps that constructivists "can help fill" and theorists are described as ready to "open up" or "embrace" a constructivist perspective. Such optimistic, change-talk language from these leaders is noteworthy. The latter, if modeled well by the next generation, is essential in creating what so many strive to see in constructivism's future: resilience.

214

REFERENCES

Baardseth, T. P., Goldberg, S. B., Pace. B. T., Wislocki. A. P., Frost, N. D., Siddiqui, J. R., ... Wampold, B.E. (2013). Cognitive-behavioral therapy versus other therapies: Redux. *Clinical Psychology Review, 33*, 395–405.

Burke, L. A., & Neimeyer, R. A. (2011). Spirituality and health: Meaning making in bereavement. In M. Cobb, C. Puchalski & B. Rumbold (Eds.), *The textbook on spirituality in healthcare* (pp. 127–134). Oxford, England: Oxford University Press.

Burke, L. A., Neimeyer, R. A., Holland, J. M., Dennard, S., Oliver, L., & Shear, M. K. (2014). Inventory of complicated spiritual grief: Development and validation of a new measure. *Death Studies, 38*(4), 239–250, doi: 10.1080/07481187.2013.810098.

Burke, L. A., Neimeyer, R. A., McDevitt-Murphy, M.E., Ippolito, M. R., & Roberts, J. M. (2011). In the wake of homicide: Spiritual crisis and bereavement distress in an African American sample. International Journal Psychology of Religion, 21, 289–307.

Burke, L. A., Neimeyer, R. A., Young, A. J., Piazza Bonin, E. & Davis, N. L. (2014). Complicated spiritual grief II: A deductive inquiry following the loss of a loved one. *Death Studies, 38*(4), 268–281, doi: 10.1080/07481187.2013.829373.

Coleman, R. A., & Neimeyer, R. A. (2010). Measuring meaning: Searching for and making sense of spousal loss in later life. *Death Studies, 34*, 804–834.

Currier, J. M., Holland, J. M. , & Neimeyer, R. A. (2012). Prolonged grief symptoms and growth in the first two years of bereavement: Evidence for a non-linear association. *Traumatology, 18*, 65–71.

Currier, J. M., Malott, J., Martinez, T. E., Sandy, C. , & Neimeyer, R. A. (2012). Bereavement, religion and posttraumatic growth: A matched control group investigation. *Psychology of Religion and Spirituality, 18*, 65–71.

Gillies, J., Neimeyer, R. A., & Milman, E. (2014). The Meaning of Loss Codebook: Construction of a system for analyzing meanings made in bereavement. Death Studies, 38, 207–216. doi: 10.1080/07481187.2013.829367

Holland, J. M., Currier, J. M., Coleman, R. A. , & Neimeyer, R. A. (2010). The Integration of Stressful Life Experiences Scale (ISLES): Development and initial validation of a new measure. *International Journal of Stress Management, 17*, 325–352.

Joiner, T. (2005). *Why People Die by Suicide.* Cambridge, MA: Harvard University Press.

Meichenbaum, D. (n.d.). Trauma, spirituality and recovery. Retreived from http://www.melissainstitute.org/documents/Spirituality_psychotherapy.pdf

Meichenbaum, D. (1977). *Cognitive behavior modification: An integrative approach.* New York, NY: Plenum Press.

Meichenbaum, D. (1992). Evolution of cognitive behavior therapy: Origins, tenets, and clinical examples. In J. Zeig (Ed.), *The evolution of psychotherapy: The second conference* (pp. 114–127). New York: Brunner/Mazel.

Meichenbaum, D. (2003). Cognitive-behavior therapy: Folktales and the unexpurgated history. *Cognitive Therapy and Research, 27*(1), 125–129.

Meichenbaum, D. (2006a). Resilience and post-traumatic growth: A constructive narrative perspective. In C.G. Calhoun & R.G. Tedeschi (Eds.), *Handbook of posttraumatic growth* (pp. 355–367). Mahweh, NJ: Lawrence Erlbaum Associates.

Meichenbaum, D. (2006b). Trauma and suicide: A constructive narrative perspective. In T. Elllis (Ed.), *Cognition and suicide: Theory, research and practice* (pp. 337–354). Washington, DC: American Psychological Association.

Meichenbaum, D. (2009, May). *Psycho-cultural assessment and interventions: The need for a case conceptualization model.* Paper presented at the 13th Annual Annual Melissa Institute Conference. Retreived from http://www.melissainstitute.org/documents/13AConferenceMay2009.pdf

Meichenbaum, D. (2011). Ways to improve political decision-making: Negotiating errors to be avoided. In F. Acquilar & M. Gallucio (Eds.), *Psychological and political strategies for peace negotiations* (pp. 87–99). New York, NY: Springer.

Meichenbaum, D. (2013). *Roadmap to resilience: A guide for military, trauma victims and their families.* Clearwater, FL: Institute Press. (See www.roadmaptoresilience.org)

Meichenbaum, D. & Fong, G. (1993). How individuals control their mind: A constructive narrative perspective. In D. Wegner & Pennebaker (Eds.), *Handbook of mind control* (pp. 473–490). Englewood Cliffs, NJ: Prentice Hall.

Murphy, V., & Neimeyer, R. A. (2014). Playback Theatre. In B. E. Thompson & R. A. Neimeyer (Eds.), *Grief and the expressive arts: Practices for creating meaning.* New York, NY: Routledge.

Neimeyer, R. A. (2000). Research and practice as essential tensions: A constructivist confession. In L. M. Vaillant & S. Soldz (Eds.), *Empirical knowledge and clinical experience* (pp. 123–150). Washington, DC: American Psychological Association.

Neimeyer, R. A. (2009). Constructions of death and loss: A personal and professional evolution. In R. J. Butler (Ed.), *On reflection: Emphasizing the personal in personal construct psychology* (pp. 291–317). London, England: Wiley.

Neimeyer, R. A. (2011). Reconstructing the self in the wake of loss: A dialogical contribution. In H. Hermans & T. Gieser (Eds.), *Handbook on the dialogical self* (pp. 374–389). Cambridge, England: Cambridge University Press.

Neimeyer, R. A. (Ed.). (2012). *Techniques of grief therapy: Creative practices for counseling the bereaved.* New York, NY: Routledge.

Neimeyer, R. A., & Burke, L. A. (2011). Complicated grief in the aftermath of homicide: Spiritual crisis and distress in an African American sample. *Religions, 2,* 145–164.

Neimeyer, R. A., Ray, L., Hardison, H., Raina, K., Kelley, R., & Krantz, J. (2003). Fixed role in a fishbowl: Consultation-based fixed role therapy as a pedagogical technique. *Journal of Constructivist Psychology, 16,* 249–271.

Neimeyer, R. A., & Sands, D. C. (2011). Meaning reconstruction in bereavement: From principles to practice. In R. A. Neimeyer, H. Winokuer, D. Harris & G. Thornton (Eds.), *Grief and bereavement in contemporary society: Bridging research and practice* (pp. 9–22). New York: Routledge.

Stanley, C. M., Glendening, Z. S., Hatfield, M. L., & Boldoser, C.A. (2012, July). *Fixed-role enactment as a pedagogical tool for personality psychology students.* Paper presented at the 15th Biennial Conference of the Constructivist Psychology Network, Arlington, TX.

Thompson, B. E., & Neimeyer, R. A. (Eds.). (2014). *Grief and the expressive arts: Creative contributions to meaning making.* New York, NY: Routledge.

217

PART IV

LOOKING FORWARD

ca 8 so

Imagining Possible Futures: Scenarios for Constructivist Psychology[1]

Jelena Pavlović

The aim of this paper is to experiment with possible answers to a demanding question: *What is the future for young constructivist scholars?* Anticipating the future of a discipline is not an easy task. Even harder is to offer personal visions of the future as some sort of a guide for young scholars. That is why I chose a propositional approach to the outlined topic. In other words, I reformulated the initial question into an experiment with possible futures for constructivist psychology.

Relatively loose boundaries of constructivist psychology have made my task even more challenging. What counts as constructivist psychology is somewhat a matter of a viewpoint. Some authors tend to unify constructivist approaches into a single paradigm, which includes (at least) personal construct psychology, radical constructivism and social constructionism (Mascolo & Pollack, 1997; Raskin, 2002; Stojnov, 2005). However, there have also been efforts to stress points of divergence between different "constructivisms" (Chiari & Nuzzo, 1996) or more strongly between "constructivism"

[1] This contribution is the result of the projects "From encouraging initiative, cooperation and creativity in education to new roles and identities in society" (No. 179034) and "Improving the quality and accessibility of education in modernization processes in Serbia" (No. 47008), financially supported by the Ministry of Science and Technological Development of the Republic of Serbia (2011–2014).

and "constructionism" (Gergen, 2001; Stam, 1998). In this paper, I will use the phrase "constructivist psychology" to point primarily to personal construct psychology (PCP). The reason for this choice of terminology is not that I find these approaches too distant to be unified. The reluctance of social constructionists to construe the similarities seems to be an issue that cannot be ignored, despite the hard work in the unification direction. However, I argue that in the future constructivist psychology may become a more unified field in practice, not only in theory.

In the first part of the paper the basic idea of future thinking and scenario methodology is briefly sketched. In line with the ideas of scenario methodology, two possible trends for psychology in general are identified: (a) marketization, and (b) unification. Based on these trends, four scenarios for constructivist psychology are constructed. The implications of each scenario are discussed as a starting point for strategic conversations about the future of constructivist psychology.

FUTURE THINKING AND SCENARIO METHODOLOGY

Quick and frequent changes have become some of the defining features of contemporary societies. The pace of human ability to transform the self and the environment has been rapidly increasing, which Kelly (1966) referred to as "ontological acceleration" almost half a century ago. Quick anticipatory actions are therefore becoming more and more important. As a response to this increasing pace of change, future thinking and scenario methodology have been developed in the social sciences.

Future studies refer to a relatively new cluster of disciplines gathered around the shared goal of exploring alternative visions for the future (Peters, 2003). While other approaches aim at prediction, future studies are based on the assumption that the future cannot be predicted because it is dependent on the choices we make in the present. The aim of future studies is to consider a number of *possible futures* (Miller, 2006). These studies analyze policies, strategies and actions that may contribute to constructing desirable futures. In other words, the discipline of future studies expands our understanding of the future and facilitates strategic conversations. One of the most developed forms of future studies is *scenario methodology*.

Scenario methodology was developed during World War II for the purpose of military strategic planning (Saussois, 2006). A couple of decades later, it became a part of the planning and decision making process in many public and private sector organizations. In this methodological frame, scenarios are defined as narratives that depict possible futures and different avenues that lead to them (Peters, 2003). Another definition points to scenarios as consistent and coherent descriptions of alternative hypothetical futures that reflect different visions of past, present and future developments (van Notten, 2006). Positive and negative scenarios are differentiated based on the desirability of the visions for the future (Ogilvy, 2006). Negative scenarios are considered easier to design because they do not require finding better solutions than the existing ones. Positive scenarios require depicting new realities, but may be rejected as too optimistic or utopian.

The main idea behind scenario methodology is to explore the future in the present. Scenarios facilitate imaginative learning (Peters, 2003), proactivity and flexibility regarding the future. Moreover, scenario methodology is a useful tool for initiating strategic dialogue and enhancing decision making about future developments (van der Heijden, 2005). Because scenarios represent a storytelling genre and are based on divergent thinking, they may promote expression of rather different opinions. Scenarios help elaborate different visions for the future and pathways to desirable developments. By facilitating strategic conversations, scenario methodology helps shape the future.

There are different approaches to designing and analyzing scenarios. The basic model for scenario development includes the following steps: (a) identifying the key theme or key question for the analysis; (b) identifying the main trends and sources of change in the future; (c) constructing scenarios; (d) evaluating scenarios and creating action plans. In the first step, the task is to formulate a question to which scenarios give an answer, as well as to define the time frame in which scenarios should be considered. Usually, the defined time frame in scenario methodology is 5–20 years (Snoek, 2003). The second step includes identifying key trends in the area of interest. These trends are often two dimensional models, based on two key areas of development. In the third step, scenarios should be depicted so that they include different versions of the future, types of positioning of the key actors and their interests in each of the scenarios. Finally, scenarios are evaluated through analysis of potential gains and losses, as well as risks and opportunities they offer (Godet, 2000). This final step may also include creating action plans according to the outcomes anticipated by different scenarios. Implementing action plans is eventually based on the authentic interest of key actors in the possible futures in a chosen area. Meetings, conferences or specific research projects may be a stage for this final step in the application of scenario methodology.

SOME FUTURE TRENDS IN PSYCHOLOGY

Many trends have influenced psychology and many more are still waiting to influence it in the future. To illustrate that the discipline of psychology is in constant flux, just imagine what Wundt would say about the developments in psychology after a century and a half! Although there are different possible trajectories, two important future trends for psychology will be elaborated in this paper: (a) marketization, and (b) unification.

The Marketization Trend in Psychology

Different labels have been coined to account for the shift away from an industrial society. It has been claimed, for example, that we now live in a *Knowledge Society* (Drucker, 1994) or *Market Society* (Fourcade & Healy, 2007). These labels stress the importance of the tertiary sector, knowledge, and the market orientation. While previous types of societies (e.g., agricultural, industrial) continue to co-exist, their dominance has been diminishing since the emergence of post-industrial societies in the second half of the 20th century.

As Kvale (2003) pointed out, each new type of society brings a different metaphor for psychological research and professional activity. The main metaphor psychology lives by in post-industrial societies is the "market" metaphor. This metaphor implies a shift from the "church" metaphor and the "factory" metaphor, as well as a shift from the themes of salvation and production to the theme of consumption.

> The visual and the symbolic landscape is no longer dominated by churches or factories; today, it is shopping malls and all-pervasive advertisements that draw our attention. The importance of augmenting industrial production has receded; the key to economic growth is increasing consumption of the abundance of commodities produced. With the exploitation of wage labor and the workers' adaptation to industrial discipline well secured in the Western countries, today it is the maximum exploitation of consumer desires that is the crux of economic growth. It is now necessary to manufacture customers as well as products. (Kvale, 2003, p. 589)

Kvale (2003) points to multiple implications of the "market" metaphor for psychology. The subject matter of psychology in post-industrial societies has been the construction of the self. In the age of consumption, the social self and the relational self replaced the substantial self of the modern epoch (Brinkmann, 2008; Kvale, 2003). Self construction and reconstruction became the goals of life, but also important pursuits of psychology.

According to Cushman (1995), the psychology of advertising and psychotherapy were two main sites for promotion of self construction. These two areas of psychology promoted expression, designing and redesigning of the self. New anti-authoritarian therapies that emerged in the second half of the 20th century considered clients as the ultimate authority in line with the proverb, "the customer is always right." Although Kvale (2003) analyzed humanistic therapies as examples of these new types of therapies, personal construct therapy (PCT) fits this quite well, too. Describing the "credulous approach" as one of the core characteristics of PCP, Kelly (1955) referred to the same proverb. This customer orientation of PCP corresponds with the descriptions of the marketization trend in psychology. Moreover, the idea of personal agency underlying PCP may be seen as a means of producing "responsibilized" persons who are well suited to serve neo-liberal economic interests (Pavlović, 2011). Kvale (2003) also refers to social constructionism as one of the new psychologies that operate under the "market" metaphor. The emphasis on social construction of a fluid self through conversations and narratives promises consumers the freedom of constructing their own identities and worlds (Brinkmann, 2008; Kvale, 2003). Finally, qualitative research, once dismissed as unscientific by academia, constitutes one of the key means of inquiry in post-industrial societies. Market research and the psychology of advertizing have been relying on qualitative research for at least a couple of decades.

In sum, post-industrial societies seem to be offering the "market" metaphor as one of the most influential metaphors for psychology. It is somewhat ironic that constructivist and constructionist psychology may be recognized as being in line with this new Zeitgeist. Is this Zeitgeist the one constructivist and constructionist psychologists would necessarily choose to be associated with? Probably not. However, throughout history, the market orientation has been associated both with liberation and oppression. As Fourcade and Healy (2007) point out, the market society may be seen as promising liberal dreams, but also as an offering of a commodified nightmare. Constructivist and constructionist psychology may choose between these two poles of the same construct. In the meanwhile, the marketization trend will probably continue to grow. According to certain analyses, even this new type of society will soon give way to another techno-economic system—the Dream Society (Jensen, 1996). In this type of society, storytelling and the ability to produce dreams for public consumption will be valued skills. What type of psychology will be best suited to support the needs of the Dream Society? Will constructivist psychologists still be there when this time comes?

The Unification Trend in Psychology

Another future trend that is even more specifically tied to psychology as a discipline is unification of its theories and approaches. Unification of psychology has been recognized as one of the recurrent themes in its history, but also as its "immunity booster" (Kazdin, 2008, p. 5). Moreover, one of the strategic goals for the American Psychological Association's 2016 governance practices and structure includes further movement towards unification (APA, 2012). Apart from the policy documents, the idea of unification has been strongly advocated in a number of theoretical papers (Calhoun, 2004; Henriques & Cobb, 2004; Sternberg & Grigorenko, 2001; Valsiner, 2007, 2009).

For example, Sternberg and Grigorenko (2001) argue that unified psychology can and should supplement traditional approaches to psychology. They point to some of the commonplace "bad habits" of psychology, such as exclusive reliance on a single methodology, identification of scholars in psychology in terms of sub-disciplines, and adherence to single underlying paradigms (e.g., behaviorism, cognitivism, constructivism). Replacing these "bad habits" and pursuing the unification trend may help overcome narrowness, isolation, false oppositions, marginalization, and largely method-driven rather than phenomenon driven approaches to research (Sternberg & Grigorenko, 2001).

Valsiner (2007) points to the need for unification of psychology in order to resolve the struggles with its self-identity. He locates these struggles in social positioning games of psychological approaches. According to Valsiner (2009), the history of psychology has been filled with fashions that discredit other fashions, rather than finding solutions to basic human problems. Methodological and epistemological orientations have taken precedence over a problem orientation, which has led to much of the ideological discourse in psychology. In line with this analysis, the future of psychology should acknowledge the "side effects" of social positioning games.

Another call for unification may be found in Harré's idea of "hybrid psychology" (Harré, 2010). This trend for unification starts from the meta-theoretical level, which could gather together neuroscience research and the study of the meaning-making processes. Integrating neuroscience and discursive psychology would cover the study of cognitive processes of the brain and the management of meaning. By treating different approaches to psychology as different grammars (Person or P-grammar, Molecular or M-grammar, and Organism or O-grammar), Harré intends to set a common discursive meta-theoretical ground for unification of psychology. In this respect, his endeavor differs from Sternberg's call for phenomenon driven unification and Valsiner's call for the end of the social positioning games.

Finally, as Stam (2004) points out, unification projects have been dominated by institutional concerns (e.g., funding, credentialing, or training) rather than epistemological concerns. Emergence of "hyphenated sciences" such as neuro-science threatens to drain grant funds that may represent resources for psychology scholars. These institutional concerns are therefore of primary interest to government regulators, university administrators, and health care managers. According to Stam (2004), implicit unity in method is already established, serving a significant gate keeping function. Although this analysis seems to convey much less enthusiasm about the unification trend, it also stresses that this trend ought to be taken seriously.

Whether constructivist psychology will ever join the unification camp probably depends on what grounds psychology is to be united. While Harré's hybrid science may seem encouraging, dismissing pluralism of approaches in favor of orientation to phenomena may be seen as undermining the very foundations of constructivist psychology. It is phenomena that are created by specific ways of seeing, rather than independent of them. As for the social positioning games of the future, will they really come to an end in psychology? And if not, how will constructivist psychologists play them in future?

WHAT SCENARIO FOR CONSTRUCTIVIST PSYCHOLOGY?

The two outlined future trends for psychology pave the way for different scenarios for constructivist psychology. We may raise the question about the future of constructivist psychology in the next couple of decades, having in mind marketization and unification trends. A useful starting point for scenario development would be a two dimensional model, based on these two trends (Figure 1).

Scenario 1. "Legacy keeping"

In this scenario, constructivist psychology remains highly differentiated and maintains a relatively low degree of market orientation.

Constructivist psychology is focused on preserving its pioneering and distinctive epistemological position (Kelly, 1955; Raskin, 2002; Stojnov, 2005; Warren, 2002). Epistemological relativism, meaning-making processes, and an agentic view of persons remain at the core of constructivist psychology. It resists unification trends, even within a group of similar approaches (e.g. social constructionism, narrative psychology, dialogical psychology). Each of the approaches within constructivist and constructionist psychology stresses its distinctiveness from, rather than commonality with, other approaches. Cross-fertilization is rather sporadic, unsystematic, and often provokes resistance. Boundary keeping between different approaches seems to serve a metaphorical function of legacy keeping. Constructivist psychologists are sensitive to the very usage of the term "constructivist" and try to restrict it to research and practice that demonstrate full appre-

FIGURE 1. FOUR SCENARIOS FOR CONSTRUCTIVIST PSYCHOLOGY.

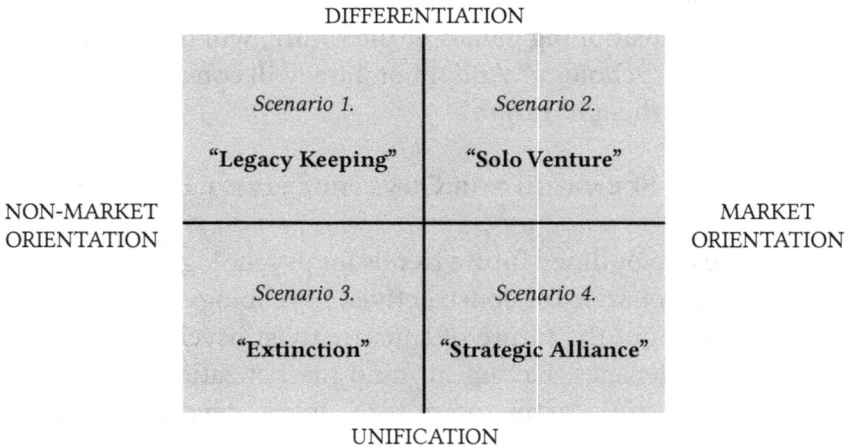

DIFFERENTIATION

	Scenario 1. **"Legacy Keeping"**	Scenario 2. **"Solo Venture"**	
NON-MARKET ORIENTATION			MARKET ORIENTATION
	Scenario 3. **"Extinction"**	Scenario 4. **"Strategic Alliance"**	

UNIFICATION

ciation of the legacy. Thus, constructivist psychology remains loyal to its roots and somewhat "frozen in history" (Butt, 2008).

The legacy is perceived as valuable enough not to be marketed. This scenario depicts constructivist psychology as waiting for the right *Zeitgeist*, when its true value and contribution will be appropriately acknowledged. In face of invalidation, constructivist scholars choose not to change the "legacy keeping" metaphor towards greater market orientation. Adherents to constructivist psychology are positioned as its loyal *guardians*, whose mission is to keep the legacy for the right times.

The main advantage of this scenario for constructivist psychology is strengthening its distinctive and unique position as a pioneer and precursor to the postmodern wave in psychology. In this scenario, constructivist psychology remains clearly delineated in terms of its identity and boundaries. The legacy is preserved and carried through the changing times in its original form.

The "Legacy" scenario imposes high responsibility and risk for embracing the future in a more experimental style. This scenario also assumes a relatively high level of resistance to change. Consequently, this scenario implies a risk that low market orientation may further move constructivist psychology towards isolation and lack of visibility. Somewhat elite positioning prevents wider infusion of constructivist psychology into society and culture. The practical demands of future societies are not properly addressed, which creates the "pragmatic paradox." Although grounded in pragmatic principles (Butt, 2006; McWilliams, 2009), constructivist psychology in this scenario fails to apply these principles for reconstructing itself in face of new market demands.

Scenario 2. "Strategic Alliance"

In this scenario, constructivist psychology moves both in the direction of unification and market orientation.

Constructivist psychology enters into strategic alliances with other approaches, while preserving its identity. Keeping the legacy is, therefore, no longer a priority, but instead the goal becomes exploring commonalities and building a network of interdependencies with other approaches. Constructionist, narrative, cognitive, or positive psychology approaches are considered for strategic partnership in relevant areas of work. For example, fruitful experiments are carried out in allying constructivist psychology and constructionist psychology (Pavlović, 2011). This alliance extends and enriches social constructionist theory and points to benefits of applying the toolkit of constructivist psychology. On the other hand, this kind of an alliance contributes to constructivist psychology and points to new ways of addressing social construction in therapeutic conversations.

The unification trend is considered as an important driver of greater infusion of constructivist psychology into society and culture. In this scenario, a highly differentiated position of constructivist psychology is considered as an obstacle to development of the approach. Stressing differentiation is perceived as a pathway to exclusion and a somewhat elitist positioning of constructivism. Instead, success in the clinical, educational, or organizational contexts is perceived as dependent on some degree of unification with more or less compatible approaches. Therefore, constructivist psychologists gain expertise in other relevant approaches to increase their ability to address emerging social needs. Also, they adapt their technical genre to make it more understandable to wider audiences.

In this scenario, constructivist scholars are positioned as *networkers*, who create appropriate alliances, through which constructivist psychology realizes its full potential. Important experiments are carried out in the ways constructivist psychology communicates to its audience. Increasing accessibility and cross-fertilization are some of the strategic activities for constructivist scholars.

This scenario has the potential to increase the outreach of constructivist psychology. Responsiveness to market needs and cross-fertilization with other relevant approaches may result in further developments of constructivist psychology. As a result, its relevance and practical utility may be validated across contexts.

A possible weakness of this scenario is further loosening of the boundaries of constructivist psychology. Unification efforts may result in over-simplification of constructivist theory, while more challenging or provocative aspects may be neglected. The distinctiveness and originality of constructivist psychology may be under threat in the "melting pot" of future market needs.

Scenario 3. "Solo Venture"

In this scenario, constructivist psychology preserves its high differentiation, while becoming more open for marketization.

Constructivist psychology is still highly differentiated from other approaches in psychology. However, its distinctiveness is not treated as a legacy, nor is it communicated as a core feature of constructivist psychology. Pragmatic underlying assumptions are applied to the positioning of constructivist psychology itself.

Constructivist scholars keep experimenting with new applications of constructivist psychology in line with the emerging market needs across various domains. They try to anticipate future trends and accommodate constructivist psychology to be as useful as possible. For example, they respond to the decline of psychotherapy's use (Olfson & Marcus, 2010) or the changing profiles of mental health service providers (Wang et al., 2007). They are especially sensitive to emerging practices in psychology (e.g., coaching, psychological services for the aging population). Using constructivist psychology to shape these new practices is considered one of the best ways of demonstrating its practical utility. Special attention is given to the way constructivist psychology communicates its values, by adapting its technical genre to be more accessible to a wider audience. Rewriting theory in a more accessible form was something Kelly also wanted to pursue in his later work (Raskin, 2002).

At the same time, adherents to constructivist psychology are open to invalidation and respond to it by redesigning their future experiments in line with the validation data at their disposal. This may be seen as a way of putting constructivist psychology again at the forefront of developments in psychology. Just as it was a precursor to postmodern psychology, this may be a way of reestablishing its pioneering role in exploring unchartered territories. As Kelly (1955, p. 17) argued, a fertile theory provokes experiments and "inspires inventions of new approaches to the solution of the problems of man and his society."

The main strength of this scenario is bringing constructivist psychology closer to the emerging needs of future societies. Consequently, new sources of validation may be available to constructivist scholars and practitioners. Positioning of constructivist scholars as *entrepreneurs* in this scenario may also expose them to risks of invalidation. The "Solo Venture" scenario for constructivist psychology may prove to be a step towards the realization of the commodified nightmare version of the marketization trend. For example, in constructivist coaching a sensitive issue could be the questions of serving organizational interests rather than the interests of individual persons (Pavlović, 2012). Finally, playing "solo" may prevent constructivist psychology from realizing the benefits of cross-fertilization.

Scenario 4. "Extinction"

In this scenario, constructivist psychology moves towards the unification trend and away from the marketization trend.

Constructivist psychology joins the unification trend without a clear rationale. Unsustainability of its isolated position leads constructivist scholars to nonstrategic and ad hoc integrations. In this version of unification, constructivist psychology faces the threat of the gradual loss of its identity.

At the same time, constructivist psychology decreases its responsiveness to market needs. Constructivist psychologists fail to learn from market invalidation, which leads them deeper and deeper into hostility and exclusion from mainstream social practices.

This scenario probably represents the worst-case scenario for constructivist psychology. In this scenario, constructivist scholars are positioned as *victims* of unfavorable circumstances. It implies gradual disappearance of constructivist psychology from the historical scene of psychological theories. At this point, the extinction scenario invokes Kelly's attitude toward the end of theories:

> A theory should be considered as modifiable and, ultimately, expendable. . . . How long one should hang on to his assumptions in the face of mounting contrary evidence is pretty much a matter of taste. . . . If we apply this principle to perseverance in a theoretical position, it would mean that we would consider any scientific theory as an eventual candidate for the trash can. Such an outlook may save the scientist a lot of anxiety, provided he has flexible overriding convictions that give him a feeling of personal independence of his theory. It may also prevent him from biasing his experimental results in favor of a theory which he dares not abandon. (Kelly, 1955, p. 22)

This quote reminds us that the extinction scenario is not only possible, but that we should also construe it permeably enough. Personal independence of any scientific theory would probably represent a healthy approach not only for the progress of the person, but also for scientific progress. Finally, from the standpoint of constructivist psychology, abandonment of a theory represents an act of daring. This applies to the abandonment of constructivist theory, too.

Scenario Implications: Strategic Conversations about the Future

The future scenarios outlined imply different visions for constructivist psychology. These scenarios assume differences in construing the role and purpose of constructivist psychology in society. "Keeping the legacy", forming "strategic alliances", or undertaking "solo ventures" are different pathways to different visions. Conversations about the scenarios are therefore strategic conversations about the future of constructivist psychology.

An important aspect of strategy underlying each scenario is the positioning of constructivist scholars. Being a loyal *guardian* may be seen as quite different from being an *entrepreneur*. An interesting tool for increasing awareness of these positions can be found in the Perceiver Element Grid technique (Procter, 2008). Table 1 presents different ways of construing the constructivist scholar from the perspective of each scenario.

From the "Legacy" scenario perspective, following marketization or unification trends could jeopardize the legacy, either by unacceptable integrations or by means of uncontrolled experiments in theory and practice. In either case, there is a threat both for the legacy and for its keepers. The "Strategic Alliance" scenario anticipates invalidation for the "legacy keepers" and points to the downsides of isolated entrepreneurial positioning. From the "Solo Venture" scenario perspective, legacy keeping is somewhat like being a "dinosaur"—it is perceived as a strategy that is no longer viable, while failing to acknowledge that may have serious consequences in future.

Finally, the "Extinction Scenario" assumes, somewhat hostilely, that constructivist scholars are undervalued in society. Movement towards market orientation is perceived as opportunistic and fundamentally questionable. Instead, waiting for the favorable *Zeitgeist* is perceived as the only acceptable choice. All other scenarios perceive this type of positioning as problematic: as a failure to keep the legacy, to integrate, or just to reconstrue the meaning and role of constructivist psychology in changing times.

This analysis elaborates on the types of dilemmas that are at stake in the different scenarios. It also sheds light on some of the conflicting perspectives regarding the future of constructivist psychology and constructivist scholars. Articulating these perspectives may not solve all the problems and secure a bright future, but it may represent a step towards perturbing the status quo in constructivist psychology.

A Personal Reflection on the Scenarios

At the time I got very curious about constructivist psychology, I was 22 years old. I came across constructivist psychology as part of the syllabus in Personality Psychology at the Department of Psychology, University of Belgrade. My mentor was Dušan Stojnov, whose mentor was one of the legends of constructivist psychology, Fay Fransella. "Legacy Keeping" was therefore something to be expected. However, Dušan's approach to teaching constructivist psychology was inclusive of personal construct psychology, social constructionism, radical constructivism, and narrative psychology. Some degree of unification was there at the beginning of my journey into constructivist psychology. This journey was strongly driven by my interest in discursive psychology (Burr, 1995; Potter & Wetherell, 1987). I found discourse analysis to be a very fruitful new methodology and I felt it offered some of the most interesting insights into traditional psychological topics. My master's thesis

TABLE 1. DIFFERENT SCENARIOS, DIFFERENT POSITIONING FOR CONSTRUCTIVIST SCHOLARS

	"Guardians" (Legacy keeping scenario)	"Networkers" (Strategic Alliance scenario)	"Entrepreneurs" (Solo Venture scenario)	"Victims" (Extinction scenario)
"Guardians" (Legacy keeping scenario)	Keeping the legacy	Negotiating the legacy	Performing uncontrolled experiments	Failing to keep the legacy
"Networkers" (Strategic Alliance scenario)	Unaware of the upcoming invalidation	Creating alliances strategically	Lacking larger networks	Failing to integrate
"Entrepreneurs" (Solo Venture scenario)	Being "dinosaurs"	Lacking innovations	Innovating	Failing to reconstrue
"Victims" (Extinction scenario)	Still fighting	Being opportunists	Being opportunists	Being undervalued

was a discourse analysis of what counts as knowledge (Pavlović, 2008). I found the metaphor of *knowledge as unnecessary hurdles* to be the most dominant discourse of knowledge, which provided some rather undesirable types of positioning both for students and their teachers.

Specialization in the field of qualitative psychology led me to something completely different. As a part time job I started facilitating focus groups and writing qualitative analysis reports for one of the major European marketing research agencies. There, I had the opportunity to meet the Market. My knowledge of discourses, constructs, positioning, and similar academic topics, was highly valued, but only as long as I did not talk about it! The market research world liked excellence in focus group moderation and qualitative data analysis, but it did not care about the fact that underlying it there was laddering, pyramiding, or grounded theory. It was a very close encounter with the marketization trend—the pragmatic dimension of constructivist psychology was highly valued, while nobody actually cared about what that psychology "was." The market research world was only interested in how constructivist psychology could be a means to some business ends. At the same time, it was quite different from stressing the elitism of epistemology and distinctive theory, as the "Legacy" scenario would suggest.

Together with academic research and part time work in the field of market research, I was also studying to become a constructivist therapist. It was a hard journey into the finest details of personal construct psychology, its terminology, principles, and techniques. In the beginning, I was not very sure whether that would actually be my profession one day. Little by little, my initial anxieties waned and years later I was enjoying the mastery of personal construct therapy very much. Some of the most inspiring aspects of constructivist psychotherapy for me were Mair's (1977, 2000) ideas about metaphorical fragmentation into the Community of Selves, as well as Procter's qualitative grids (Procter & Procter, 2008).

However, I received most validation for my work with people who would not be given any diagnosis, even in the ever-expanding DSM repertoire. Gradually, I started to think of constructivist psychology as an ideally suited theoretical basis for coaching. In a series of papers, I elaborated on *constructivist coaching* (Pavlović, 2010; Pavlović & Stojnov, 2011; Stojnov & Pavlović, 2010). Kelly's (1970) experience cycle was placed at the center of constructivist coaching as a model for learning/changing. Eventually, that led me to a Ph.D. in which I developed, implemented, and evaluated a coaching program ("Developmental Laboratory") based on the principles of constructivist psychology (Pavlović, 2012). I wanted my Ph.D. to be in line with the market trend of increased interest in coaching and employee health. One could say it was to some extent in line with the unification trend, because I combined a personal construct theory of change with constructionist ideas about positioning (Davies & Harré, 1990; Harré et al., 2009) and appreciative inquiry (Cooperrider, 1986; Cooperrider, Barret & Srivastva, 1995; Cooperrider & Whitney, 2005).

As this personal story shows, constructivist psychology has been playing a central role in my career so far, providing a common ground for some diverse professional choices, such as educational research, qualitative market research, psychotherapy, and coaching. At the moment of writing this text I am 34 years old and I count as a young constructivist scholar. I consider it a great privilege having had an opportunity to learn about constructivist psychology very early in my career. And I am even happier that constructivist psychology proved to be so fruitful for me in diverse areas of psychological practice. In my personal experience, constructivist psychology has offered me a structured and comprehensive outlook on major psychological phenomena, while stimulating my creativity. I expect it to be a source of experimentation for at least another decade and wish it will continue to be such a confident guide for professional experimentation.

As I see it, the *market orientation* has worked for me very well so far. I have taken constructivist psychology with me wherever the market demanded and validation has been the result. Some degree of *unification* has also worked for me, especially in terms of integrating constructionist and constructivist approaches. I would say that underlying my practice most of the time there was something between the "Solo Venture" scenario and the "Strategic Alliance" scenario. Keeping the legacy was not my professional choice and at the point of reading this text I suppose some constructivist colleagues would perhaps frown upon this. In the spirit of constructivist psychology, we all have the choice between different scenarios. Probably the worst case scenario would lead us to the *victim positioning*. And at that point, George Kelly's ghost would probably frown and remind us that no one needs to paint themselves into a corner (Kelly, 1955).

CONTINUING THE STRATEGIC CONVERSATIONS

The very title of this book implies some degree of dissatisfaction with the status quo in constructivist psychology. One possible source of dissatisfaction among constructivist scholars may be that constructivist psychology fails to be appropriately appreciated by its potential audiences. The audience may have never heard of constructivist psychology, or they may find it too conceptually demanding and difficult to learn, or they may think that learning constructivist psychology is just not worth the effort. As the postmodernist *Zeitgeist* spreads among younger generations, only the minority of the potential new audience would likely disagree with constructivism's epistemological claims.

This line of thinking leads me to a hypothesis that making constructivist psychology more visible and more approachable would in turn improve its current positioning among various audiences, including academics, practitioners, and clients. And at this point, we are actually moving constructivist psychology towards a greater market orientation. I would also say that we are moving constructivist psychology into future experiments with its relevance and utility. Another hypothesis is that the unification trend may add to the usability of constructivist psychology. However, it remains a matter of striking the right balance between unification and differentiation. Defining the boundaries of constructivist psychology certainly is not a finished project yet.

Four proposed future scenarios for constructivist psychology point to some of the possible directions for perturbing the *status quo*. The "Legacy" scenario is perhaps closest to maintaining the *status quo* in constructivist psychology. It may prove to be the right strategic direction for constructivist psychology in future. However, the "legacy keeping" metaphor may also prove to be a source of invalidation. Both the "Strategic Alliance" and "Solo Venture" scenarios may perturb the *status quo* in constructivist psychology. By inviting experimentation with the market orientation, these two scenarios may provide useful strategic directions for constructivist psychology.

Testing the proposed scenarios within the constructivist community could be an exciting experiment in itself. Which of the scenarios would be assessed as most desirable and why? What kind of actions could be provoked by these scenarios? Conferences and scientific meetings could provide perfect venues for constructivist scholars to engage in these sort of strategic conversations.

The proposed trends and scenarios are only some of the ways of imagining possible futures for constructivist psychology. Different trends and scenarios can be constructed to point to different strategic directions. The main purpose of the scenarios offered in this paper is to provoke strategic conversations about the future of constructivist psychology. As Stam (2004, p. 1261) reminds us, academic disciplines require a common stand regarding three important issues.

> Academic disciplines, sociologists of the professions argue, require three things to manage their institutional existence: (a) a marketplace in which they can disseminate their symbolic capital, (b) a recognizable manner of producing and reproducing a knowledge base, and (c) a scholastic system of training to produce new members of the discipline.

Do constructivist scholars have a common stand regarding these issues? Where do we think constructivist psychology is going? Where do we want it to go? How do we get there? Constructivist psychology definitely deserves answers to these questions.

REFERENCES

APA (2012). *Report of GGP project team*. Retrieved from http://www.apa.org/about/division/officers/dialogue/2012/02/governance-report.pdf

Brinkmann, S. (2008). Changing psychologies in the transition from industrial society to consumer society. *History of the Human Sciences, 21*(2), 85–110.

Burr, V. (1995). *Introduction to social construction*. London, England: Routledge.

Butt, T. (2006). Personal construct theory and its history in pragmatism. In P. Caputi, H. Foster, and L. Viney (Eds), *Personal construct psychology: New ideas* (pp. 20–34). Chichester, England: John Wiley.

Butt, T. W. (2008). Kelly's legacy in personality theory: Reasons to be cheerful. *Personal Construct Theory & Practice, 5*, 51–59. Retrieved from http://www.pcp-net.org/journal/pctp08/butt08.html

Calhoun, L. (2004). The unification of psychology: A noble quest. *Journal of Clinical Psychology, 60*(12), 1283–1289.

Chiari, G., & Nuzzo, M. L. (1996). Psychological constructivisms: A metatheoretical differentiation. *Journal of Constructivist Psychology, 9*, 163–184.

Cooperrider, D. (1986). *Appreciative inquiry: Toward a methodology for understanding and enhancing organizational innovation*. Unpublished Doctoral Dissertation, Case Western Reserve University, Cleveland, Ohio.

Cooperrider, D., Barret, F., & Srivastva, S. (1995). Social constructionism and appreciative inquiry: A journey in organizational theory. In D. Hosking, K. Dachler, & K. Gergen (Eds.), *Management and organization: Relational alternatives to individualism* (pp. 157–200). Aldershot, England: Averbury Press.

Cooperrider, D., & Whitney, D. (2005). *Appreciative Inquiry: A positive revolution in change*. San Francisco, CA: Berrett-Koehler Publishers.

Cushman, P. (1995). *Constructing the self, constructing America: A cultural history of psychotherapy*. Cambridge, MA: Perseus Publishing.

Davies, B., & R. Harré. (1990). Positioning: the discursive production of selves. *Journal for the Theory of Social Behaviour, 1990, 20*(1), 43–63.

Drucker, P. (1994). Knowledge work and knowledge society: Transformations of this century. *Edwin L. Godkin Lecture,* John F. Kennedy School of Government, Harvard University. Retrieved from http://cmap.bradercomm.net:8001/servlet/SBReadResourceServlet?rid=1168308523370_415312417_40162

Fourcade, M., & Healy, K. (2007). Moral views of market society. *Annual Review of Sociology, 33*, 285–311.

Gergen, K. (2001). *Social constructionism and pedagogical practice.* Retrieved from http://www.swarthmore.edu/Documents/faculty/gergen/Social_Construction_and_Pedagogical_Practice.pdf

Godet, M. (2000). The art of scenarios and strategic planning: Tools and pitfalls. *Technological Forecasting and Social Change, 65*(1), 3–22.

Harré, R. (2010). Hybrid psychology: The marriage of discourse analysis with neuroscience. *Athenea Digital, 18*, 33–47.

Harré, R., Moghaddam, F., Cairnie, T., Rothbart, D., & Sabat, S. (2009). Recent advances in positioning theory. *Theory & Psychology, 19*(1), 5–31.

Henriques, G., & Cobb, H. (2004). Introduction to the special issues on the unified theory. *Journal of Clinical Psychology, 60*(12), 1203–1205.

Jensen, R. (1996). The dream society. *The Futurist, 30*(3), 9–13.

Kazdin, A. (2008). Unity: Psychology's immunity booster. *Monitor on Psychology, 39*(3), 5.

Kelly, G. A. (1955). *The psychology of personal constructs* (2 vols.). New York, NY: Norton.

Kelly, G. A. (1966). Ontological acceleration. In B. Maher (Ed.), *Clinical psychology and personality: The selected papers of George Kelly* (pp. 7–45). New York, NY: John Wiley.

Kelly, G. (1970). A brief introduction to personal construct psychology. In D. Bannister (Ed.), *Perspectives in Personal construct theory* (pp. 1–30). London, England: Academic Press.

Kvale, S. (2003). The church, the factory and the market: Scenarios for psychology in a postmodern age. *Theory & Psychology, 13*(5), 579–603.

Mair, J. M. (1977). The community of self. In D. Bannister (Ed.), *New perspectives in personal construct theory* (pp. 125–149). London, England: Academic Press.

Mair, J. M. (2000). Psychology as a discipline of discourse. *European Journal of Psychotherpay and Counselling, 3*(3), 335–347.

Mascolo, M., & Pollack, R. (1997). Frontiers of constructivism: Problems and prospects. *Journal of Constructivist Psychology, 10*(1), 1–5.

McWilliams, S. (2009). William James' pragmatism and PCP. *Personal Construct Theory & Practice, 6*, 105–110. Retrieved from http://www.pcp-net.org/journal/pctp09/mcwilliams091.html

Miller, R. (2006). Future studies, scenarios and the "possibility space" approach. In OECD, *Think scenarios, rethink education. Schooling for tomorrow series* (pp. 93–105). Paris, France: OECD.

Ogilvy, J. (2006). Education in the information age: Scenarios, equity and equality. In OECD, *Think scenarios, rethink education. Schooling for tomorrow series* (pp. 69–92). Paris, France: OECD.

Olfson, M., & Marcus, S. (2010). National trends in outpatient psychotherapy. *American Journal of Psychiatry, 167*(12), 1456–1463.

Pavlović, J. (2008). Pozicije subjekata i diskursi o znanju: analiza govora nastavnika i učenika. Magistarska teza. Univerzitet u Beogradu: Filozofski fakultet. [*Subject positioning and discourses of knowledge: analysis of teachers' and students' talk*. Master's Thesis. University of Belgrade: Philosophical Faculty].

Pavlović, J. (2010). Koučing kao tačka susreta ličnog i profesionalnog razvoja. U Polovina, N. i J. Pavlović (ur.), *Teorija i praksa profesionalnog razvoja nastavnika*. Beograd: Institut za pedagoška istraživanja. [Coaching as the point of intersection between personal and professional development. In N. Polovina & J. Pavlović (Eds.), *Theory and practice of teacher professional development*. Belgrade, Serbia: Institute for Educational Research].

Pavlović, J. (2011). Reframing the relationship between personal construct psychology and social constructionism: Exploring some implications. *Theory & Psychology 20*(6), 396–411.

Pavlović, J., & Stojnov, D. (2011). Personal construct coaching: "New/old" tool for personal and professional development. In D. Stojnov, V. Džinović, J. Pavlović, & M. Frances (Eds.), *Personal construct psychology in an accelerating world* (pp. 37–147). Belgrade, Serbia: EPCA Publishing.

Pavlović, J. (2012). *Konstrukcija identiteta u diskursu kontinuiranog profesionalnog obrazovanja*. Doktorska disertacija. Univerzitet u Beogradu: Filozofski fakultet. [*Identity construction in the discourse of continuous professional education*. Doctoral thesis. University of Belgrad: Philosophical Faculty].

Peters, M. (2003). Education policy futures. *Journal of Future Studies, 8*(1), 39–52.

Potter J., & Wetherell, M. (1987). *Discourse and social psychology: Beyond attitudes and behavior*. London, England: Sage Publications.

Procter, H., & Procter, J. (2008) The use of qualitative grids to examine the development of the construct of Good and Evil in Byron's play "Cain: A mystery." *Journal of Constructivist Psychology 21*(4), 343–354.

Raskin, J. D. (2002). Constructivism in psychology: Personal construct psychology, radical constructivism, and social constructionism. In J. D. Raskin & S. K. Bridges (Eds.), *Studies in meaning: Exploring constructivist psychology* (pp. 1–25). New York, NY: Pace University Press.

Saussois, J. M. (2006). Scenarios, international comparisons and key variables for educational scenario analysis. In OECD, *Think scenarios, rethink education. Schooling for tomorrow series* (pp. 53–67). Paris, France: OECD.

Snoek, M. (2003). The use and methodology of scenario making. *European Journal of Teacher Education, 26*(1), 9–19.

Stam, H. (1998). Personal construct theory and social constructionism: Difference and dialogue. *Journal of Constructivist Psychology, 11*(3), 187–203.

Stam, H. (2004). Unifying psychology: Epistemological act or disciplinary maneuver? *Journal of Clinical Psychology, 60*(12), 1259–1262.

Sternberg, R., & Grigorenko, E. (2001). Unified psychology. *American Psychologist, 56*(12), 1069–1079.

Stojnov, D. (2005). *Od psihologije ličnosti do psihologije osoba: konstruktivizam kao platforma u obrazovanju i vaspitanju.* Beograd: Institut za pedagoška istraživanja. [From *Personality psychology to Psychology of the Person: Constructivism as the platform for Education.* Belgrade: Institute for Educational Research].

Stojnov, D., & Pavlović, J. (2010). Invitation to personal construct coaching. *International Coaching Psychology Review 5*(2), 129–139.

Valsiner, J. (2007). Becoming integrative in science: Re-building contemporary psychology through interdisciplinary and international collaboration. *Integrative Psychological & Behavioral Science, 41*, 1–5.

Valsiner, J. (2009). Integrating psychology within the globalizing world: A requiem to the post-modernist experiment with Wissenschaft. *Integrative Psychological & Behavioral Science, 43*, 1–21.

van der Heijden, K. (2005). S*cenarios: The art of strategic conversation.* Chichester, England: John Wiley.

van Notten, P. (2006). Scenario development: A typology of approaches. In OECD, *Think scenarios, rethink education. Schooling for tomorrow series* (69–92). Paris, France: OECD.

Wang, P., Demler, O., Olfson, M., Pincus, H., Wells, K., & Kessler, R. (2007). Changing profiles of service sectors used for mental health care in the U.S. *American Journal of Psychiatry, 163*(7), 1187–1198.

Warren, B. (2002). *Philosophical dimensions of Personal construct psychology.* London, England: Routledge.

⚉ 9 ⚉

What Would an Integrative Constructivist Psychology Look Like?

Michael F. Mascolo, Michael Basseches, and Amanda El-Hashem

Constructivism has a long history in psychology and related fields. Throughout that history, constructivist thinking has flourished, but has often occupied the margins of mainstream psychology. One of the central organizing questions for this volume states: "Do constructivist theories offer genuinely practical and scientifically-grounded models for conducting psychological research and psychotherapy?" Herein, we argue that constructivist approaches have much to offer to psychological theory, research and practice. Several issues, however, have obscured fulfillment of their promise. In what follows, we first describe circumstances that have made it difficult for mainstream psychologists to embrace constructivist thinking. To address these concerns, there is a need to create an integrative constructivist psychology—one that offers a promise of transcending different versions of constructivism, and that shows the relevance and importance of constructivist thinking for psychology. In so doing, we describe (a) an embodied, coactive systems model of the development of persons within socio-cultural contexts (Mascolo, in press; Mascolo & Fischer, 2010), and (b) a set of conceptual and empirical tools for analyzing the construction of integrative patterns of thinking, feeling, and action as they arise in joint interaction over time (Basseches & Mascolo, 2010). We illustrate the model by tracking the construction of modes of acting in a variety of different domains, including the development of everyday skills in young children and the development of affectively charged meaning systems over the course of psychotherapy.

THE CONCEPT OF CONSTRUCTION IN CONSTRUCTIVIST THEORY

Constructivists use the term *construction* in a variety of ways. First, constructivists invoke the concept of construction as an epistemological principle that describes (the perception of) reality as a human construction. A second use simply states that patterns of meaning, feeling, and acting are structures that are *built, formed* or *put together* over time. Third, scholars differ in their conceptions of the processes by which humans construct the meanings that mediate action. Some maintain the primacy of individuals in the process of constructing meaning (Kelly, 1955; Piaget, 1954; von Foerster, 1988); others ascribe to primacy to dyads and sign-mediated cultural processes (Gergen, 2009; Vygotsky, 1978). Some senses of *construction* are more controversial than others. Mainstream psychologists tend to object to aspects of the first and third uses of the term. The second sense—the notion of construction as a dynamic process of building structures—is largely silent with respect to the latter more contentious uses. We suggest that the idea of *construction as building* can provide a point of entry for an integrative constructivist psychology.

The Construction of Reality

The first meaning of the concept of *construction* has to do with the idea that what we take to be *real* or *true* is something that humans *create* rather than something that is found or discovered (von Forester, 1988). One can offer many examples to support the constructivist claim that what humans take to be real (or true) relies upon the constructive processes of persons. However, there is a world of difference between saying, on the one hand, that the knower (scientific or otherwise) *participates* in the known, and saying, on the other, that "reality" is a human *creation*. For example, it is true that an intact visual system is essential in the construction of the experience of color; however, such experiences also rely upon the (colorless) waves of light, in relation to which color receptors evolved (Valberg, 2005). Similarly, humans represent what appear to be naturally organized events in terms of temporal-causal narrative structures organized around human meanings and interests (Brockmeier, 2012; Bruner, 1991); however, narrative modes of knowing are nonetheless fashioned out of concrete experiences within an existing physical and social world. Further, while scientific theories are constructed using metaphors, metonyms and systems of pre-theoretical assumptions (L'Abate, 2012), they are not, of course, constructed willy-nilly. The objects our inquiries fight back and resist our categories of interpretation (Sargent, 1997). If they did not, we would be unable to speak of scientific progress at all.

The idea that reality is simply a human construction arises from adopting an overly sharp distinction between subject and object (Mascolo, 2012; ter Hark, 1990). The subject/object dichotomy casts the world as something that is separate, distinct or foreign to the "inner" world of the experiencing subject. The tearing asunder of person and world creates a self-inflicted wound that becomes difficult to heal. The theorist now faces the task of building a bridge between an unbridgeable chasm. At its most extreme, the parsing away of the active subject from a passive object fosters epistemological and moral solipsism. The idea that individuals (or human collectives) are the sole authors of (their perceptions of) reality is ultimately incoherent: There can be no category of *individual* without the category of *other*. However, the moment we acknowledge the Other, we are forced to take both *her* and her *world* seriously (Levinas, 1985). Thus, we are not self-encased entities locked within our own experiences, forever barred from the world and experiences of others (Oveergard, 2006; ter Hark, 1990). Instead, humans are, as reflected in Heidegger's

(1927/2008) notion of *Dasein*, beings who are always already in the existent world (Stenner, 1998). The fact that there is no such thing as a God's eye view of an independently existing world does not mean that there is a barrier between person and world. Our knowledge claims are neither reflections of personal subjectivity nor mirrors of an independent world; instead, they are products of our *experiences-in-the-world* (Clark, 1997).

An integrative constructivism would examine how human knowledge, experience and action arise as a result of the inherent embeddedness of embodied persons within their physical, personal and socio-cultural worlds. In so doing, an integrative constructivism need not embrace either epistemological or moral relativism (Evanoff, 2005). It would justify its knowledge claims in terms of the *corroboration* and *convergence* of multiple forms of mediated evidence rather than through appeals to so-called objective data. It would work to answer the call for rigorous and accountable methodologies that are capable of producing corroborated, if not Real or True, knowledge about the world (Madill, Jordan & Shirley, 2000). Further, an integrated constructivism would acknowledge the embeddedness of all psychological theory in systems of social-cultural and moral values (Shotter, 1975). In so doing, however, it would work to articulate those values and submit them to the continuous scrutiny of public discourse and personal reflexivity (Gilbert & Sliep, 2009).

Non-Constructive Reductionisms: Individual and Social Construction

Constructivism has its origins in the idea that meaning arises not as a mirror of nature, but instead as the result of individual action on the world. This view has its origins at least as far back as Kant, who argued that our experience of the world would be unintelligible in the absence of a priori categories (e.g., *causality*, *substance*). In the 19th century, building upon the foundation erected by Kant and others, Piaget maintained that the schemes we use to organize experience are not innate properties of the mind, but instead arise through sensori-motor action on objects in the world (Piaget, 1954). For example, according to Piaget, the symbolic concept of object—a bounded entity that exists independent of an observer—is not a given; instead, it arises from the successive differentiation and integration of sensorimotor actions over the first years of life. Developmental changes in the structure of action and thought occur as events conflict with a child's existing knowledge structures (schemes). Such conflicts prompt a reorganization of existing knowledge in order to adapt to novel events (Piaget, 1985). While social experience is important in promoting development, for Piaget, the individual attempt to restore internal equilibrium in the face of conflict is the primary source of development.

For Piaget, knowledge had its origins primarily (but by no means exclusively) on the active and coordinating processes of individual actors. While acts of individual construction are essential for the development of knowledge to occur, they are nonetheless insufficient. Higher-order forms of knowledge and skill—understanding concepts like *inertia, democracy* and *beauty*—have their origins in cultural practices accruing over long historical periods. Individuals do not construct such concepts on their own; instead, they are culled from the repositories of cultural wisdom and communicated using the cultural tool of *language* (Wertsch, 2007). Language has special properties; it allows humans to represent and communicate more-or-less arbitrary, socially shared and communally constructed meanings. Without the use of language, children would not acquire higher-order cultural concepts like *democracy*. Children even learn that basic conceptual relations like *in, on,* and *above* contain considerable cultural content (Bowerman, 2007); such relations are not simply semantic primitives that are acquired through individual action on objects.

Some constructivist approaches tend to privilege the individual actor in the construction of the meanings that mediate human action (Piaget, 1954; Kelly, 1955); others privilege social (Gergen, 2009), semiotic (Wertsch, 2007) and cultural-historical processes (Arnason, 2010; McHoul & Rapley, 2005). It is increasingly clear, however, that the construction of meaning is not a process that can be reduced to acts of individual construction or the internalization of cultural forms. The constructivist/social constructionist antinomy rests on a false premise, namely that acts of individual construction can operate independent of social relations, and vice-versa (Cole & Wertsch, 1996; Pavlović, 2011; Raskin, 2002). An integrated constructivist psychology would be one that can account for the ways in which self, other, culture and world operate in relation to each other in the dynamic construction of meaning and action.

The Metaphor of Construction as Building

A third meaning of the term *construction* is organized with reference to the metaphor of *building* or *forming a structure*. Drawing upon this metaphor, one can understand any given instance of human action and experience as exhibiting some type of structure. A *psychological structure* (Mascolo & Fischer, 2010) consists of the *organization* of goal-directed meaning, feeling and motor action as they arise in any given context. The concept of psychological structure implies that persons do not function as series of isolated parts; all psychological acts necessarily involve some integration of motivational, affective, experiential, representational and sensorimotor activity. To the extent that psychological life is structured, the task of identifying the ways in which psychological structures formed, made or constructed over time becomes a central one.

This use of the concept of *construction* is most congenial to a developmental analysis of origins of psychological structures, especially those organized around the concepts of *epigenesis* (Gottlieb & Lickliter, 2007) and *orthogenesis* (Werner & Kaplan, 1984). Epigenetic models of development maintain that anatomical and psychological structures are neither pre-formed nor predetermined, but instead *emerge* in development. Epigenetic approaches examine the ways in which anatomical and psychological structures emerge over time as products of vertical (gene-cell; cell-organ; organ system-organism; organism-environment, etc.) and horizontal (gene-gene; cell-cell; organism-organism, etc.) coactions that occur within a complex developmental system. Orthogenesis refers to the idea that developmental changes can be understood in terms of principles of differentiation and integration (Raeff, 2011; Siegler & Chen, 2008; Werner & Kaplan, 1984). Drawing upon the metaphor of the developing embryo, development involves the successive *differentiation* of the parts of developing systems (e.g., cells, different types of cells), the *integration* of its parts to form systems and subsystems (e.g., the cardiovascular system; the respiratory system), and finally the *hierarchic* integration of systems to form a single unified whole (e.g., an organism). The analysis of development in terms of increasing differentiation and integration is central to many psychological analyses, including Piagetian and neo-Piagetian theory (Case & Mueller, 2001; Piaget, 1954), organismic-developmental theory (Raeff, 2011; Werner & Kaplan, 1984), personal construct theory (Kelly, 1955), dynamic skill theory (Fischer & Bidell, 2006), and dynamic systems models of development (Camras, 2011).

Toward More Constructive Constructivisms

Most theory and research in psychology continues to be dominated by positivist and realist epistemologies. In an effort to fashion itself as a science, psychology continues to embrace *objectivity* as a central value. Ideally, from a positivist view, an objective description is one that is (a) based on publically observable evidence, (b) records only what is observed (without adding or subtracting), and (c) describes events as they truly are. However, despite its ubiquity, the quest for objective observation is a quixotic one. All observation necessarily occurs against the backdrop of some form of pre-understanding; without a conceptual lens to focus the eye of inquiry, observation is simply unintelligible. The failure to achieve objectivity is not a technical problem that researchers can solve simply by refining their methods. To the extent that the knower participates in the known, objectivity is unachievable in principle. Constructivist approaches face this philosophical problem head on. If constructivist models of inquiry and personhood have not entered the mainstream of psychology, it is most likely because of psychology's continued commitment to the positivist methodology (Cupchik, 2001; Gadenne, 2010). However, it is also likely that some versions of constructivism are marginalized because they have been organized around extreme positions (Boden, 2010; Schmidt, 2001), or because they have not yet demonstrated that methodological rigor can be achieved outside the context of a positivist epistemology. In what follows, in broad strokes, drawing upon constructivist, social constructionist, and embodied systems approaches, we propose an Embodied Coactive Systems account of what an integrative and methodologically rigorous constructivist psychology would look like.

THE COACTIVE CONSTRUCTION OF MEANING: AN OVERVIEW

The following principles provide an overview of the basic principles of a coactive system model of the nature and development of human action and experience.

Human Actions Operate as Meaning-Mediated Control Structures

1. Humans act with reference to the *meaning* that events have for them. Actions are meaning-mediated, goal-directed operations. As such, any act necessarily involves an integration of cognition, conation and emotion.
2. Human actions function as hierarchically-organized *control structures* (Carver & Scheier, 2002; Powers, 1971). In any given context, higher-order goals and meanings activate lower level operations directed toward bringing perceptual experience in line with those higher-order goals.
3. Although they regulate lower-level operations, higher-order conscious representations are themselves coactive

products of non-conscious processes. Non-conscious emotion-generation plays a central role in organizing the conscious representations that drive human action (Freeman, 2000).

Higher-Order Meanings Develop through the Coordination of Lower-Level Action and Experience

1. *Action* and *experience* are ontogenetically prior to symbolic or reflective *thought*. In development, symbolic thought develops through the coordination of lower-order elements of action into higher-order representations. Thinking operates as a kind of interiorized goal-directed activity.
2. Drawing on dynamic skill theory (Fischer, 1980; Fischer & Bidell, 2006), integrated structures of meaning-mediated action develop through 13 hierarchical levels of complexity. Skill theory provides a set of conceptual and empirical tools for identifying the integrative structure of meaning-mediated action as it emerges within particular contexts and conceptual domains.

Novel Meaning Structures Are Jointly Constructed but Individually Consolidated Over Time

1. Although individuals exert control over their actions, persons are not autonomous in doing so. Individual actors function as a part of a larger *person-environment system* (Gottlieb & Lickliter, 2009; Mascolo & Fischer, 2010). In social exchanges, partners mutually regulate each other's thoughts, feelings and actions. The actions of others thus function as an integral part of the process of the actions of the self (Fogel, 1993).
2. Higher-order meanings develop in social interactions through the use language and cultural tools. Language is a special type of cultural tool (Wertsch, 1998). Because of

its capacity to represent *shared social meanings*, language is a vehicle for communicating cultural meanings that pre-exist any particular individual and for generating new meanings between individuals.

3. Through their participation in discursive activity, individuals gain the capacity to use language to mediate higher-order modes of thinking, feeling and action. In this way, language functions as a vehicle for the higher-order construction of the self and social relationships (Mascolo, 2004).

THE DYNAMIC AND INTEGRATIVE STRUCTURE OF HUMAN ACTION AND EXPERIENCE

Action consists of any *goal-directed, meaning-mediated process.* Acting consists of the goal-directed manipulation of meaning for the purpose of regulating perceptual experience. The execution of any given *action* implies some sort of integration of cognition, affect and conation. It follows that meaning and experience are part of the very process of acting. As a result, *action* is not a synonym for "overt behavior" or "motor movement." There is not a separate or autonomous sphere of "mind" or "mental action" that exists behind and controls (motor) action. Instead, acting itself is a type of meaning-mediated doing. When humans advance their goals by operating on their environments, actions involve motor movement; other times, as when individuals engage in private contemplation, psychological activity action occurs without motor action. Figure 1 provides a schematic diagram of the dynamic structure of individual action.

Action and the control of perception. We begin with the observation that psychological acts are *intentional* processes (Searle, 1983). Psychological acts are intentional in the sense that they are performed *on* something, directed *toward* something or are *about* something, real or imagined. Ted does not simply swing an axe; he swings the axe *toward the tree*; Nancy does not simply calculate; she calculates *how long it will take to reach her desti-nation*. Todd is not simply thinking; he is thinking *about what he will have for lunch*. There is an intimate relationship between acts and their objects; the object of an action is part of the process of acting. When Ted chops down the tree, the tree has a role in Ted's chopping. Ted will adjust the intensity, angle and direction of his swing to the shifting height, density, and position of the tree (Bateson, 1973). Thus, all actions are best understood as actions-on-objects. The action-object relation is represented in Figure 1 by the large arrow (a) directed toward its "object" (b).

To say that humans are actors implies that persons have *agency*: individuals are able to exert control over their behavior. The concept of control implies that action is goal-directed. We use the term *goal* to refer to valued *reference standards* against which the outcomes of action are judged. The goals that regulate psycho-logical functioning are constructed representations of some desired state of affairs. When we act, our goal-directed behavior is directed toward producing changes in our experience. In this way, human action proceeds as an attempt to control *perception*. We act in order to bring the flow of perception in accordance with representations of how we *want* the world to be or how we believe the world *should* be. When we act, we are essentially saying, "Make my *experience* look like *this*." As he chops the tree, Ted does so with reference to his image of the final desired state of the tree. His chopping actions function to bring his perception of the tree in line with his image of how he wants the tree to be.

It is helpful to think of action as a kind of control system (Mascolo, Fischer & Neimeyer, 1999; Powers, 1973). Miller, Galanter and Pribram's (1960) early TOTE model of action describes the basic structure of a control system. The acronym TOTE stands for Test-Operate-Test-Exit. From this approach, any given act is regulated by a goal (e.g., chop down the tree). To complete the act, the system first *tests* the goal against goal-relevant sources of input (e.g., "Is the tree lying on the ground?"). If the goal has not been met, the system *operates* (e.g., "Chop the tree"). The system continues to test

FIGURE 1. THE ARCHITECTURE OF INDIVIDUAL ACTION

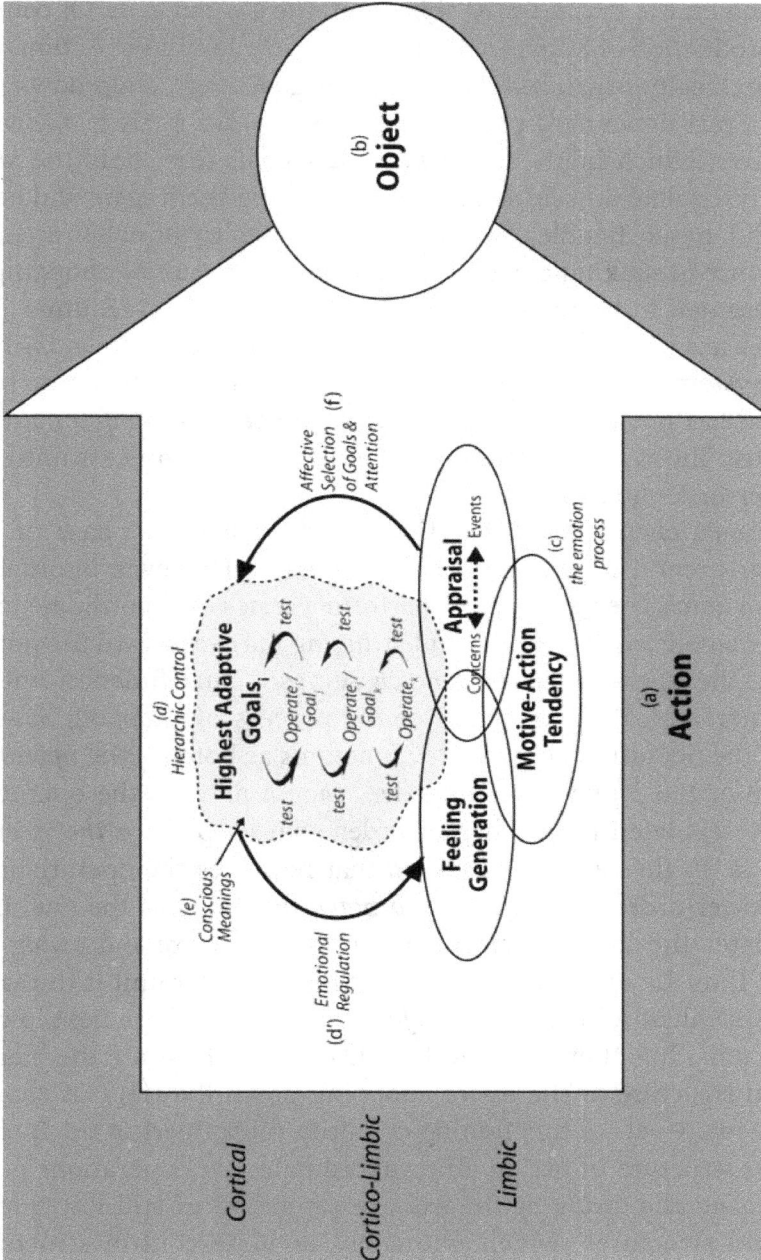

relevant input against the goal until the goal is met (e.g., "the tree is lying on the ground"). At this point, the system *exits*. Of course, the production of human action is not nearly so simple. Actions are hierarchically organized. Higher-order goals (e.g., chop down the tree) exert downward control over lower-order goals (e.g., swing the axe), which imply still lower-order goals (e.g., hold the axe), which regulate muscle action (e.g., squeezing the fingers and hand around the axe handle). Figure 2 describes two levels in hierarchical structure of making a chop in a tree. The structure of chopping is represented in terms of two levels of embedded TOTE units. The higher level TOTE unit is governed by the goal: *chop down the tree*. The system tests the goal against the current position of the tree. If goal has not yet been met, the system *operates: Chop a notch in the tree*. The system continues the *test-operate-test* process until the higher-order goal is met.

Thus, *chop a notch* functions as the *operation* phase of the higher-order TOTE unit: *chop down the tree*. However, in order to *chop a notch*, the person must perform a series of subordinate level acts, namely *raising the axe* and *swinging the axe* toward the notch. Thus, the operation *chop a notch* serves a dual function within the hierarchical organization of the process of *chopping down a tree*. The operation *chop a notch* functions as both (a) the *operation* phase of the *higher-order* unit (i.e., *chop a notch* is the operation phase regulated by the higher-order goal *chop down the tree*) as well as (b) the *reference standard* that regulates the operations of the lower-order unit (i.e., *chop a notch* functions as the goal that regulates the lower-level operations *raise the axe* and *swing the axe*). Thus the *operation* phase of the higher-order unit is the same as (equivalent to) the *goal* or *reference standard* of the next lower-level unit. Together, these nested TOTE units illustrate the hierarchical structure of the act of chopping down the tree. Of course, these two levels of functioning comprise only a part of the hierarchical structure of action. The subordinate level operations/goals of *raising* and *swinging* the axe are composed of still lower-level control structures, which ultimately regulate control structures

FIGURE 2. THE HIERARCHICAL CONTROL OF ACTION

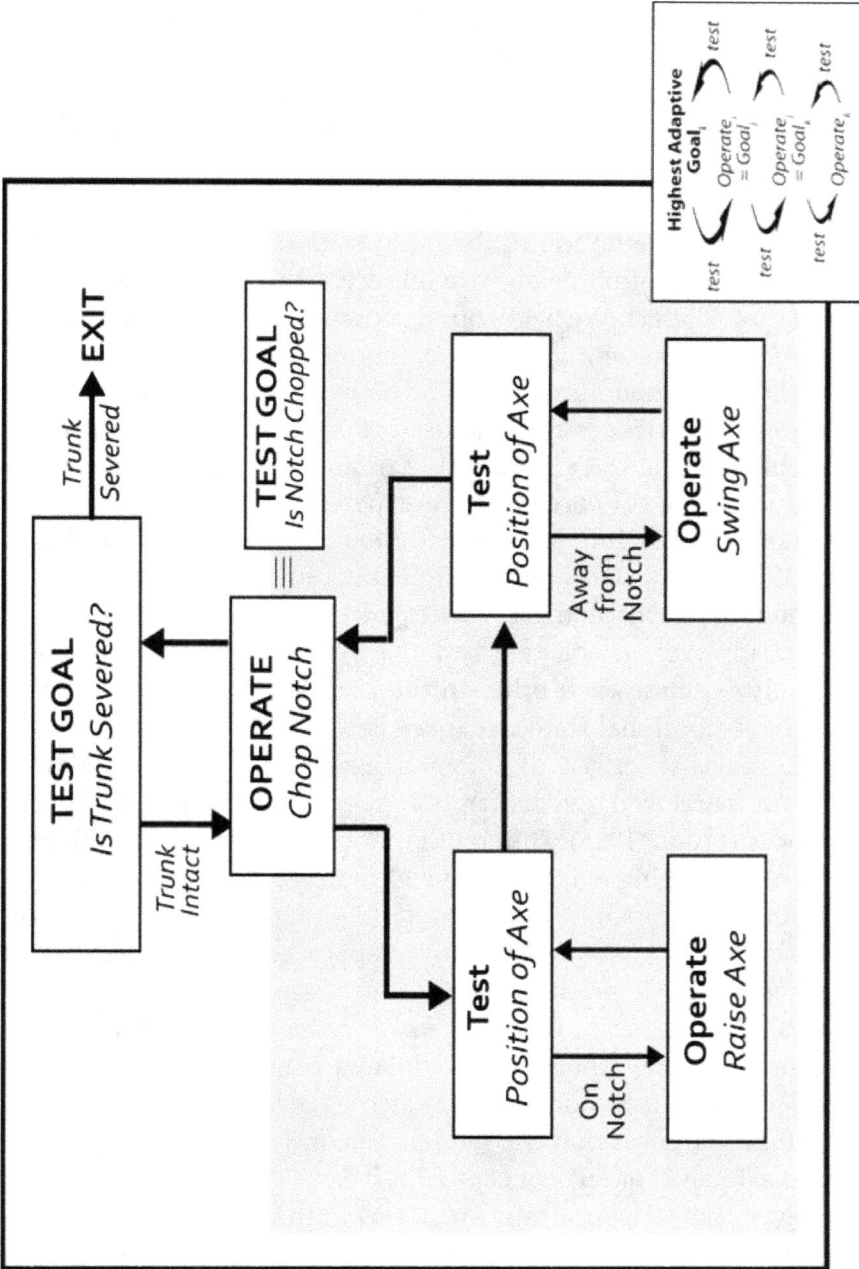

that regulate the operation of specific muscle movements. Moving upward to higher-levels of activity, the act of *chopping down the tree* is itself embedded within higher-order control structures. *Chopping down a tree* can be part of the higher-order activities of *gathering firewood* or *building a hut*. The hierarchical regulation of action is indicated in Figure 1 at Point (d).

Affect and the organization of consciousness. To appreciate the role of emotion in the organization of action and development, it is helpful to elaborate on recent theory and research on the nature of affect. We begin our discussion with an analysis of the operation of fast-acting, intuitive, emotion-generating processes. Current theory and research on the nature of emotion suggest that emotional experiences are composed of three component processes (Mascolo, Fischer, & Li, 2003): (a) motive-relevant *appraisals* (Lazarus, 1991), (b) core affective experience or *phenomenal tone* (Bermond, 2008) and (c) *motive-action tendencies* (Frijda, 1986). Appraisal, affect, and motor action function as coactive systems. Individually, each of these classes of processes is continuously active. However, as coactive systems, appraisal, affect, and action mutually regulate each other in the constructive organization of any given emotional state or experience.

Appraisals consist of ongoing assessments of the relation between perceived events and a person's motives, goals and concerns (Frijda, 1986). Different emotional states reflect different ways of appraising events relative to motives and desires. Positive emotions accompany motive-consistent appraisals (i.e., getting something that is wanted); negative experiences arise when events clash with one's motives, goals, and concerns (i.e., unwanted events). For example, a person experiences anger upon making the appraisal that someone has violated conditions that *ought* to exist; joy with the sudden experience of wanted outcomes; guilt with the awareness that the self has performed some wrongdoing. Appraisals are often conceptualized as "cognitive" processes. However, while appraisals *involve* cognition (and increasingly so with psychological development), they are *motive-relevant* processes. They are assessments of changes in the *status of one's motives* (Roseman, 1984); they reflect changes in one's relation to the experienced world. Thus, although "cognitive" processes mediate appraisal activity, appraisals function in the service of a person's motives

The processes that generate conscious appraisals are fast-acting, automatic and occur *primarily outside of conscious awareness*. We experience fear, for example, when we are immediately aware *that* an automobile is passing into our lane; however, we are not aware of the processes by which we become aware of the looming vehicle. Indeed, when viewed from the standpoint of conscious activity, the question of why we become aware of certain classes of events over others is a puzzling one. Most drivers, for example, have had the experience of operating their vehicle for long periods of time without being consciously aware of their driving actions. During this time of largely non-conscious driving, the driver may be aware of the radio, the scenery, or the discussion she is having with passengers. Why does the driver become aware of the threat of the oncoming car? Although we experience our consciousness as shifting seamlessly from our interlocutor to the automobile, we cannot explain the shift from the *lack* of awareness of driving conditions to *awareness* of those conditions by appealing to conscious experience (e.g., "the driver saw the ongoing car"). We cannot consciously shift awareness to an oncoming car if we were not already previously aware of road conditions.

Thus, *non-conscious* processes must participate in organizing the driver's awareness of the oncoming automobile. The emotion process plays a central role in organizing such awareness. At any given point in time, appraisal processes non-consciously monitor the status of a person's entire system of motives, desires, standards, or concerns. Appraisals that identify changes in events that are relevant to the fate of a person's motives generate *affective changes* (i.e., feeling tone, bodily transformation) and *motive-action tendencies* (i.e., voluntary and involuntary action patterns that function in the service of one's newly activated motives).

For example, as she travelled along routine roads and conditions, non-conscious appraisal processes monitored a variety of different classes of motive-relevant input (e.g., "Is the coast clear?"; "Is my car on the left hand side of the middle lane?"; "Am I sitting up straight?"; "How will I respond to my interlocutor's last comment?"). As the errant automobile swerved into her lane, non-conscious appraisals began to register the threat. The appraisals thereupon began to generate affective changes, which result in feeling states that we ordinarily identify as "fear" or "horror." Thereupon, these affective changes provide immediate, fast-acting feedback to the very same appraisal processes that precipitated the affective changes. *This internal affective feedback functions to select, amplify and organize the driver's conscious awareness of the threat of the oncoming automobile.* From the thousands of concurrently monitored events undergoing appraisal, affective processes select processing of the oncoming car for conscious awareness. The participation of the feeling tone of fear amplifies the importance of that event in consciousness. In this way, appraisal and affect-generating processes mutually regulate each other in the production of emotional experience.[1] Although initial appraisal activity occurs primarily out of consciousness, as they are active, emotions amplify and organize the content of motive-relevant appraisals in consciousness. In this way, *emotion plays a role in the organization of all psychological activity* (Freeman, 2000; Mascolo, Fischer & Li, 2003). The lack of independence among affect, action and appraisal activity suggests there are no purely "cognitive" or "affective" actions; psychological actions are necessarily integrative structures.

The meaning of meaning. Psychological acts are predicated on the meaning that events have for individuals. The same outstretched arm can function as a *reach*, a *point*, or a *request* depending upon the meaning that it has for the person within her

---

[1] Similar patterns of mutual regulation occur, on the one hand, between affect and action, and on the other, between affect and action (see Mascolo, Fischer & Li, 2003).

social community. From a coactive perspective, meaning is neither something that exists "in the head" nor "in the external world." It is neither an innate property of the mind nor a product of the registration of sensory experience. Instead, meaning is a product of constructive activity that occurs between an individual and her physical and social worlds. At its most general level, meaning can be understood as the *structuring of experience*. Meaning is both a part of the process of constructive activity and its product. To the extent that meaning has its origins in action, there as many forms of meaning as there are modes of acting on and structuring our experience of the physical and social world.

Several examples illustrate the different ways in which meanings function as both parts and products of action. First, consider the process of forming images. Imagine that you are in front of the Eiffel Tower. Imagine seeing the top of the tower. Imagine seeing its base. Now, shift your focus from the bottom to the top again. As you do so, attend to the movement of your eyes. If you are like most people, you will find your eyes moving up and down as you shift the focus of your imagining from the top to the bottom of the Tower. This simple experiment suggests that, contrary to the conventional notion that images are "mental pictures," imagining is a form of constructive action. The process of imagining the Eiffel Tower is similar to the processes that occur when one actually looks at the Eiffel Tower—except the actual Tower is absent. Based on this view, one would predict that imagining the Eiffel Tower involves abbreviated patterns of sensorimotor activity (e.g., movement of the eyes) and brain activity that are similar to those that occur when one actually looks at the Eiffel Tower. In this case, the visual-motor meaning of the Eiffel Tower is a product of reconstructive activity—reconstructing what is done when one looks at the Eiffel Tower (or looks at a picture or video of the Eiffel Tower).

As a second example, imagine an infant learning how to point. At first, the infant stretches her hand in an attempt to reach for a wanted Teddy Bear. The child's mother interprets the child's gesture as a manifestation of her desire for the Teddy Bear. The child's mother might say to the still preverbal infant, "Do you want the Teddy Bear? Here it is." In this interaction, the mother treats the child's *reach* as if it was a *request*. In so doing, the mother recasts the meaning of the child's reach for the child. Over time, with many permutations of this interactive routine, the child will be able to abstract or generalize a common social meaning from these social routines. Appropriating the meaning that her outstretched arm has for her *mother*, the child will gain an understanding of the social function of this action-turned-gesture. She will come to use this gesture as a social request rather than as a personal attempt to grasp the object. The child's ability to abstract regularities from such joint interactions provides a second example of how higher-order meanings are constructed through the structuring of experience. Unlike the imagining of the Eiffel Tower, which involves the reconstruction of individual acts of looking and seeing, the child's constructive abstraction of the social meaning of his reach-turned-request is born from jointly structured intersubjective experience.

A third example highlights the ways in which language operates as a tool for creating meaning through the structuring of experience-in-action. A father takes his son to the park. As the boy begins to climb up the ladder of the slide, a little girl attempts to squeeze in front of him. The boy's father says, "Be a gentleman. Let the little girl go first." The word "gentleman" has cultural meaning that precedes both the child and the father. In this situation, the father's use of the socially-shared concept of "gentleman" structures the meaning of the child's experience. The child is being encouraged to identify himself in terms of the cultural meaning of "gentleman." He might be encouraged to act in accordance with the rule "ladies before gentleman," to hold the door for women and so forth. When the child learns the meaning of the word "gentleman," he can now use it to structure his experience. Of course, because, the meaning of the word "gentleman" is part of a larger system of discursive meanings available to structure a child's experience, the child will learn that the connotations of the word may differ depending on whether he is speaking with his grandfather or his feminist aunt.

The Developmental Construction of Meaning in Action

How does meaning develop? What does it mean to say that meanings are constructions? How are meanings coactively constructed over time? In this section, we examine how psychological structures—integrative structures of thinking, feeling and action—undergo constructive developmental change over time. In so doing, we focus first on how psychological structures develop within individuals through the coordination of lower-level components of action into higher-order meaning structures. In a later section, we more fully examine the coactive processes by which higher-order meanings are created in joint action that occurs between individuals within socio-cultural contexts. Meaning has its origins in contextualized action. We draw upon dynamic skill theory (Fischer & Bidell, 2006; Mascolo & Fischer, 2010) to understand how meaning structures develop over time through the coordination of action. Dynamic skill theory provides a set of conceptual and empirical tools for tracking the development of psychological structures—integrated structures of acting, thinking, and feeling—as they arise within particular contexts and conceptual domains (Mascolo & Fischer, 2010). According to skill theory, skilled activity develops as individuals actively coordinate lower-level actions into higher-order structures of meaning. Within any given context, a skill or psychological structure consists of an integrated structure of acting, thinking, and feeling. Consistent with the arguments articulated above, skills operate as *control structures*. A skill refers to those elements of acting, thinking, and feeling that are under the control of an individual within a given context. Using dynamic skill theory (Fischer & Bidell, 2006; Fischer, 1980), one can identify the structure of any type of controlled activity as it arises within particular contexts and domains.

According to skill theory, within any given domain of action, structures of action and meaning develop through four broad tiers: *reflex* activity (i.e., innate action elements that require direct stimulation for their activation, emerging at birth), *sensori-motor* actions (i.e., controlled actions directed toward objects and people, emerging around 4 months), *representations* (i.e., concrete symbols and ideas, emerging around 2 years), and *abstractions* (i.e., abstract meanings, emerging around 10 years). Within each tier of development, skills develop through four basic levels: single *sets, mappings, systems,* and *systems of systems.* Within each tier, the last level of skill – *systems of systems* – is the equivalent of the *first* level of the next broad tier of development (single sets). The progression of skill levels from the sensorimotor[2] through the abstract tiers is depicted in Figure 3. Any particular skilled action is represented by a base term and a modifier enclosed in brackets. A single set is represented in terms of a single skill element. Mappings consist of relations between at least two skill sets. Mappings are indicated by a line between two skill sets: one skill set is mapped onto another. Systems consist of the integration of two (or more) mappings.

Reflexive Intersubjectivity: Foundations for Individuation and Social Relations

The first tier of development (not indicated in Figure 3) consists of reflexes. A reflex is an innate action pattern that requires direct stimulation for its evocation. In skill theory (Fischer, 1980; Fischer & Hogan, 1989), a reflex is not the equivalent of a simple knee-jerk or eye-blink; a reflex is a pattern of behavior over which the infant is able to exert some control. Such action patterns include sucking a nipple placed in the mouth; orienting to a noise; closing fingers around an object placed in the hand. Further, reflexes are not simply actions evoked by objects. They also include social actions,

---

[2] To preserve space, although it is discussed in the text, we have omitted reference to the reflex tier from Figure 3.

such as actively looking at someone's face and even imitating facial actions produced by others.

The finding that neonates are capable of imitating facial actions is an important one with deep implications for how we understand the problem of how we come to know "other minds" (Melzoff & Moore, 2005; Overgaard, 2005). In order to imitate facial actions in others, an infant must be able to connect her own facial actions—actions that she cannot herself observe—with the facial actions of others. Further, the infant must have some sense—however primitive—that her caregiver's facial actions are in some way "like me." How could this be possible? One answer comes in the form of the discovery of "mirror neurons" in monkeys (Gallese, Eagle, & Migone, 2007; Rizzolatti, 2005). Mirror neurons are those that are activated both when a monkey *performs* a given action as well as when the monkey *observes* that same action being performed by conspecifics. This duality of function suggests that neurons involved in the production of an act can also mediate the process of observing that same action in others. This finding provides the neurobiological grounding for understanding neonatal imitation. To the extent that the same neural systems mediate both the observation and production of certain facial actions, neonates may be able to imitate facial actions in a reflexive fashion.

More important, these findings suggest a radical *inversion* of the ways in which we think about the problem of "other minds." Rather than conceiving of infants as socially isolated beings who must "break into" social interaction by learning how to take the perspective of others, these findings suggest that the capacity for social interaction and perspective taking *builds upon* an already *existing* capacity for establishing primitive forms of intersubjectivity with others (Meltzoff & Brooks, 2007). As such, "social development" is not a derivative product of "cognitive development;" instead, a primitive capacity for coordinating experience with others, given at birth, provides the intersubjective foundation for psychological and socio-emotional development (Overton et al., 2007). We are not individuals first and social beings second.

267

Instead, both individuation and connectedness are built upon a primitive foundation for coordinating experience (Matsov, 2003). We take the inherent capacity for intersubjectivy as the foundation for later development.

The Sensori-Motor-Affective Roots of Meaning[3]

In infancy, beginning around four months of age, infants gain the capacity to control *single sensori-motor-affective acts* (Level 4/SM1). At this level, an infant can direct an act of *looking* at or *seeing* his mother's smiling face. The mother's smile is not something that is separate from the infant's actions. By four-months of age, infants and their caregivers are engaged in complex emotional exchanges. A caregiver's smile is often sufficient to evoke a smile in the infant—as well as the accompanying state of positive affect. In this way, a caregiver's smile is part and parcel of the socio-affective regulation of a child's experience (Shore & Shore, 2011). In the world of objects, an infant can direct the act of *looking* or *tracking* the movement of a toy placed in front of him. An infant can *reach* for a bottle placed before him. The structure of such single sensori-motor acts is indicated at Level 4/SM1 in Figure 3. Although four-month-old infants can exert smooth control over a single sensorimotor act, it is not until about 7-8 months of age that they can seamlessly coordinate two or more such acts in relation to each other. This is achieved at the level of *sensorimotor mappings* (Level 5/SM2). At this level, for example, an infant can reach for a bottle *in order* to look at it, or, alternatively, look at a bottle *in order* to reach for it. In the socio-affective world, a child can actively look at his mother's face *in order* to see her smile. Alternatively, the infant can smile at the mother in order to evoke a smile in return. The shift from single sets to mappings illustrates how higher-order actions are constructed from the coordination of lower-level acts.

---

[3] In light of the centrality of affect in the social organization of infant action, these early psychological structures might be better understood as *sensori-motor-affective* rather than simply *sensori-motor.*

Beginning around 12 months of age, infants gain the capacity to construct skills at the level of sensorimotor systems (Level 6/SM3). A sensorimotor system emerges from the inter-coordination of two or more sensorimotor mappings (i.e., it is a mapping of mappings). At this level, children are capable of a variety of coordinated socio-affective interactions involving treating others as social agents. These involve pointing (Tomasello, Carpenter & Liszkowski, 2007), establishing joint attention (Corkum & Moore, 1995), and other forms of secondary intersubjectivity (Fogel & DeKoeyer-Laros, 2007; Trevarthen & Aitken, 2000). Prior to about 9–10 months of age, infants are able to direct their attention to objects in the world or to other people. They cannot yet share attention on an object with a caregiver. This skill requires the capacity to coordinate one's own intended actions toward an object with another person's awareness of that object. The structure of this skill is depicted at Level 6/SM3 in Figure 3. In this situation, a 1-year-old is able to coordinate *looking at mom* and *reaching toward a toy* in order to prompt his mother to shift from *looking at me to looking at the toy*. At this level, children are capable of pointing toward objects in order to attempt to influence the psychological states of others (Tomasello, Carpenter & Liszkowski, 2007).

Representations and the Origins of Symbolic Meaning

Beginning around 18–24 months of age, children gain the capacity for single concrete representations, which is the first step of the next broad tier of development. Using representations, a child is able to use one thing (e.g., an object, an image, a picture, words, etc.) to refer to an absent object or concrete meanings that go beyond the information given in sensori-motor-affective experience. Linguistically, a simple single representation corresponds to a simple declarative sentence. Single representations emerge as children gain the capacity to coordinate multiple sensori-motor action systems into a *system of sensori-motor systems*. In this way, the *fourth* level of the sensori-motor tier of development (systems of sensori-motor systems) is the equivalent of the *first* level of the *representational* tier of development (Level 7 ≡ SM4 ≡ RP1). Children construct single representations by abstracting across what is common (or typical) to multiple sensori-motor-affective experiences within a given psychological or social domain. For example, abstracting across multiple cooperative exchanges with caregivers, a child can construct single representations of the *concrete meaning* of those interactions. This process is represented in Figure 2 at Level 7/Rp1. At this level, a child is able to coordinate multiple sensori-motor action systems (Level 6/SM3) for participating in cooperative exchanges with caregivers into a *system of sensori-motor systems*, which is the equivalent of a single *representation*. As indicated in Figure 3, a child can construct concrete representations related to self ("I like my Teddy Bear"), other ("I love mommy"), and social interactions ("Mommy plays with me"; "Mommy gives me a toy") and related meanings.

The form of representational activity that emerges between 18-24 months of age differs from sensori-motor action in many ways. Prior to 18-24 months of age, children are able to construct images, are able to produce and understand speech, and are able to use gestures to communicate meanings. However, these capacities are largely tied to the sensori-motor-affective contexts in which they occur. An 8-month old can hold an image of his mother in mind after she leaves the room; but that image is tied to the sensori-motor experience of the mother's leaving. A 12-month old child points to objects that are present or within his sensori-motor sphere; a 15-month old child is able to recognize herself in the mirror; but her recognition is tied to the presence of her reflection in the mirror. In contrast, by the end of the second year, children can begin to construct concrete images and meanings in the absence of the objects and people that those meanings are about. In this way, the child gains control over the representational activity, whether it be speech, imagery, pretend play, or other symbolic acts.

Although infants both understand and produce words at earlier phases in infancy, the capacity to use language in a fully representational way arises between 18–24 months. The capacity to use language to represent meaning is one of the single most important milestones in the development of a person (as well as in the evolution of our species). This is because language allows the child to acquire shared, socially constructed meanings that are the products of cultural history. With the capacity for language, a child can begin to use sign systems (e.g., words, mathematical notion, etc.) not simply to express needs, thoughts, and feelings to others, but also to formulate higher-order meanings that have their origins in cultural history rather than in personal experience. In a later section, say more about the role of language (sign systems) in the joint construction of meaning in development. At present, we bracket the question of how language fosters development and continue our analysis of how psychological structures undergo structural transformation over time.

Prior to about three and a half years of age, a child is only able to hold in mind one concrete idea at any given time. Beginning around three and a half to four and a half years of age, children gain the capacity to construct *representational mappings* (Level 8/Rp2). Using mappings, children can form representations embodying various forms of relations between ideas (e.g., cause and effect; part-whole; sequence; reciprocity; size; quantity; etc.). Figure 3 shows how representational mappings build from the intercoordination of lower-level single representations. Abstracting across multiple interactions with caregivers, a 4-year old can begin to build mapping-based "working model" of his relationship with a caregiver. For example, coordinating single representations such as "My mommy plays with me" and "playing with my Teddy Bear is fun," a child can construct a mapping like "Mommy plays with me so that we can have fun." Similarly, abstracting across multiple occasions of having received gifts, a child can form a representation like "I love Mommy because she buys me presents." Around 6–7 years, children begin to coordinate two or more lower-level mappings into a higher-order representational *system* (L9/Rp3). For example, as indicated in Figure 3, at this level, a child is capable of development of what makes life meaningful, when asked what was most important in his life, one 8-year old boy said, "My mom and dad are important to me because they let me play hockey. They buy me stuff to play hockey with my friends. They take me to my hockey games and they come to see me play." One precocious 5-year old girl produced the following systems level articulation of what is most important in her life: "ourselves ... people are more important than toys because toys are not real and people are real."

Adult Development through the Abstract Tier

The next broad tier of skill development consists of the development of *abstractions.* Abstractions consist of ideas about intangible, hypothetical, generalized, or unimaginable meanings. Abstractions are the product of "abstracting" what is common or typical to multiple concrete instances of a concept. For example, because the statement, "My mom is important to me because she takes me to hockey" contains reference to concrete, imaginable, and tangible content, it functions at the representational tier of development. However, the statement "My family is important to me because without them, I couldn't do all of the things that I do" makes reference to generalized rather than concrete events (i.e., "all the things that I do"). As such, it begins to operate within the abstract tier of development. Development within the abstract tier begins to occur around 10–11 years of age in social contexts that support its development. However, as skills move into the abstract tier, attainting higher levels of skill becomes increasingly difficult. This is because each new level of development requires the integration of increasingly large amounts of meaningful information within particular conceptual domains. Higher levels of development are attainable only after a great deal of active and integrative experience within particular conceptual domains. As such, although pre-teens gain the capacity to construct single abstractions around 10–11 years of age, much of *adult* development occurs through the abstract tier of development (Mascolo & Fischer, 2010).

FIGURE 3. DEVELOPMENT OF CORE GOAL REPRESENTATIONS FROM INFANCY THROUGH ADULTHOOD

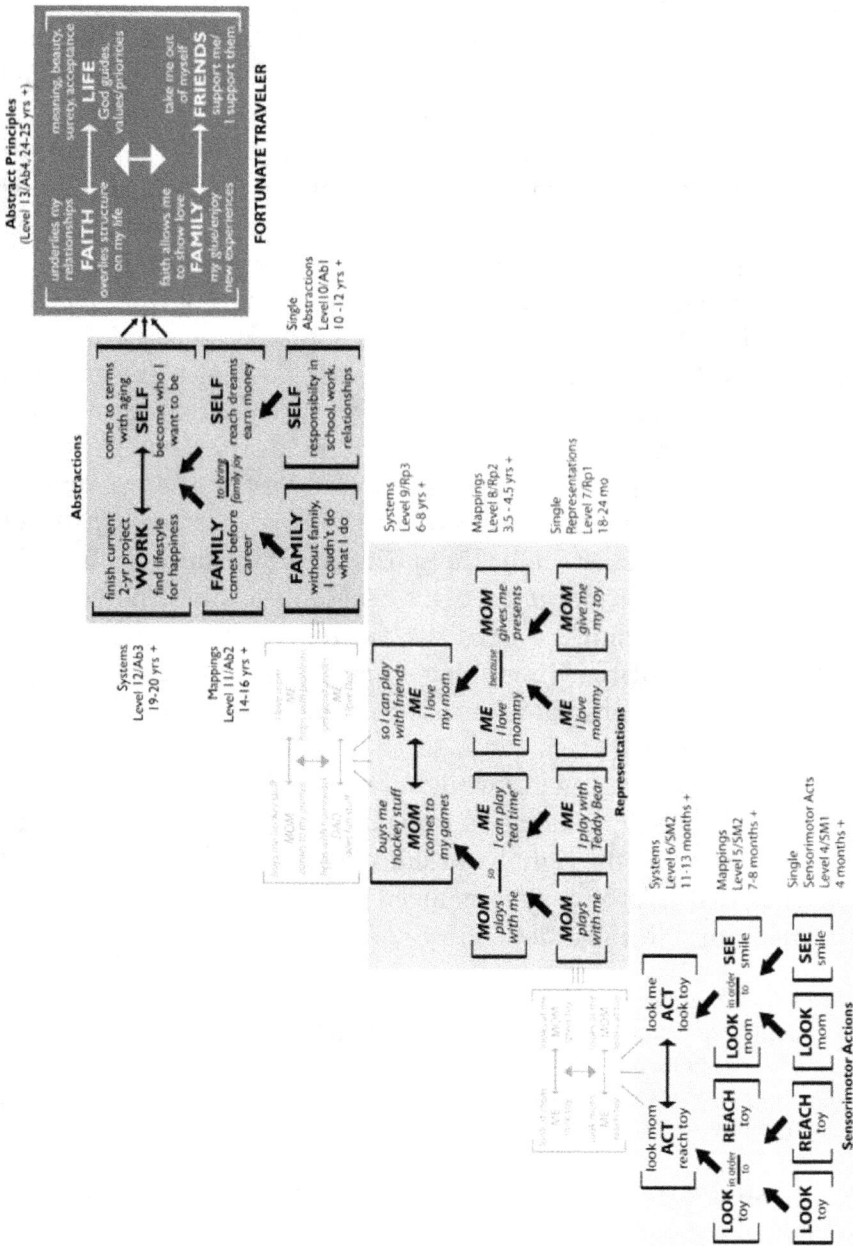

Abstract Principles
(Level 13/Ab4, 24-25 yrs +)

underlies my relationships

meaning, beauty, surety, acceptance

FAITH — God guides, values/priorities — **LIFE**

faith overlies structure on my life

take me out of myself

FAITH allows me to show love — faith allows me to show love — **FRIENDS** support me/ I support them

FAMILY my glue/enjoy new experiences

FORTUNATE TRAVELER

Abstractions

Single Abstractions
Level 10/Ab1
10 -12 yrs +

finish current 2-yr project — come to terms with aging

WORK find lifestyle for happiness — **SELF** become who I want to be

FAMILY *to bring family joy* comes before career — **SELF** reach dreams earn money

FAMILY without family, I couldn't do what I do — **SELF** responsibility in school, work, relationships

Systems
Level 12/Ab3
19-20 yrs +

Mappings
Level 11/Ab2
14-16 yrs +

Systems
Level 9/Rp3
6-8 yrs +

Mappings
Level 8/Rp2
3.5 - 4.5 yrs +

Single Representations
Level 7/Rp1
18-24 mo

MOM gives me presents

MOM give me my toy

ME *because* I love mommy

ME I love mommy

so I can play with friends

ME I love my mom

Representations

buys me hockey stuff

MOM comes to my games

ME I can play "tea time"

ME I play with Teddy Bear

MOM so plays with me

MOM plays with me

Systems
Level 6/SM2
11-13 months +

Mappings
Level 5/SM2
7-8 months +

Single Sensorimotor Acts
Level 4/SM1
4 months +

look me **ACT** look toy

LOOK *in order to* **SEE** smile

SEE smile

look mom **ACT** reach toy

REACH toy

LOOK mom

LOOK mom

Sensorimotor Actions

LOOK *in order to* toy

REACH toy

LOOK toy

273

To illustrate the developmental construction of meaning over the course of adulthood, we draw upon a study exploring developmental changes in *what makes life meaningful* over the lifespan (Mascolo & Fischer, 2010). To explore this question, we asked individuals between the ages of 18 and 80 to respond to the question, "What are the most important things in your life?" Our intention was to extract higher-order integrative representations of the self that we call *core goal representations*. Core goal representations identify the higher order goal structures that superordinate, drive, and give meaning to a person's local life projects. For example, the first level of the abstraction tier of development consists of *single abstractions* (L10/Ab1). Abstractions develop as pre-teens gain the capacity to coordinate and abstract over at least two lower-level representational systems to form a single abstraction. The transition from the representational to the abstract tier of development is shown in on the left hand side of the *single abstractions* level Figure 3. When asked about the most important thing in his life, one 12-year-old boy organized his response around the concept of **family**: "My family. I need my family. Without my family, I couldn't do all of the things that I am able to do." This budding abstraction "superordinates" over lower-level concrete examples of this statement, such as "I get to act in plays", "my parents give me advice" and "without them, I wouldn't have my computer." A second example of a single abstraction was provided by an 18–25 year-old man (indicated on the right hand side of the *single abstractions level* in Figure 3). This individual organized the most important things in his life around the abstract concept of **responsibility**:

> School, work and relationships. I think that the general idea is responsibility. In school, you have to be responsible and study to keep up with assignments. At work, you have to be on time and be focused on what needs to be done. In relationships, you have to give time and attention to the other person.

Abstractions do not function as mere ruminations that occur outside of the context of action. Abstractions *mediate* higher-order modes of thinking, feeling and acting. We use abstractions to organize and regulate thinking, feeling and acting within particular contexts. For example, in stating, "Without my family, I couldn't do all of the things that I am able to do," the boy expresses a type of *enduring gratitude* toward his parents. Such an emotional state is organized by the boy's capacity to use abstractions to organize and regulate his feelings and actions toward his parents.

As indicated in Figure 3, the next level within the abstract tier, abstract mappings (L11/Ab2), begins to develop between 15–16 years of age in contexts that support their construction. Abstract mappings are representations of relations between two or more independent abstractions. The abstract mapping depicted in Figure 3 describes a core goal structure of a 26–35 year-old woman:

> Family is most important and it comes ahead of your career or money. However, you must reach your dreams and earn money in order to be a fulfilled person and bring joy to the family. If you are disgruntled, then you would not be an asset to your family.

This individual identifies her core goals in terms of the relationship between the abstract concepts of **family** and **career/selfhood**. For this woman, the route to *"bringing joy to one's family"* requires *"reaching your dreams"* and *"earning money"* in order to become a fulfilled person."

The next level within the abstract tier consists of abstract systems (L12/Ab3) and begins to develop around 17–18 years of age. Abstract systems arise from the coordination of two or more lower level abstract mappings. The next protocol was articulated by a 55–65 year-old woman, and provides an example of a core goal representation at the level of abstract systems (L12/Ab3).

> Completing my current two-year project, finding work and a life-style that will give me happiness, coming to terms with getting older. These things put together the person I want to/can become. The first two fit together chronologically. I will complete the first goal and by that time my second goal will be completed, and who knows what will be most important at that time? The third . . . arcs above the first

two, because finding your place in life is important. Once you find your niche . . . you can be prepared to face the fact that you're getting older. While things seem to get more stable as you age, they do still change, and you have to be flexible.

As indicated in Figure 3, this core goal representation is composed of integrated relations involving various aspects of **work** and **self**. The individual sees the goal of *completing his long-term project* (**work**) as the chronological precursor to *finding meaningful work* and a *lifestyle that will bring happiness* (**self**). These two processes will provide the vehicle through which the speaker *can be the person* (**self**) *he wants to become.* As time passes, finding a niche in life will provide the preparation for *coming to terms with getting older* (**self**) *and finding a place or niche in life* (**work, self**). This complex goal representation coordinates and gives meaning to a suite of major and minor life projects.

At the highest level of skill development, an adult is able to bring together multiple abstract systems into a single coordinated principle (L13/Ab4). The following principled-based core goal representation was provided by a 65–75 year-old woman, and is organized around the faith-based principle that *"I am the fortunate [spiritual] traveler."*

My faith . . . underlies all other important relationships in my life. It connects me to other people and events and overlies a structure on my entire life. My faith has deepened as I have aged, and I turn over everything stressful to God. [Faith gives me the belief that] this journey is guided and is meaningful. It imbues my life with a surety, with love, and with acceptance. This has helped me to put loss in perspective, and to understand the importance of friends and families over material possessions. My faith defines my values and priorities, and allows me to demonstrate love to my family and my friends. My family is my glue! I enjoy being with them, doing things, enjoying new experiences. . . . I have a hierarchy of friends. Friendships are so important because they take me out of myself. I feel they support me, and I support them. These things cannot be separated. They are all guiding forces in my life, instill meaning to my life, and define who I am. My faith reinforces my belief that I am traveling on a journey of purpose, and my family and friends are my guides on that journey. This [is what] makes for a spiritual life. My faith gave me the path, my children forged it, and my friends illuminate it. I am the fortunate traveler.

As indicated in Figure 3, this complex protocol brings together two abstract systems into a single coordinated structure. This woman's organizes her core goal representation around four inter-coordinated abstractions: **faith, life, family** and **friends**. Her **faith***"underlies other important relationships"* and *"overlies a structure on my life."* Her **faith** defines the *"values and priorities"* in her **life**, and imbues it with *"surety, love and acceptance."* Her **family** is her *"glue"* to whom she shows *"love"* through her **faith**. She also enjoys a "hierarchy" of **friends** with whom she gives and receives *"support."* Her **family** and **friends** are "guiding force" that "instill meaning in my life, and define who I am." Using her **friends** and **family** as guides, she *"travels on a [spiritual] journey of purpose."*

Beyond the Individual: Coaction within the Person-Environment System

Up until this point, the discussion has focused on the processes involved in the construction of meaning as it occurs within individual actors. However, at best, this describes only part of the process by which meanings are constructed. A more complete model of process of meaning construction must *include* but go *beyond* individual acts of construction. Individual acts of construction operate only as a part of a larger *coactive person-environment system* (Gottlieb & Lickliter, 2007; Mascolo & Fischer, 2010). Figure 4 displays a model of the person-environment system. The coactive-person environment system is composed of five categories: (a) an individual actor; (b) other people, (c) the objects of joint action; (d) cultural tools and meditational means; and (e) broader socio-cultural systems. We have already discussed the functioning of individual actors and the ways in which the elements of action mutually regulate each other. In elaborating the nature of the person-environment system, it is necessary to examine how various elements of the system co-act in the production of individual and joint action. The primary assumption of coactive system theory is the lack of independence among systems and system components: *Although the components of the person-environment system are conceptually distinct, they are inseparable as causal processes in the construction of meaning and action.*

Communication and the Co-Regulation of Social Action

The key to understanding how processes regarded as distinct can nonetheless be *inseparable* as causal processes lies in the ways in which we conceptualize the process of human communication. We often think of human communication as a discrete and sequential process. From this view, in order for communication to occur, there must be a *sender*, a *receiver*, and a *message*. The process begins with the sender, who constructs a thought that functions as the basis of the message. The sender translates the thought into a language or code and then passes the resulting message through a communication channel. When the message reaches its destination, the receiver must first decode it, translating it into thought so that it can be understood. At that point, the receiver and the sender can switch roles; the sender becomes the receiver and vice-versa. The process continues as the former receiver adopts the role of sender and thereupon sends a new message. The defining feature of the discrete state model of communication is that at any given time, an individual can only operate as a sender *or* a receiver; a person cannot be a sender and a receiver at the same time. Further, each step in the transmission process is discrete and separable from each other step. The sender autonomously creates the message. Once constructed, the message remains fixed until it passes through a set communication channel. Only after receiving the message can the receiver switch roles and become the sender.

This model works well for understanding communication systems such as mail, email, texting, or similar systems. However, it breaks down when applied to an analysis of direct communication. In face-to-face communication, individuals continuously operate *as senders and receivers at the same time.* In face-to-face interaction, interlocutors communicate continuously in a variety of verbal and nonverbal ways. For example, when Sally begins to speak, Harry looks into her eyes and waits. As Sally speaks, Harry nods his head to indicate his understanding. Seeing that Harry understands her point, Sally decides to consolidate what she is saying. As she does so, Harry momentarily shifts his gaze away from Sally's eyes. Seeing this as an expression of Harry's desire to speak, Sally concludes her statement. In this example, both Harry and Sally are simultaneously "senders" and "receivers" of meaning. In this example, while Sally communicates verbally, Harry uses verbal (e.g., uh huh) and nonverbal action to communicate his understanding. In so doing, Sally's "message" changes during the course of both its *construction* and *communication.* In this way, the "message" is constructed *jointly* as a product of processes that occur *between* Harry and Sally. Harry's actions are an *inseparable part of the process* of Sally's communication, and vice-versa. As a result, concepts such as "sender," "receiver," "transmission," and "message" begin to lose their meaning in analyses of face-to-face communication.

The continuous nature of face-to-face communication has important implications for the ways in which we think about the control of individual action. In face-to-face communication, social partners simultaneously and continuously adjust their thoughts, feelings, and actions to the ongoing and anticipated actions of each other. As a result, neither partner is autonomous in the regulation of his or her actions; instead, joint interaction is *co-regulated* (Fogel, 1993). Social partners function as part of the process of each other's actions. This transforms but does not diminish the idea that humans are active agents. Although humans are active agents, they are not autonomous agents. As such, rather than

FIGURE 4. THE COACTIVE PERSON-ENVIRONMENT SYSTEM

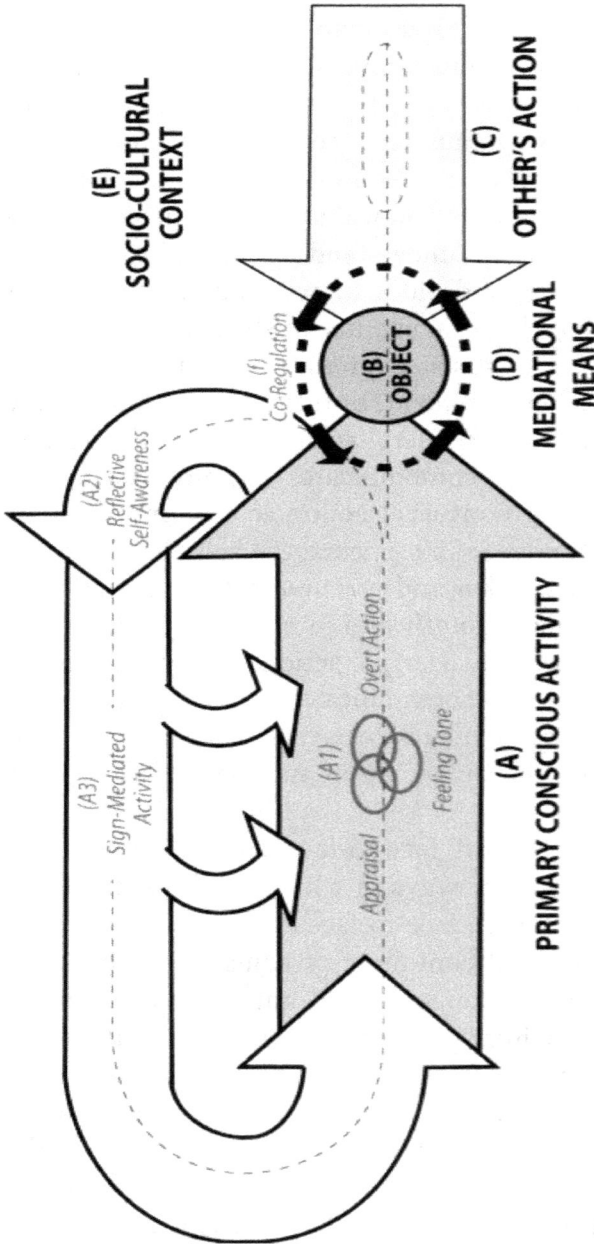

The Person-Environment System. The person-environment system is composed of five categories of interlocking processes. The base gray arrow (**A**) represents a person's primary conscious activity. The gray circle toward which the base arrow points represents (**B**) the objects of intentional action. The intentional object of action can be either real or representational, and represents the focus of a persons' attentional activity. Many interactions involve (**C**) another person or persons. In face-to-face interaction, individuals co-regulate each others actions both verbally and non-verbally. Higher-order co-regulation occurs using some form of mediational means (**D**) the most significant of which is language. All interaction occurs within a particular socio-cultural-historical context (**E**) consisting of socially shared meanings, practices and artifacts.

saying that humans *control* their actions, it is perhaps better to say that humans *exert control* over their actions. Although we exert control over our thoughts, feelings, and actions, we exercise control *through our relations* to objects, persons, and semiotic systems that extend beyond the skin, just as our capacity for control operates and emerges within the medium of our physical bodies.

The Concept of Mediational Means

Mediational means are the cultural tools that we use in order to complete individual and joint projects (Wertsch, 1998). The role of mediational means in the co-regulated construction of action is indicated at Point D in Figure 4. We use an axe to chop wood; a fireplace to hold the wood; and a book of matches to light the fire. In social action, our most useful tool for constructing and communicating higher-order meaning is *language*. Language is a system of arbitrary signs that we use for constructing, representing, and communicating shared social meanings. When we use language, we draw from our collective cultural repertoire of meanings in order to represent and regulate our experience in socially useful ways. In the example described above, responding to Harry's nodding head, Sally began to modify her communication even before Harry had an opportunity to speak. The generative potential of joint construction explodes as meanings collide and combine within verbal exchanges. When we use language to communicate meaning, we are essentially saying, "in this interaction, imagine that the world like this." Through language use, we do not simply share meanings, we play a role in the joint construction of novel meaning. There are few richer illustrations of how language mediates the joint construction of meaning than an analysis of psychological change over the course of psychotherapy.

TRACKING INDIVIDUAL CHANGE IN JOINT ACTION: THE DEVELOPMENTAL ANALYSIS OF PSYCHOTHERAPY PROCESSES

In this section, we illustrate the processes by which meanings are co-created as a result of sign-mediated co-regulation that occurs between people in joint action. In so doing, drawing on the methods elaborated by Basseches and Mascolo (2010), we describe tools for tracking fine-grained changes in integrative psychological structures as they develop over the course of discourse and joint action. The basic tool for analyzing how individual development occurs within joint action is the *discursive map*. For any given unit of social interaction, a discursive map tracks how each partner's psychological structures change in relation to each other in real time. To illustrate the richly textured ways in which social partners co-construct novel meanings in social interaction, we examine moment-by-moment changes and jointly-produced patterns of thinking, feeling, and acting as they evolve over the course of psychotherapy. Psychotherapy is a particularly rich area for exploring how individual development occurs through joint action. Psychotherapy provides a microcosm of psychological development. Basseches and Mascolo (2010) have suggested that psychotherapeutic change functions as a developmental process. Clients enter psychotherapy as a response to some sort of adaptive conflict in their lives. When psychotherapy works, it promotes transformation in the structure of a client's thoughts, feelings, and actions. Over time, successful psychotherapy functions to create higher-order structures of thinking, feeling, and action that allow clients to manage, resolve, or transcend the adaptive conflicts that brought them into therapy.

In what follows, we provide a series of snapshots of key developmental moments in a single pivotal session of short-term "anxiety-regulating" dynamic therapy (McCullough, 1999). In so doing, we identify different developmental change process and the particular ways in which they result in key developmental changes over the course of the therapy session. The case used involves "The Lady Cloaked in Fog," a 42-year-old depressed woman who reported a long history of difficulty experiencing feelings of closeness (McCullough, 1999). The client had been in therapy for the last 24 years and had been seriously depressed for the entirety of her adult life. The client entered therapy experiencing deep depression over her sense of "not mattering" in the world. Specifically, the client experienced a sense that she "mattered on stage"—that is, at work when she was acting in the service of others—but did not matter when she was "off stage," that is, at home alone in her personal relationships.

Significant transformation in the structure of the client's thoughts, feelings and actions occurred over the course of the fifteenth session. During this session, the client was able to construct a higher-order emotionally-charged representation of her relationship to her therapist. In particular, the client was able to experience her therapist as a "harbor light"—a beacon of light that expressed the therapist's care for the client whether or not the client was "on shore" or "off shore," feeling "foggy" in "stormy seas." In this way, the client was able to experience herself as mattering to her therapist whether or not the client was "on stage" or "off stage":

> A harbor light is really helpful. [T:Yeah, so there is a storm?] Storms and fog...It's the fog that is bothering me the most right now . . . Yeah and it, right now I'm not feeling like that skulpy thing of being oarless in the boat. But sometimes I do, and how nice to think that if I just perk my little head up, that there's going to . . . be a harbor light somewhere. And that we can . . . we can talk about the bad stuff . . . But, at the same time I don't have to go in that particular direction. A harbor light is useful because you know where it is and you can decide where you want to go relative to it . . . So I don't have to aim right for you. You can just be there.

The transition from the initial to the final state of the client's conflict is indicated in Figure 5. In what follows, we present a series of snapshots of four important episodes that occurred over the course of this single therapy session that set up the client's "harbor light insight." In so doing, we not only identify changes in integrative structures of thinking, feeling, and acting, but we also identify change processes that operate within and between client and therapist that result in the observed changes.

Episodes 1 & 2: Challenging Feelings of Not Mattering

Our analysis starts with the following dialogue between client and therapist:

> C: Yeah. I guess that's it. It's like I, it's like when I'm at work, I matter, and when I go home, am by myself, I don't matter. It's sort of on or off. Um, on stage or off stage.
> C: It blows my mind to think that there were a lot of days like that when I'd go home and, my God, you and Carol [client's previous therapist] were talking on the phone. It blows me away.
> T: Yeah, that you might have been at home while Carol and I were talking about you . . . those were heartfelt conversations. Now, how did that feel, thinking about that?
> C: Well, it's new and different and . . . and, um, shakes something very deep. Some real deep core belief.
> T: Uh-huh. Put some words on it?
> C: That I don't matter—and there I was mattering and I didn't even know it.

Figure 6 identifies the major structural changes that occur over the course of this episode. At the beginning of the episode (1), with expressed sadness the client represents her problem in terms of a conflictual relation (mapping) between "I matter 'onstage'" (at work, when doing things for others) but "I don't matter 'offstage'" (after hours; at home alone). Soon after articulating this distinction, shifting to a more ironic tone, the client (2) *differentiated* (DIFF) a concrete counter-example to her experience of "not mattering off stage"—namely that her present and previous therapists would talk about the client when the client was home alone ("off stage"). After a simple request by the therapist (3) to "put some words on

Figure 5. Comparison of Initial and Final Representations
the Client's Relational Self

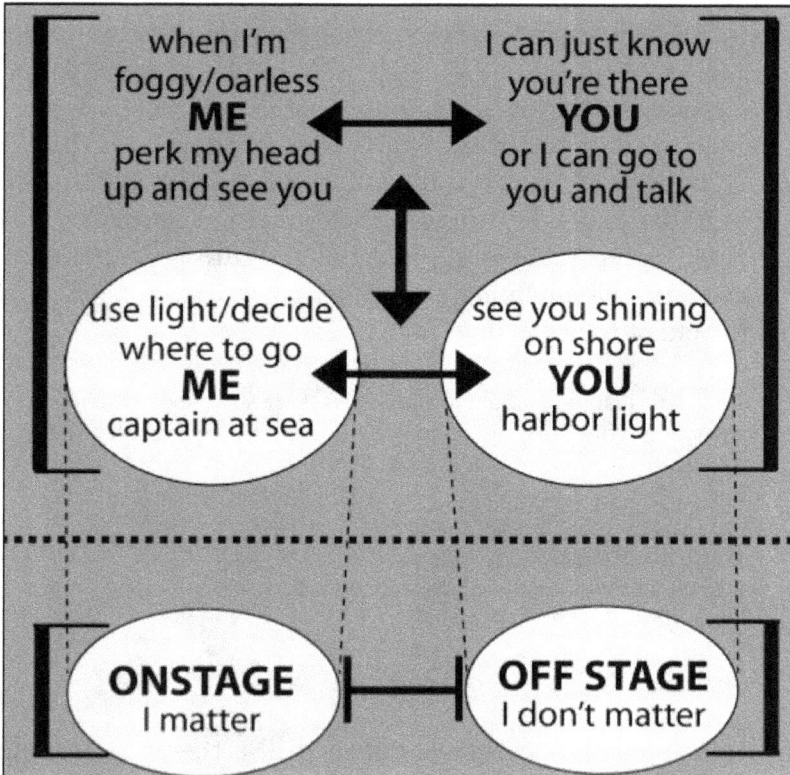

it," the client brought together (*integrated*) (INT) two previously articulated meaning elements (i.e., "I matter" and "off stage") into the representation "I was mattering 'offstage.'" This representation stands in conflict with the previously articulated "I don't matter 'offstage.'"

Episodes 3 & 4: Do I Really Matter "Off Stage"?

Immediately after the client challenged her own sense of not mattering, she began to marginalize it. In reflecting on whether or not the client felt that her previous therapist cared about her "in her thoughts and in her heart," with anxiety and sadness the client said, "Thoughts, yeah. Heart, oh well, I don't know about heart." The client's initial anxiety about "mattering in her previous therapist's heart" is represented at point (1) in Figure 7. Responding to this statement, the following dialogue occurred as the therapist (2) asked the client to perform a thought experiment:

> T: Well, let's just think about it this way. Is there somebody whom you work with in your job that you know is hurting or in pain, someone . . . and then that you've gotten involved with and really want to see feel better, or feel sad about their pain? And when you think about them off hours you feel it in your heart?
> C: (With positive affect and empathic concern) Yeah.
> T: It's not some act—or just intellectual thought.
> C: (Empathically) Oh yeah.
> T: So you know that and so it's important.
> C: Yeah and I do feel and I do know that.

In affirming the scenario implied in the therapist's thought experiment, the client (2 and 3) makes a *differentiation* between her sense of "not mattering in her previous therapist's heart" and her own capacity to feel empathically for co-workers who are in pain. In stating, "Yeah, I do feel and I do know that," the client entertains the possibility that her prior therapist may indeed have cared about the client "in her heart." The shift from (3) to (4) requires acts of coordination and *inversion* (INV). The client must *coordinate*

Figure 6. Challenging the Feeling of Not Mattering

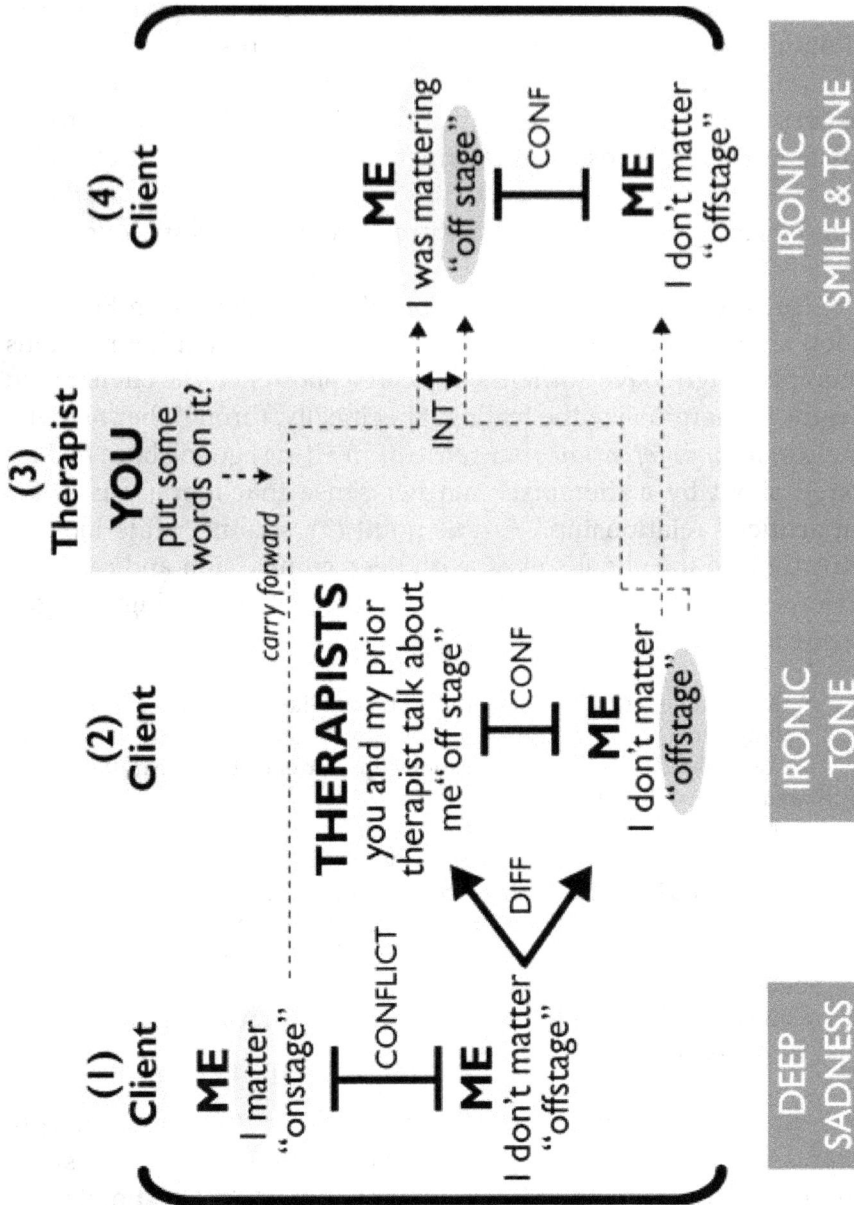

her experience (i.e., "my co-workers matter to me offstage") with her conflicting representation of her therapist's experience (i.e., "I didn't matter to my therapist offstage"). To resolve this contradiction, the client must *invert* (i.e., "reverse" or "take the inverse") her representation of her therapist: "If my co-workers matter to me offstage, then it is possible that I mattered to my therapist offstage."

Episodes 5: Questioning the Reality of Care from Professionals

The discursive structure of Episode 5 is indicated in Figure 8. Soon after (1) the client entertains the possibility that her previous therapist might have authentically cared about her, the client again begins to marginalize the feeling. Specifically, through her anxiety, the client (2) *differentiates* her sense of "feel[ing] good about feeling cared about by a therapist" and her sense that therapy is "such an artificial relationship." At this point (3), smiling while looking directly into the client's eyes, with deep compassion and care, the therapist said, "Do I seem artificial to you?" The following dialogue ensued:

> C: No, but the relationship and the . . . it's not like we're friends, I was paying her.
> T: Yes, this is a professional relationship. But does that mean there aren't human feelings?
> C: No.
> T: People are paying you. I mean you're working for a salary, but you, just you know the feelings you have, there's human involvement there and . . . and somehow when it comes toward you, you want to push it away . . . I'm saying open wide (laugh), don't spit it out. Don't throw it off the plate . . . It's hard isn't it?
> C: It is . . . it is hard, it's yeah . . . It feels . . . I-I-I could go to beating up on myself and making it wrong.

In this situation, in the context of the therapist's deeply expressed *emotion*, and through her expressions of positive emotion, anxiety, and embarrassment, the client acknowledges the authenticity of the therapist's feelings of care. The thera-

FIGURE 7. CREATING POSITIVE FEELINGS ABOUT MATTERING TO THERAPIST

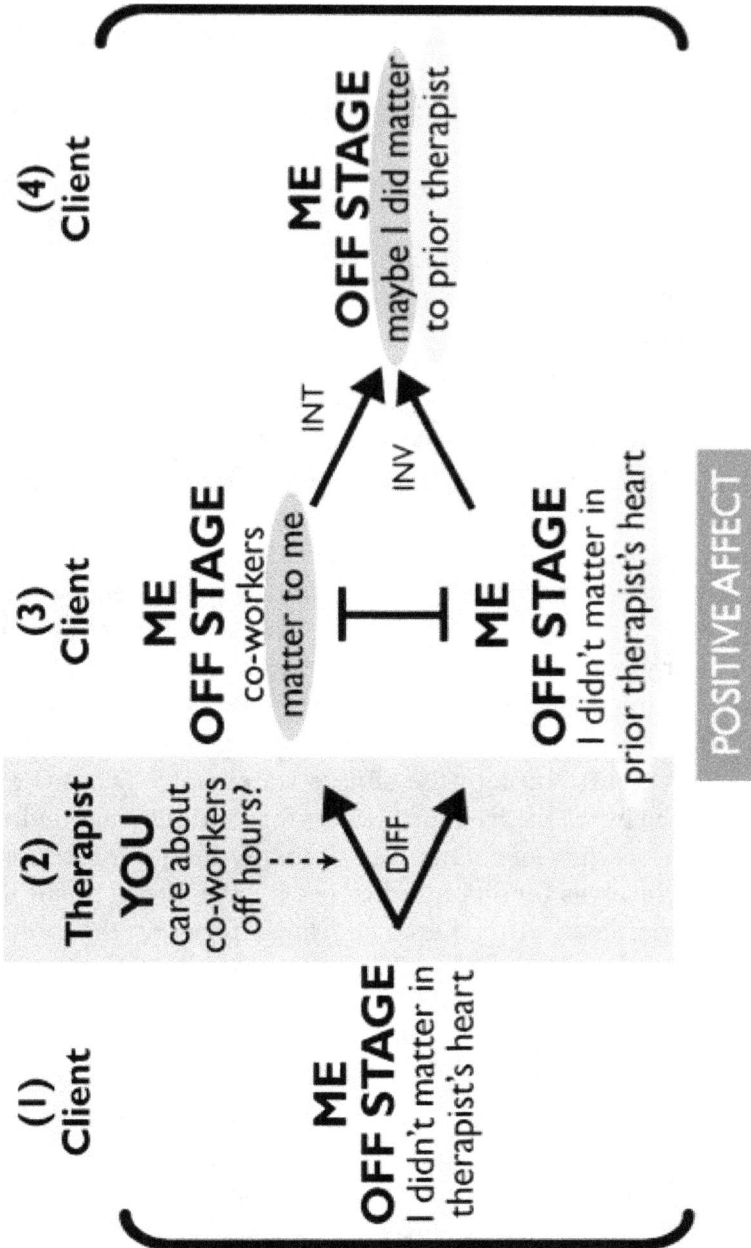

pist's (4) expressed emotion conflicts with the client's sense that care expressed in the context of therapy is artificial. To resolve this contraction, the client (5) must begin the process of inverting (reversing) her emotionally-charged belief that care in therapy is artificial.

Episode 6: Accepting Care from the Therapist as Genuine

Figure 9 displays the discursive structure of Episode 6. This episode marks one of several pivotal points in the therapy session. Still questioning the artificiality of the therapeutic relationship, the client (1) says, "And you're telling me that this is real, and I'm saying, 'Well, it is real and I can really feel it.' Oh, but then it's also not really real and, in that it's bounded. You're not going to invite me for dinner, and I'm not going to invite you for dinner. You know." The therapist (2) responds with a seemingly simple statement, "That's right. Our experience will be here." The client responds with renewed positive emotion and says, "*Yeah, right and that is very real, and I don't mean . . . but it is also not out in the world.* So my real thing will . . . my next challenge will be to find whatever thing is here out in the world."

Figure 9 displays the subtly and discursive force of the therapist's statement. Through the simple statement, "Yes, our experience will be here," the therapist brings forward several previously conflicting meaning elements into a single, integrated representation that resolves their contradictions for the client. In speaking of "our experience," the therapist brings forward the previous reference to shared feelings of care between the client and the therapist. In locating that experience in the here-and-now of the therapy room, the therapist suggests a differentiation between the *realty* of feelings of *care* and the *space* within which such feelings would be experienced. In so doing, the therapist *differentiated* three *undifferentiated* statements put forth by the client. Specifically, the therapist affirmed the client's statement that the therapeutic relationship was bounded (i.e., "our *experience* will be *here*"). However,

FIGURE 8. PRESSING CLIENT TO EXPERIENCE FEELINGS OF BEING
CARED ABOUT

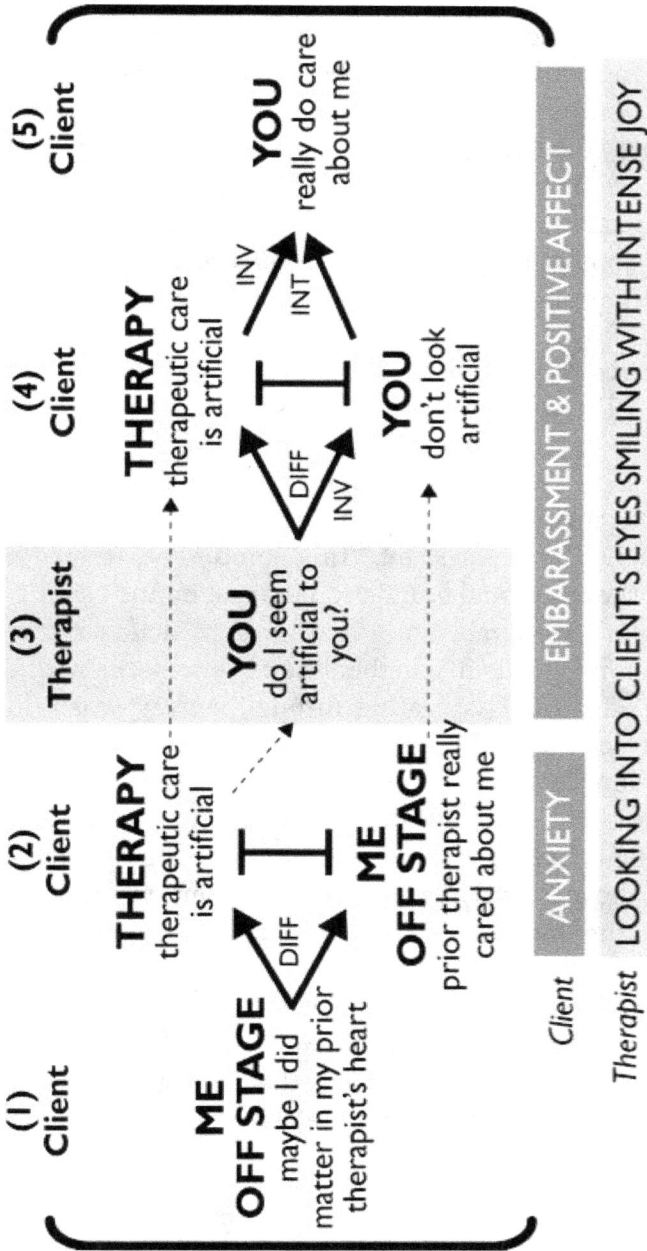

in affirming the reality of the dyad's experience (i.e., "our *experience* will be here"), the therapist rejected the idea that the feelings of care were not real. Finally, by identifying their shared experience as occurring within therapy (i.e., "our experience will be *here*"), the therapist differentiated between therapeutic relationships and other types of relationships. The client (4) was able to appropriate the distinction between the *reality of care* and the *location of care*, and *integrate* them into a meaning structure that resolved the apparent conflict between them: "*Yeah, right and that is very real, and I don't mean...but it is also not out in the world.*"

The Coactive Construction of Meaning Both within and between Client and Therapist

The client's hard-won capacity to experience herself as genuinely mattering to her therapist functioned as a central emotional achievement in the session. This jointly-constructed meaning provided the emotional foundation that set up the client's capacity to represent her therapist as a "harbor light" who shines a beacon of care upon the client whether she is "on shore" with the therapist or "off shore" navigating through stormy seas without the therapist (see Figure 5). However, what is most important in the analyses described above is the subtle nature of the co-constructive processes that mediated the developmental changes observed in the client. Even a casual examination of the discursive maps describe above reveals the futility of attempting to separate the client and the therapist as independent causal forces in accounting for the client's development. To be sure, the client and the therapist exist as distinct individuals. However, the developmental changes observed are the result of coactive processes that occur within and between the client and therapist as they adjust the pattern of their thoughts, feelings, and actions in relation to each other in moment-to-moment exchanges.

FIGURE 9. ACCEPTING THE LEGITIMACY OF BEING CARED ABOUT BY THERAPIST

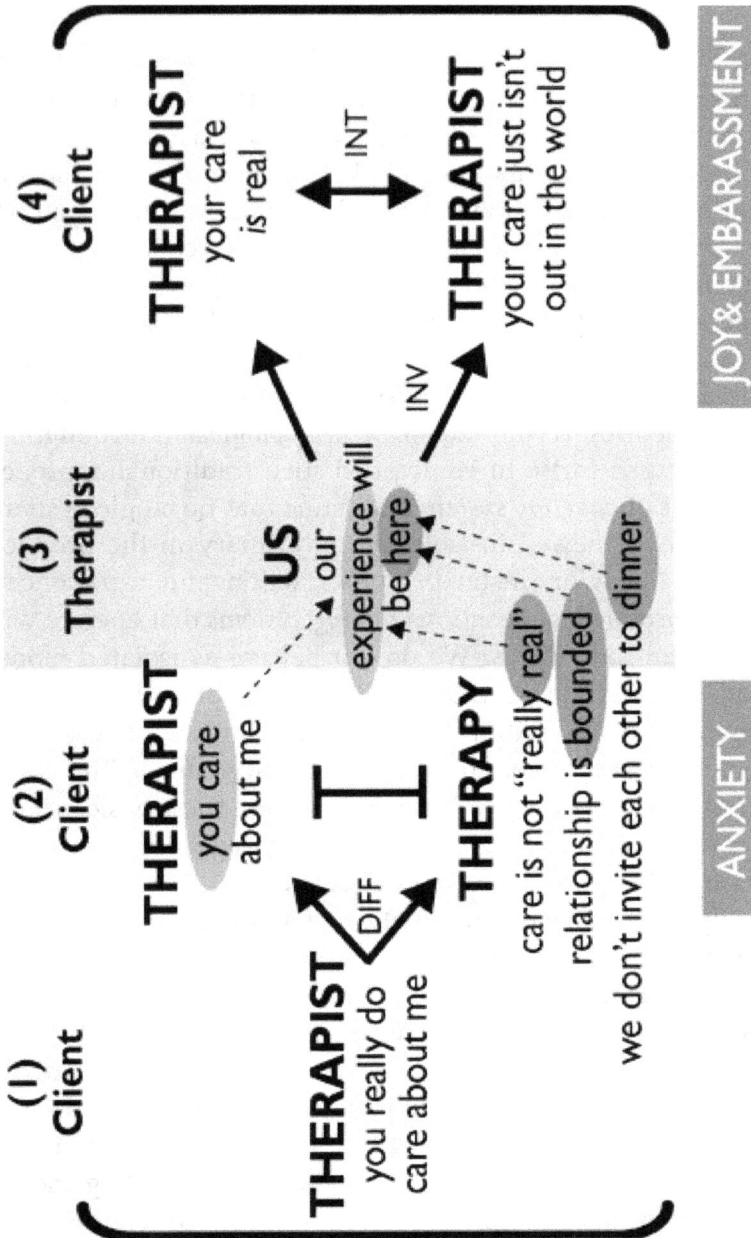

COORDINATING DIVERGENT CONSTRUCTIONISMS

The concept of coactive systems is congenial to the task of elaborating an integrative constructionism. Traditionally, psychology has conceived its subject matter as a set of discrete processes. Psychologists have tended to study distinct aspects of human behavior as if they operate in isolation from one another. The chapters in introductory textbooks aptly reflect the resulting fragmentation that occurs when psychological processes are studied as distinct modules. When psychologists do work toward integration, one set of psychological processes is often identified as primary. Thus, we have *cognitive* theories (Lazarus, 1991), *motivational* theories (Fiske, 2004), *neurobiological* (DeYoung, 2010) theories and so forth. In contrast to such traditional approaches, the concept of *coactive system* maintains that no single system (or set of systems viewed in isolation) is primary in the production of human behavior; instead, human action and experience are emergent products of coactions *among systems* that operate within and between individuals. We do not behave as isolated modules; instead, we operate as integrated systems of action and experience that function within the medium of the body and which are embedded in still larger social and cultural systems. The coactive systems approach described here builds upon these basic principles and works toward the goal of building an integrative constructivist psychology that elaborates a set of conceptual and empirical tools for studying the coactive production of action and experience.

Although the differences among alternative versions of constructionism can be subtle, they reflect meaningful differences in conceptions of the origins and significance of meaning construction. These include differences in the relation between meaning and "reality;" the importance of individual, social, and cultural-historical processes; the primacy of language versus thought; the role of the body and world in grounding meaning; the role of the internal/private versus the external/public, and so forth. Many have suggested the need to move beyond the various "isms" that divide constructivist thought. This is an important goal. However, in working to move beyond distinctions, we must be careful to avoid the temptation to gloss over important theoretical distinctions or simply mix divergent claims into an eclectic theoretical soup. An integrative constructivist psychology must synthesize divergent theoretical approaches in ways that resolve the contradictions between them. If advocates of different versions of constructionism cannot recognize their own positions in any given synthesis, then either the synthesis is inadequate or the failed synthesis indicates a need to sharpen the distinctions among conflicting viewpoints. However, if sharpening differences is to be constructive, we need continued rigorous dialogue. Intellectual isolation is the enemy of scientific progress.

REFERENCES

Arnason J. (2010). The cultural turn and the civilizational approach. *European Journal of Social Theory, 13*(1), 67–82.

Basseches, M., & Mascolo, M. (2010). *Psychotherapy as a developmental process.* New York, NY: Taylor & Francis.

Bateson, G. (1972). *Steps to an ecology of mind.* New York, NY: Aronson.

Bermond, B. (2008). The emotional feeling as a combination of two qualia: A neurophilosophical based emotion theory. *Cognition & Emotion, 22,* 897–930.

Bowerman, M. (2007). Containment, support, and beyond: Constructing topological spatial categories in first language acquisition. In M. Aurnague, M. Hickmann, & L. Vieu (Eds.) , *The categorization of spatial entities in language and cognition* (pp. 177–203). Amsterdam, The Netherlands: John Benjamins.

Brockmeier, J. (2012). Narrative scenarios: Toward a culturally thick notion of narrative. In J. Valsiner (Ed.), *The Oxford handbook of culture and psychology* (pp. 439–467). New York, NY: Oxford University Press.

Bruner, J. (1991). The narrative construction of reality. *Critical Inquiry, 18*(1), 1–21.

Camras, L. A. (2011). Differentiation, dynamical integration and functional emotional development. *Emotion Review, 3*(2), 138–146.

Carver, C. S., & Scheier, M. F. (2002). Control processes and self-organization as complementary principles underlying behavior. *Personality and Social Psychology Review, 6*, 304–315.

Case, R., & Mueller, M. P. (2001). Differentiation, integration, and covariance mapping as fundamental processes in cognitive and neurological growth. In J. L. McClelland & R. S. Siegler (Eds.), *Mechanisms of cognitive development: Behavioral and neural perspectives* (pp. 185–219). Mahwah, NJ: Lawrence Erlbaum.

Clark, A. (1997). *Being there.* Cambridge, MA: MIT Press.

Cole, M. & Wertsch, J.V. (1996). Beyond the individual-social antimony in discussions of Piaget and Vygotsky. *Human Development, 39*, 250–256.

Corkum, V., & Moore, C. (1995). Development of joint visual attention in infants. In C. Moore, P. J. Dunham (Eds.), *Joint attention: Its origins and role in development* (pp. 61–83). Hillsdale, NJ: Lawrence Erlbaum.

Cupchik, G. (2001). Constructivist realism: An ontology that encompasses positivist and constructivist approaches to the social sciences. *Forum: Qualitative Social Research, 2*(1), 29–39.

DeYoung, C. G. (2010). Personality neuroscience and the biology of traits. *Social and Personality Psychology Compass, 4*, 1165–1180.

Evanoff, R. J. (2005). Universalist, relativist, and constructivist approaches to intercultural ethics. *International Journal of Intercultural Ethics, 28*(5), 439–458.

Fischer, K. W. (1980). A theory of cognitive development: The control and construction of hierarchies of skills. *Psychological Review, 87*, 477–531.

Fischer, K. W., & Hogan, A. (1989). The big picture for infant development: Levels and variations. In J. Lockman & N. Hazen (Eds.), *Action in social context: Perspectives on early development* (pp. 275–375). New York, NY: Plenum.

Fischer, K. W., & Bidell, T. R. (2006). Dynamic development of action, thought, and emotion. In W. Damon & R. M. Lerner (Eds.), *Theoretical models of human development. Handbook of child psychology* (6th ed., Vol. 1, pp. 313–399). New York: John Wiley.

Fiske, S. T. (2008). Core social motivations: Views from the couch, consciousness, classroom, computers, and collectives. In J. Y. Shah & W. L. Gardner (Eds.), *Handbook of motivation science* (pp. 3–22). New York, NY: Guilford Press.

Foerster, H. von. (1988). On constructing a reality. In S. C. Feinstein, A. H. Esman, J. G. Looney, G. H. Orvin, J. L. Schimel, A. Z. Schwartzberg, & M. Sugar (Eds.) , *Adolescent psychiatry: Developmental and clinical studies, Vol. 15* (pp. 77–95). Chicago, IL: University of Chicago Press.

Fogel, A. (1993). *Developing through relationships.* Chicago, IL: University of Chicago Press.

Fogel, A., & DeKoeyer-Laros, I. (2007). The developmental transition to secondary intersubjectivity in the second half year: A microgenetic case study. *Journal of Developmental Psychology, 2,* 63–90.

Freeman, W. (2000). Emotion is essential to all intentional behaviours. In M. D. Lewis & I. Granic (Eds.) *Emotion, development, and self-organization* (pp. 209–235), New York, NY: Cambridge.

Frijda, N. H. (1986). *The emotions.* Cambridge, England: Cambridge University Press.

Gadenne, V. (2010). Why radical constructivism has not become a paradigm. *Constructivist Foundations: An Interdisciplinary Journal, 6*(1), 77–83.

Gallese, V., Eagle, M. N., & Migone, P. (2007). Intentional attunement: Mirror neurons and the neural underpinnings of interpersonal relations. *Journal of the American Psychoanalytic Association, 55,* 131–176.

Gergen, K. J. (2009). *Relational being: Beyond self and community.* New York, NY: Oxford.

Gilbert, A., & Sliep, Y. (2009). Reflexivity in the practice of social action: From self- to inter-relational reflexivity. *South African Journal of Psychology, 39*(4), 468–479.

Gottlieb, G., & Lickliter, R. (2007). Probabilistic epigenesis. *Developmental Science, 10,* 1–11.

Heidegger, M. (2008). *Being and time* (J. Macquarrie & E. Robinson, Trans.). New York, NY: Harper Perennial. (Original work published 1927)

Kelly, G. (1955). *The psychology of personal constructs* (2 vols.). New York, NY: Norton.

L'Abate, L. (2012). *Paradigms in theory construction.* New York, NY: Springer.

Lazarus, R. S. (1991). *Emotion and adaptation.* New York, NY: Oxford University Press.

Levinas, E. (1985). *Ethics and infinity.* Pittsburgh, PA: Duquesne University Press.

Madill, A., Jordan, A., & Shirley, C. (2000). Objectivity and reliability in qualitative analysis: Realist, contextualist and radical constructionist epistemiologies. *British Journal of Psychology, 91*(1), 1–20.

Mascolo, M. F. (2013). Developing through relationships: A coactive systems framework. To appear in R. Lerner, R. & J. Benson (Eds.), *Embodiment and epigenesis: Theoretical and methodological issues in understanding the role of biology within the relational developmental system.* New York, NY: Elsevier.

Mascolo, M. F. (2012). The internal-external dichotomy. In T. Teo (Ed.) *Internet encyclopedia of critical psychology.* Retrieved from www.springerreference.com/docs/edit/chapterdbid/306996.html

Mascolo, M. F., (2004). The coactive construction of selves in cultures. In M. F. Mascolo, & J. Li (Eds.), *Culture and self: Beyond dichotomization* (pp. 79–90). San Francisco, CA: Jossey-Bass.

Mascolo, M. F., & Fischer, K. W., (2010). The dynamic development of of thinking, feeling and acting over the lifespan. In R. Lerner & W. Overton (Eds.) *Handbook of lifespan development* (pp. 149–194). New York, NY: John Wiley.

Mascolo, M. F., Fischer, K. W. & Neimeyer, R. A. (1999). The dynamic co-development of intentionality, self and social relations. In J. Brandstadter & R. M. Lerner (Eds.) *Action and development: Origins and functions of intentional self-development* (pp. 133–166). Thousand Oaks: CA: Sage.

Mascolo, M. F., Fischer, K. W., & Li, J. (2003). The dynamic construction of emotions in development: A component systems approach. In N. Davidson, K. Scherer & H. Goldsmith (Eds.), *Handbook of affective science* (pp. 375–408). New York, NY: Oxford University Press.

McCullough, L. (1999). Short-term psychodynamic therapy as a form of desensitization. Treating affective phobias. *In Session: Psychotherapy in Practice,* 4, 35–53.

McHoul, A., & Rapley, M. (2005). Re-presenting culture and the self (dis)agreeing in theory and in practice. *Theory & Psychology, 15*(4), 431–447.

Meltzoff, A. N., & Brooks, R. (2007). Intersubjectivity before language: Three windows on preverbal sharing. In S. Bråten (Ed.), *On being moved: From mirror neurons to empathy* (pp. 149–174). Philadelphia, PA: John Benjamins.

Meltzoff, A. N., & Moore, M. K. (1999). Persons and representation: Why infant imitation is important for theories of human development. In J. B. G. Nadel (Ed.), *Imitation in infancy: Cambridge studies in cognitive perceptual development* (pp. 9–35). New York, NY: Cambridge University Press.

Miller, G. A., Galanter, E., & Pribram, K. H. (1960). *Plans and the structure of behavior.* New York, NY: Henry Holt.

Overgaard, S. (2006). The problem of other minds: Wittgenstein's phenomenological perspective. *Phenomenology and the Cognitive Sciences, 5,* 53–73.

Overton, W. F. (2007). A coherent metatheory for dynamic systems: Relational organicism-contextualism. *Human Development, 50,* 154–159.

Pavlović, J. (2011). Personal construct psychology and social constructionism are not incompatible: Implications of a reframing. *Theory & Psychology, 21,* 396–411.

Piaget, J. (1953). *The origins of intelligence in children.* London, England: Routledge and Kegan Paul.

Piaget, J. (1954). *The construction of reality in the child.* New York, NY: Basic. Books.

Piaget, J. (1985). *The equilibration of cognitive structures.* Chicago, IL: University of Chicago Press.

Powers, W. T. (1973) *Behavior: The control of perception,* Chicago, IL: Aldine

Raeff, C. (2011). Distinguishing between development and change: Reviving organismic-developmental theory. *Human Development, 54*(1), 4–33.

Raskin, J. D. (2002). Constructivism in psychology: Personal construct psychology, radical constructivism, and social constructionism. *American Communication Journal, 5*, 1–25.

Rizzolatti, G. (2005). The mirror neuron system and imitation. In S. Hurley & N. Chater (Eds.), *Perspectives on imitation: From neuroscience to social science* (Vol. 1) (pp. 55–76). Cambridge, MA: MIT Press.

Sargent, R-M. (1997). The social construction of scientific evidence. *Journal of Constructivist Psychology, 10*, 75–96.

Siegler, R. S., & Chen, Z. (2008). Differentiation and integration: Guiding principles for analyzing cognitive change. *Developmental Science, 11*(4), 433–448.

Schmidt, V. H. (2001). Oversocialised epistemology: A critical appraisal of constructivism. *Sociology, 35*(1), 135–157.

Searle, J. (1983). *Intentionality.* New York, NY: Cambridge.

Shore, J. A., & Shore, A. N. (2008). Modern attachment theory: The central role of affect regulation in development and treatment. *Clinical Social Work Journal, 36*, 9–20.

Shotter, J. (1975). *Images of man in psychological research.* London, England: Methuen.

Stenner, P. (1998). Heidegger and the subject: Questioning concerning psychology. *Theory & Psychology, 8*(1), 59–77.

Ter Harke, M. (1990). *Beyond the inner and the outer: Wittgenstein's philosophy of psychology.* Dordrecht, The Netherlands: Kluwer Academic.

Tomasello, M., Carpenter, M., & Liszkowski, U. (2007). A new look at infant pointing. *Child Development, 78*, 705–722.

Trevarthen, C., & Aitken, K. J. (2000). Infant intersubjectivity: Research, theory, and clinical applications. *The Journal of Child Psychology and Psychiatry and Allied Disciplines, 42*, 3–48.

Valberg, A. (2005). *Light, vision, color.* New York, NY: John Wiley.

Valsiner, J. & Rosa, A. (Eds.), *Cambridge handbook of sociocultural psychology.* New York, NY: Cambridge.

Vygotsky, L. (1978). *Mind in society.* Cambridge, MA: Harvard University Press.

Werner, H., & Kaplan, B. (1962/1984). *Symbol formation.* New York, NY: Norton.

Wertsch, J. V. (1998). *Mind as action.* Cambridge, MA: Harvard.

෪ 10 ෨

Constructivism: Where Do We Go from Here?
Jonathan D. Raskin, Sara K. Bridges, and
Jack S. Kahn

The contributions to this volume all address, in one way or another, the issue of constructivism's future. What are the challenges that constructivists face going forward? While there are many issues worthy of consideration, in this concluding contribution we take up four. Our focus in discussing these issues is often directed specifically at the personal construct psychology (PCP) and Constructivist Psychology Network (CPN) communities, of which we are longtime members and with which we are most familiar. However, we hope that the radical constructivist and social constructionist communities may also resonate with the themes addressed. The four issues raised can be playfully described as (a) resisting "epistobabble," (b) herding the Groucho Marx Brigade, (c) harnessing our "mojo," and (d) using it instead of losing it.

RESISTING "EPISTOBABBLE"

Recently, one of the authors (Jack) was implored by a friend to watch a YouTube video about video gaming (Cosmo Speedrun, 2013). As someone who has played video games much of his life, Jack usually appreciates such videos. Jack's friend thought this particular video would be interesting because it focused on some young people who learned how to beat "The Legend of Zelda:

Ocarina of Time (OoT)" on the Nintendo 64 (a mid-1990s gaming system) in under 25 minutes, even though the task should take a minimum of 5-6 hours. The video nicely illustrates emergent gameplay, or how gamers find creative and alternative ways to approach presumably deterministic systems of gameplay so as to thwart predefined ground rules in ways that either were not intended to work in that manner or should not be possible in the first place (Kleinrock, n.d).

The video takes place at a charity event hosted by Speed Demos Archive (SDA), a group that conducts video game events called "speedruns," in which participants, under an agreed upon time constraint (which may include attempting to beat an established record), try to complete specific requirements of a video game (Speed Demos Archive, n.d.). There are different versions of these speedruns, with various rules about permissible player behavior and what constitutes success. In the video, a young man in his early twenties plays OoT from start to finish while describing to a group of (mostly) young men how he is doing what he is doing. While Jack admits to having some "street cred" in video gaming, he has never played the Zelda series and is unfamiliar with the specific challenges it poses. However, he has a general appreciation for the task, which involves identifying aspects of a video game that its developers did not realize could be exploited in order to defeat the game much more quickly. This video is interesting because it shows a player doing things in the game that its designers never intended (for example, running backwards instead of forward because it is actually faster) and creatively finding ways to do things that are supposedly impossible—in this case defeating OoT more quickly than ever imagined.

What Jack found most notable was the specialized language and communication patterns of the gamers' social group. Given that Jack is a person who plays video games and knows some of the basics involved in them, he expected to be able to follow the conversation. Yet he was unable to keep up with much of what was being said. A great deal of his confusion was due to the jargon and culture-specific language used by the gamers. At times the only reason why Jack was able to get the general gist was because the whole group laughed, applauded, and cheered at various points as the protagonist progressed toward his goal of defeating the game. The conversation itself was sometimes nearly unintelligible to him; much of the exchange became almost like listening to another language.

The issue of impenetrable jargon is not unique to video gamers. A challenge faced by contributors to this volume is that constructivists often have difficulty communicating their ideas in ways that those outside their immediate community can comprehend (Efran & Clarfield, 1992; Neimeyer, 1997). Neimeyer (1997) pointed out that psychotherapy practitioners are often bewildered by constructivism's intimidating and super-specialized language—its tendency toward what Coyne (as cited in Neimeyer, 1997) referred to as "epistobabble." Said Neimeyer (1997):

> The encounter with a lexicon of terms such as *constructive alternativism, second order cybernetics, autopoietic entities, narrative deconstruction, subjugated knowledges,* and *morphogenic nuclear structure* can prove daunting to the psychotherapy practitioner, not to mention the beleaguered graduate student who trudges through courses in history and systems of psychology only to wade into still murkier waters upon embarking on coursework in the applied area of psychotherapy! (p. 53)

"Epistobabble" entails using terms, phrases and culture-specific references to describe and create meaning within a social group with little attention to how others who may not have the requisite knowledge or background are affected. Constructivist epistobabble is often steeped in philosophy, presuming extensive knowledge in areas such as epistemology, phenomenology, existentialism, and linguistics (among others). Mastery of these areas then becomes a prerequisite for entrée into the constructivist arena—even as it pertains to applied practices such as diagnosis, assessment, treatment planning, and psychotherapy. Much like those gamers conquering OoT, we constructivists seem to have created ways of communicating that, if observed by others outside our group, might have the same impact on them that watching the conquering of the Ocarina had on Jack.

Not only is constructivism too-often steeped in epistobabble, it also has a tendency toward proliferating an ever-increasing number of theoretical variations, each with its own often over-whelming array of concepts. Efran and Cohen (2015, this volume) use George Kelly's work as one example of this tendency:

> In addition to those who considered Kelly's approach overly intel-lective, some complained about what might be called an embar-rassment of riches. They were put off by the prospect of studying Kelly's "ten types of weeping," "nine techniques for reducing anxiety," "twelve techniques" for prompting movement, and "fifteen criteria" for establishing client readiness. . . . By the same token, they had difficulty figuring out how to integrate his eclectic list of techniques. (pp. 158–159)

So not only is there a lot of epistobabble, but it rapidly multiplies—often leading to greater confusion about constructivism among "non-club members." The unfortunate result may be that fewer people wind up paying attention because doing so becomes increas-ingly daunting. The amount of material to learn is vast and often impenetrable, thus it seems irrelevant to their everyday concerns.

In fairness, some of the language and detail is necessary. After all, if Jack spoke with the young man conquering the OoT game, the man might say that many of the terms used within the gaming community are essential to conveying certain ideas. If one wants to be a part of this community, one must learn the broader cultural language necessary for engaging. One must know what is meant by a speed run, trial skip, boss, Navi-Dive, glitch, bombchu, warp, exploit, or hack if one wants to "get it." A shared discourse is a necessary part of every community. Besides, beating a video game in record time involves a highly detailed and idiosyncratic set of processes and procedures. It isn't gamers' fault that the nature of the process is so complicated. Likewise, why should we blame constructivists if human psychology is so complex? Much like gamers who cannot decide on what constitutes a win, Winter (2015, this volume), Strong (2015, this volume), and Pavlović (2015, this volume) all independently point out that constructivists often cannot agree on what constructivism is. All communities have their own unique conundrums, which spring from their shared relational practices. As one of us (Jon) vividly recalls, a prominent member of the constructivist community once responded to complaints that his presentations were laced with technical jargon by combatively asserting, "It took me many years to become well-versed in constructivist ideas, which I did so I could partake in the conversation. If you want to talk to me, learn my language!"

Therefore, "babbling" (whether epistobabble or Nintendobabble) seems to serve an important function. It clearly helps to support a within-group identity. Having a specialized lexicon gives a group a way of identifying itself as distinct and separate from other groups. When the OoT gamers laugh knowingly on the video at a comment made by the person playing the game, we see how excited and engaged members are as they participate in this gaming community event—even though without context it isn't clear to us why what was said is funny. We have experienced something quite similar at constructivist psychology conferences. There is this wonderful feeling we get when attending these conferences. We are able to relate to colleagues in a way that we do not with others. We talk to them about Kelly's corollaries, rep grid analyses, structure determinism, social discourses, and other constructivist notions and they understand and are interested in these ideas! It's empowering, exciting, and leads to a sense of belongingness—which can feel pretty amazing.

The downside to this bonding, of course, is that it can be alienating to outsiders. It can be very hard to understand what it is we are trying to convey. We surmise that even some of the wonderful contributions to this volume will prove bewildering to many readers. The technical jargon that feels so clear and precise to us often poses a barrier to those beyond our theory group. Consequently, they fail to see the exciting and creative ideas that constructivism has to offer.

Now some may suggest that the "epistobabble" complaint is applicable to all areas of academia, not just constructivism. Telling academics that they are obtuse and difficult to understand is certainly not new. A recurring stereotype of academics is that we sit in our ivory towers, communicating in ways that most cannot (or do not care to) understand. Why should constructivism be held to a higher standard?

We agree that sometimes epistobabble *is* an issue in academia in general and this should be addressed. So why not commit ourselves to a higher standard? After all, we are not only theoreticians; we believe constructivism has many practical applications and therefore we want to see constructivist ideas utilized in everyday life. However, while the Zelda gaming community enjoys a degree of popularity and general interest, it does not always appear that people are clamoring to climb onto the constructivist bandwagon. The gaming video we referred to had been viewed 928,771 times as of December 29, 2013; the most popular video on the Constructivist Psychology Network's YouTube channel had a little more than 800 views. Clearly, we are no Zelda. Perhaps our epistobabble helps us to cope with feelings of marginalization. After all, having expert knowledge of a specialized professional discourse that few grasp may make us feel important. This may perpetuate feelings of connection to fellow theoretical travelers, but may not always help us to grow beyond our constructed borders. It is to those borders and how clearly demarcated they should or shouldn't be that we turn next.

Herding the Groucho Marx Brigade

"I don't want to belong to any club that will accept me as a member," Groucho Marx famously quipped (Quote Investigator, 2011). This remark has previously been applied to the personal construct community (Fisher, 2003) and nicely captures a long-standing attitude within it, namely that formal organization is anathema to many adherents of the theory. Neimeyer (1985) vividly captured this sentiment back in the 1980s when he interviewed prominent personal construct psychologists about whether it was time for the theory group to establish a formal organization. Jack Adams-Webber was among those who did not wish to see a formal organization, contending that "organizations may promote the status of a theory's adherents, but they do not foster the intellectual integrity of the people involved" (Neimeyer, 1985, p. 131). Steve Duck added to this, noting that formal organizations can prove isolating:

> As soon as you set up a separate organization, you're asserting a separate identity . . . and not being incorporated in things that people are doing. And it seems to me that one of the main problems with being a PCP person at this moment is that outsiders regard us as a separate group who are not to be dealt with necessarily. (Neimeyer, 1985, p. 131)

James Mancuso expressed the anti-organization stance most fervently, stating bluntly: "Institutions kill, and if they don't kill, they change the emphasis to the preservation of the institution rather than the development of that for which the institution was formed" (Neimeyer, 1985, p. 131). Sounding remarkably Groucho-esque, he declared that "the minute this organization will become formal, the minute they talk about electing a president, that's when I quit" (p. 131). How's that for not wanting to be part of any club that would have you as a member?

Despite being rather vocal, those espousing an anti-organization perspective have nevertheless seen the PCP community become increasingly organized over the past three decades—not surprising, since those supportive of organization tend to proceed with organizing while those against it tend to step aside or reluctantly come along for the ride. The argument for organization was expressed nicely by Franz Epting, who explained that an effective institution "could promote the elaboration of construct theory, and I really think we can't avoid formalizing it" (Neimeyer, 1985, p. 132). Ray Holland expanded on this, observing that

> it is a common problem for networks and social movements, that they reach a point where they are so big that it is difficult to go on in an informal, haphazard, fashion. So I think that [PCP] is now beginning to organize. (Neimeyer, 1985, p. 132)

There is ample evidence of increasing organization and institutionalization in the PCP community. In the United Kingdom, The Centre for Personal Construct Psychology (part of the School of Psychology at the University of Hertfordshire) has approved and validated formal training in PCP, although implementation of this training was on hold at the time of this volume's publication. This allows newcomers to learn PCP methods and applications, thus propagating the theory. In North America, the informal North American Personal Construct Network—despite some resistance—changed its name to the more inclusive Constructivist Psychology Network, devised bylaws, established itself as a non-profit organization, and began regularly electing officers.

We generally favor organization, though we are sympathetic to many of the arguments made by what we affectionately call PCP's "Groucho Marx Brigade." Our main counterarguments to their concerns are that (a) identity preceded organization, (b) democratic and transparent organization is more, not less, inclusive, and (c) organization is not at odds with theoretical integrity. Let us examine these one at a time.

Identity Preceded Organization

Duck stated that "As soon as you set up a separate organization, you're asserting a separate identity." We contend that the PCP community had a "separate identity" long before it formally started organizing itself. We have overheard many conversations at PCP conferences where attendees, even those opposed to organizing, seem to divide the world into "us" and "them." We realize that framing things in terms of "us" and "them" grows from a need for solidarity and connection with like-minded people rather than a desire to demonize others. Coming from work settings where constructivists are usually in the minority, finding sympathetic colleagues creates an artificial focus on "us vs. them" that is simply a passing manifestation blossoming out of relief rather than a focus on difference. Yet accompanying this connection with like-minded colleagues there is sometimes a sense of intellectual superiority—with the "them" in "us vs. them" being those in the wider world of professional psychology who have yet to recognize the brilliant, ahead-of-his-time insights of George Kelly (1955/1991a, 1955/1991b). In our view, it is this implicit sense of superiority that often keeps us separate—not having officers, bylaws, and an organizational website. We find it noteworthy that other specialized subgroups within psychology have organized themselves while simultaneously engaging with the wider world more than PCP'ers often have. We do not believe organization is central to why PCP has often remained aloof from the rest of professional psychology. Organization does not breed a separate identity, although it may at times reflect such an identity. The challenge for constructivists is to foster an identity that encourages engagement rather than demonization of those from alternative (and often more dominant, or "mainstream") perspectives.

Democratic and Transparent Organization Is More Inclusive, Not Less Inclusive

One of the strongest reasons for organizing is that it formalizes what is already occurring informally. Greg Neimeyer expressed this idea three decades ago in explaining his support for formal organization in the PCP community:

> The reason I would stand behind, or back, formalizing an . . . organization is that . . . I would see that as doing little more than making

explicit what's already happening on an implicit level. There's a
natural course of formalization going on, and I think that turning our
attention to it and making that explicit may enable us to make some
decisions consciously that otherwise we might just take for granted
or make unconsciously. (Neimeyer, 1985, p. 132)

Expanding on these sentiments, we respectfully point out that
remaining informally organized is not the same as lacking organization. All systems have organization. However, when a system
fails to make its organization explicit, it risks its leadership
consciously or unconsciously becoming an exclusive "clique." That
is, the same small group of "insiders" informally runs the group,
without democratic input. Those outside the leadership ring lack
say in the group's direction, often feeling excluded. This is the
old "Kelly cult" criticism (H. Desai, 1995)—namely, the argument
that PCP is a closed club. In principle (if not always in practice), a
clear organizational structure and bylaws allow anyone to become
involved in a group without having to discern Byzantine and often
unarticulated rules of participation. Thus, in our view, organization does not keep us separate; it actually invites others in by
modeling transparency and making the rules explicit so that the
grounds for participation are clear to all. This, of course, does not
address whether the group's focus of study is of sufficient interest
that outsiders wish entrée into the organization, but that question
is tackled in the other sections of this paper.

Organization Is Not at Odds with Intellectual Integrity

Adams-Webber expressed a viewpoint we have heard often
from the Groucho Marx Brigade: that organization is inherently
corrupting because sustaining the group takes precedence over
intellectual integrity. We imagine that those opposed to turning
the North American Personal Construct Network (NAPCN) into
the Constructivist Psychology Network (CPN) may have seen the
name change as a desperate move to sustain the organization at
the expense of its members' intellectual integrity—exemplified

by failing to keep the group's focus exclusively on Kelly's theory. We understand this sentiment, although we do not see a group's degree of institutional organization as necessarily indicative of its members' intellectual integrity because group membership need not reflect intellectual agreement. Rather, it merely implies a broad shared intellectual interest, in this case interest in (rather than agreement about issues pertaining to) personal construct psychology and/or constructivism. Ideally, all people interested in PCP and constructivism are welcomed into CPN—regardless of their particular perspectives on and uses of these theories. There is no intellectual litmus test for membership. Though we understand that any kind of group—formally organized or not—can easily morph into a mutual admiration society in which each member successively preaches to the choir, we question whether having a formal organization is what produces this. Concern that formal organization compromises intellectual integrity seems equally as misguided as concern that formal organization fosters a separate identity; how people formally organize usually reflects preexisting community views on such issues. This is why some organizations welcome diverse viewpoints and others do not. If the constructivist community has failed to effectively include others or insisted that its members share similar views (criticisms we are open to considering, however painful doing so may be), then this is a problem—but a problem that predated establishing a formal organization. Maintaining intellectual integrity is a wonderful thing, but only when combined with a tolerance for intellectual diversity. Otherwise, an organization plants the seeds of its own extinction— a question we turn to next in thinking about why CPN has so few members and how this perhaps can be remedied by sharing the practical uses of constructivism with the wider psychology and counseling communities.

HARNESSING OUR "MOJO"

So if we use language that is more accessible and create an organization that supports a constructivist identity while also being invitational and inclusive of people from more divergent perspectives, we should be inundated with people clamoring to join up, right? Not exactly. Apparently "If you build it they will come" works in movies, but not so much in organizations. Yet there are organizations built on specific theories and practices of psychology and psychotherapy that are flourishing. We would be hard pressed to say that constructivism is flourishing, but it is not quite floundering either. What makes constructivism different? What has happened and what, if anything, do we need to be doing differently? What do other organizations and theories have that we don't? We contend that it is often difficult for constructivists to feel confident in what they have to offer and to share it aggressively with others. Stated colloquially, constructivists often struggle to harness their own "mojo." There are a variety of reasons for this, but two that come to mind are that constructivists often have an aversion to proselytizing and, even if they didn't, what they are offering is often a tough sell.

Constructivists Don't Like to Proselytize

Other successful theorists and practitioners of psychotherapy don't seem reluctant to advertise or publicize their approaches. Marketing and the confidence that comes from believing that their way is the one right and true way can accomplish a great deal. If a group of people truly believes that they are right, and their rightness is also true for everyone else regardless of individual preferences or contextual factors, then loudly advertising what they believe and using marketing strategies to sell it are completely permissible, and in some cases central to their mission. Yet proselytizing is often construed by constructivists as antithetical to what it means to be a constructivist. That is, constructivists sometimes get caught in a kind of propositional construing in which committing to a tightly defined vision is seen as problematic. In this line of thinking, valuing the belief and meaning-making systems of others requires us to be, at most, invitational (and more often reticent and reserved about our own unique sense of what is right or meaningful). Thus it becomes inconsistent to recruit new constructivists in any way that looks or feels like we are imposing our own beliefs or ways of making meaning on them. However, as one of us (Jon) has been saying in recent years, constructivism does not require an "anything goes" acceptance that precludes commitment and belief (Raskin & Debany, 2012)—or, in this case, even proselytizing. When it comes to marketing constructivist ideas, we need not feel ambivalent simply because we realize that our view is but one view. There is nothing wrong with strongly advocating a constructivist perspective. Doing so need not be seen as insisting ours is the one and only way. In encouraging her PCP colleagues to initiate a "take-over bid" for the discipline of psychology, Fay Fransella (1978) strongly challenged personal construct psychologists' ambivalence toward proselytizing. Her prescient viewpoint on this issue offers a constructive alternative that may be worth putting to the test.

Practically speaking, reticence about imposing ideas on others means that constructivists have not traditionally been natural sales people. This is particularly true for one of our authors (Sara), who has often found it nearly impossible to sell anything—including things that people actually wanted to buy. Girl Scout cookies are a good example. Instead of selling them, Sara took extra babysitting jobs to pay for the cookies she was supposed to sell and then gave the cookies away. Imposing on others by "guilting" them into buying something they may not have wanted was simply out of the question for Sara. This aversion to selling has often seemed to be a "core construct" of the PCP community—manifesting itself in avoiding things like fund raising activities, deliberately recruiting students, or working to broaden or expand the membership in constructivist organizations. This does not mean that new members wouldn't be welcomed—they would, but only if they really wanted to be there and joined on their own initiation. While this stance may be understandable, it certainly does nothing to grow constructivism.

However, as Fransella's (1978) example suggests, there are exceptions to this rule. There are people who have effectively marketed constructivist ideas without being self-conscious about it. Some of these efforts have even entered mainstream pop culture. Several years ago, we were surprised to turn on an episode of "Oprah" and see psychotherapist Bill O'Hanlon talking about his latest self-help book, *Do One Thing Different* (O'Hanlon, 1999). What he seemed to be selling was fixed-role therapy marketed to the masses in simple and straightforward language that anyone could understand. Oprah seemed duly impressed. More recently, Lara Honos-Webb (a.k.a., "Dr. Lara") has become well-known for her "Gift of" book series ("The Gift of ADHD," 2007; "The Gift of Depression," 2007). These books, which provide alternative constructions of disorders like ADHD and depression, are rooted in Honos-Webb's earlier academic writings on experiential personal construct psychology and narrative (Honos-Webb & Leitner, 2001; Honos-Webb, Sunwolf, & Shapiro, 2004). Our point is not to say that we should all write a self-help tome in an effort to secure a booking on "The View" (although this might be fun!), but that it is possible to confidently advocate for and market complex construc-tivist ideas in ways that fellow psychologists and the general public can comprehend without violating our core principles.

Constructivism is a Tough Sell

We are impressed whenever someone effectively conveys constructivist ideas to colleagues or the general public because, put simply, constructivism is a tough sell. It is challenging to new-comers, not just because it tends to be jargon-heavy, but also because its ideas run counter to what most of us have been previously taught. Throughout history, thinkers espousing ideas consistent with constructivism have found it difficult to win people over because their viewpoint often seems to contradict traditional ways of understanding. In radical constructivist Ernst von Glasersfeld's (1995) words, philosophers with constructivist-consistent ideas have often encountered difficulty:

> By renouncing the quest for certain knowledge about reality, they had deprived themselves of the very argument that philosophers use to distinguish knowledge from mere opinion or belief. Consequently, these wayward thinkers were for the most disregarded in the history of philosophy. (p. 25)

Despite this difficulty, "today the philosophy of science teems with ideas that subvert the millenary tradition of realism and its goal of objective knowledge" (von Glasersfeld, 1995, p. 25). The challenge for constructivists is how to convey their position without seeming "kooky." It is our position that a fully articulated constructivist perspective does not reject science or existing knowledge paradigms. It merely places them within a framework that sees all knowledge schemes as human endeavors. Hence, one of us (Jon) warned in his opening contribution to this volume about the perils of "careless constructivism," described as the unfortunate tendency of many constructivists to make provocative statements (e.g., "Reality is invented") without thoroughly explaining the underlying stance being adopted (Raskin, 2015, this volume).

It is our contention that although constructivism can be difficult to convey, it can be done. For instance, one of the authors (Jon) sometimes teaches an undergraduate course in constructivist psychology at his university. He spends the first third of the class covering three different theories: personal construct psychology, radical constructivism, and social constructionism. The second part of the class shifts to practical and research applications, with the third part examining critiques and controversies. What Jon has found is that even students who end up disagreeing with some of constructivism's main tenets generally come to (a) appreciate and understand the perspective, and (b) see it as a meta-framework that does not require them to give up on the quest for truth, but merely recognize that any time they are on such a quest, they are always venturing forth from within a perspective that opens up some ways of knowing and forecloses others—a la Kelly's (1977) playful insistence that the truths we seek inevitably lie just beyond the horizon. That is, when students come to understand in full the distinction described in the opening contribution to this volume about ontological versus epistemological modes of construing (Raskin, 2015, this volume), they find themselves less threatened— and thereby more amenable—to the constructivist position. Our take home message here is that communicating constructivism is hard, but can be done. We may never have swarms of people clamoring for constructivism like they do to learn the intricacies of the Legend of Zelda, but we can certainly do a better job than we have at making constructivism understandable and relevant to a wider audience.

USING IT INSTEAD OF LOSING IT

Of course, one of the keys to constructivism's future is how well we share our approach with the wider world. Although it often seems like we are alone in the universe, there are instances where research and practice rooted in constructivism have had a broader impact. We highlight three examples of this: the repertory grid, coherence therapy, and Robert Neimeyer's work on grief and loss. In each of these instances, practitioners have been "using it instead of losing it" and in so doing show how constructivism can be effectively disseminated in an impactful way.

Repertory Grid

The repertory grid (rep grid) is a notable example of an application of constructivist theory that has gained widespread attention; it is as close as PCP comes to having a "gimmick" capable of garnering widespread attention in the field (Efran & Cohen, 2015, this volume). As many of our readers know, the repertory grid (or repertory grid technique) is a methodology that helps elicit idiosyncratic personal constructs through a systematic step-by-step protocol. The protocol can be done via pen and paper or through a variety of computer applications such as Rep 5, GRIDSUITE, and GRIDCOR (PCP Portal, 2010). The derived personal constructs in any given protocol can be analyzed in a variety of contexts and be used to promote insight and proactive social action.

The rep grid is rooted in George Kelly's personal construct theory. While other tools may elicit opinions based on *others'* constructs (such as a traditional survey methodology), the rep grid assumes that the individualized ways that people give meaning to their constructions must be the focus of attention if one desires to understand their lived experiences (Blundell, Witkowski, Wieck, & Hare, 2012). People's bipolar personal constructs often interact with one another to contribute to a complex personal negotiation of meaning. The rep grid process yields a kind of "construct map," which provides a means of mapping individuals' personal meanings (Blundell et al., 2012). Kelly's original use of this methodology was primarily in clinical psychology settings, an area still popular for those interested in repertory grid analysis. For example, researchers have examined topics including therapists' perception of patients (Blondell, et al., 2012; Ralley, 2009), career counseling (Mackay, 2004), treatment approaches (Neimeyer, 2004) and the overall use of the tool as a form for clinical research (Ralley, 2009).

However, the use of rep grids has expanded far beyond the realm of psychotherapy. One of the most well-known areas of application is in the field of human resources, marketing, and customer service. For example, researchers have used rep grid analyses to understand (a) branding of merchandise (Henderson, Iacobucci, & Calder, 2002), (b) management techniques (D. Desai & Sahu, 2008, Hodgkinson, 2002, Napier, Keil & Tan, 2009), (c) consumer behavior (Zinkhan & Biswas, 1988), and (d) product development (Crawford, Taylor, & Li Wan Po, 2001). Repertory grid analysis seems to be a well-used research tool in this field. In addition, it has been used in a diverse array of cultures all over the world. The rep grid has been used to address a range of topics—including understanding spirituality (deGuzman, Dalay, de Guzman, de Jesus, de Mesa, & Flores, 2009), reactions to healthcare (Adams, 2011), tourism (Schweizenberg, Wearing, & Darcy, 2012), film analysis (Blowers & McCoy, 1986), and even fingerprint technology (Davis & Hufnagel, 2007). As such, the repertory grid is a nice example of a constructivist methodology that has not only proven to be useful among constructivists, but also has made the leap into several other disciplines. It has been able to traverse the epistobabble and find a common language that people from all over the world can use and share. While personal construct psychologists, including apparently Kelly himself, have lamented that grid methodology has sometimes been adopted by methodologists without ample attention to the theory behind it (Fransella, 1995), the method's popularity nonetheless offers a potential opportunity for personal construct psychologists to share their theory more widely.

Coherence Therapy

Coherence therapy provides another example of a constructivist approach that has garnered significant attention from mainstream psychology—as evidenced by publications (Ecker & Hulley, 1996, 2008), presentations, and national and international workshops (Coherence Psychology Institute, 2013). Coherence therapy broadens the scope of constructivist psychotherapy by viewing *all* problems or difficulties a client experiences as directly related to preexisting unconscious constructs. Constructivist psychotherapy broadly aims to take a valuing position with clients and places emphasis on the validity and intelligibility of the client's distress rather than labeling symptoms as a disease or an enemy. Yet knowing that distress is valid and understandable only takes us so far. When clients arrive at the therapy office they already view their troubles or symptoms as senseless, dysfunctional and irrational, even if we as their therapists believe their troubles have their own internal rationality. Clients arrive wanting change, and although they usually appreciate the humanistic conviction that they are valid as persons even in their distress, they still want change.

Further, while having insight into "why" behavior is happening is interesting, it doesn't truly address the underlying issue—wanting the behavior to stop. Wanting troubling behaviors, thoughts or emotions to stop is usually what brings clients to therapy. Understanding or having insight into why the behaviors, thoughts or emotions are happening can be helpful, but usually insight alone is not enough. Thus, believing that reality is personally constructed may help build insight and understanding, but what happens to the personal constructs once they are elicited is what separates constructivist psychotherapy from other approaches. Coherence therapy intentionally works to discover and transform unconscious personal constructs.

As a humanistically-oriented constructivist approach, coherence therapy views presenting symptoms as part of the client's solution to some other worse suffering. This is not "secondary gain" or a form of malingering. In coherence therapy the client is viewed as always having the ability to dispel the presenting symptom by accessing and revising the unconscious constructions of reality that require it (Ecker & Hulley, 1996). Coherence therapy is uniquely constructivist in viewing clients as masters of their own experiencing—not because they can "handle" the symptom or trouble that is upon them, but rather because the symptom itself is already an unconscious manifestation of their own protective action taken in response to a core way of understanding the world. Coherence therapy aims for retrieving the unconscious, coherent personal themes or constructs that are generating problematic moods, thoughts, or behaviors (Ecker & Hulley, 1996). Coherence therapists experientially help elicit the client's unconscious constructs that necessitate the existence of the presenting problem. Thus, the client's lucid experience of the symptom as an expression of deeply meaningful personal constructs dispels previous self-pathologizing construals of the symptom as indicating a defect of self (Ecker & Hulley, 1996).

Coherence therapy is another excellent example of constructivists "using it" instead of "losing it." With a certificate program and variety of other training resources available to clinicians (Coherence Psychology Institute, 2013) and a way of presenting constructivist ideas without necessarily ensnaring newcomers in lots of technical jargon to scare them off, coherence therapy is an example of how to effectively share constructivist ideas with a wider, non-constructivist audience.

Grief and Loss

Bob Neimeyer's work on grief and loss provides a final example of constructivist ideas being applied in ways that have had a significant impact on psychology and related disciplines. Neimeyer has combined aspects of personal construct psychology, narrative therapy, and social constructionism into a meaning-based approach to conceptualizing and working with people experiencing grief and loss (Neimeyer, 2001). One of his central premises is that people often lack the meaning-making structures necessary to effectively make sense of things when faced with grief and loss. Therapy therefore becomes an arena to help people in this very difficult endeavor.

While rooting his work firmly within a constructivist epistemology, Neimeyer identifies in clear and accessible language three activities that are important in successful meaning reconstruction following loss: *sense making, benefit finding,* and *identity change* (Gillies & Neimeyer, 2006). These ideas provide a firm foundation for psychotherapeutic applications and have gained widespread attention in books (Neimeyer, 2001), training videos (American Psychological Association, 2004), and workshops. Additionally, Neimeyer has applied constructivist ideas to research on complicated grief, which involves long-term struggle in meaningfully integrating a loss into one's life (Neimeyer, 2005/2006, 2006). In understandably and accessibly applying constructivist ideas to grief and loss, Neimeyer's work provides an excellent example of a constructivist "using it" instead of "losing it."

CONCLUSION

Must constructivism continue to exist? No. As Kelly (1955/1991a, p. 22) himself said, every theory is an "eventual candidate for the trash can" once its utility has been exhausted. However, we don't believe that constructivism has come close to reaching its expiration date. Therefore, what is our responsibility to keep constructivism active in a field where the "latest" and "greatest" tend to get the most attention from practicing clinicians? Must we continue to work to keep constructivism in the mainstream of academia, to have it taught in theories courses, and be included in textbooks? Has the "good word" been spread enough that we can rest on our heels and stop attempting to help constructivism be front and center in psychological theory and practice?

Both fortunately and unfortunately, we believe that constructivists do have a responsibility to keep constructivism relevant to the larger field of psychology and psychotherapy. Constructivism has just enough popularity and coverage in most psychology and counselor education programs to capture the interest of students who are drawn to perspectives that support meaning making and non-objectivist stances. If, with further study and reflection, these students find that constructivism is a good fit for them, then having journals, organizations, and conferences—which all signify legitimacy in academic circles—is necessary for them to be taken seriously for both internships and future employment. Additionally, having outlets for constructivist research and theory (in journals, at conferences, in educational and training settings, and in the wider popular culture more generally) helps to build community and a body of literature that can sustain constructivism into the future.

While having the desire and seeing the logic in keeping constructivism viable in an ever-changing professional landscape, few of us have the time, energy, or skill set to make this happen on our own. While understanding the risks and downsides of organizing, without an organization that is responsible for keeping constructivism going, the diffusion of responsibility usually means that very little action is taken. Yet having an organization with an official membership is not enough to create a generative process that promises the continuation of the ideas and intellectual integrity of constructivism. Practical guidelines, treatment of topical issues through a constructivist lens, opening our circles more to dissolve the appearance of having a closed insider networker, being open to new ideas that stretch the current notions of constructivism, and being willing to advocate for constructivist perspectives in ways both understandable and appealing to those outside our tight nit community are all important as we move forward.

There is a necessary amount of time, energy and commitment that comes with perfecting a new skill. For one of the authors (Sara), learning to play Zelda would be truly difficult (although she did have a great aunt named Zelda). However, she might be able to do it if the directions were clear and there were others there to help her. Further, if the guidelines were written in very simple "non-video game-esque" language, there is even a chance she might find herself enjoying what she was doing. Similarly, if practical guidelines and "real world" applications for constructivist therapy and research could be written in clear language, simply and lucidly explaining complex theoretical ideas and the practices they lead to, there is a good chance that many people—even those who never would have thought themselves interested—might find ways of incorporating constructivist ideas into their work. We challenge the constructivist community to take up just such a task. If behavior is indeed an experiment—as Kelly (1969) himself suggested—then we are quite curious to see where such experimentation and perturbing of the status quo ultimately leads.

REFERENCES

American Psychological Association. (Producer). (2004). Constructivist therapy [DVD]. In *Systems of psychotherapy video series*. Washington, DC: Author.

Blowers, G. H., & McCoy, M. M. (1986). Perceiving cinematic episodes: A cross-cultural repertory grid study of a narrative film segment. *International Journal of Psychology, 21*, 317–333.

Blundell, J., Wittkowski, A., Wieck, A., & Hare, D. J. (2012). Using the repertory grid technique to examine nursing staff's construal of mothers with mental health problems. *Clinical Psychology & Psychotherapy, 19*, 260–9.

Coherence Psychology Institute. (2013). Coherence therapy [website]. Retrieved December 29, 2013 from http://www.coherencetherapy.org

Cosmo Speedruns. (2013, January 14). *The Legend of Zelda: Ocarina of Time speedrun in 22:38*, live at AGDQ2013 [Video file]. Retrieved from http://youtu.be/0M7IINwTFVw

Crawford, J. O., Taylor, C. & Li Wan Po, N. (2001). A case study of on-screen prototypes and usability evaluation of electronic timers and food menu systems. *International Journal of Human-Computer Interaction, 2*, 187–204.

Davis, C., & Hufnagel, E. (2007). Through the eyes of experts: A sociocognitive perspective on the automation of fingerprint work. *MIS Quarterly, 31*, 681–703.

de Guzman A. B ., Dalay N. J. Z., de Guzman A. J. M., de Jesus L. L. E ., de Mesa J. B. C., & Flores J. D. D. (2009). Spirituality in nursing: Filipino elderly's concept of, distance from, and involvement with God. *Educational Gerontology, 35*, 929–44.

Desai, D., & Sahu, S. (2008). CRM change management in an emerging country context: An exploratory study in India. *Global Journal of Flexible Systems Management, 9*(2/3), 41–53.

Desai, H. (1995, May). Ways in which personal construct psychology has (and has not) turned into a religion. *NAPCN News*, 4–5.

Ecker, B., & Hulley, L. (1996). *Depth-oriented brief therapy*. San Francisco, CA: Jossey-Bass.

Ecker, B., & Hulley, L. (2008). Coherence therapy: Swift change at the core of emotional truth. In J. D. Raskin & S. K. Bridges (Eds.), *Studies in meaning 3: Constructivist psychotherapy in the real world* (pp. 57–84). New York, NY: Pace University Press.

Efran, J. S., & Clarfield, L. E. (1992). Constructionist therapy: Sense and nonsense. In S. McNamee & K. J. Gergen (Eds.), *Therapy as social construction* (pp. 200–217). London: Sage.

Efran, J. S., & Cohen, J. N. (2015, this volume). Where's the gimmick? Future prospects for constructivist psychotherapy. In J. D. Raskin, S. K. Bridges & J. S. Kahn (Eds.), *Studies in meaning 5: Perturbing the status quo in constructivist psychology*. New York, NY: Pace University Press.

Fisher, J. M. (2003). Fraggle Rock: A study in isolationism. In G. Chiari & M. L. Nuzzo (Eds.), *Psychological constructivism and the social world* (pp. 98–104). Milan, Italy: FrancoAngeli.

Fransella, F. (1978). Personal construct theory or psychology? In F. Fransella (Ed.), *Personal construct psychology 1977* (pp. 1–6). London, England: Academic Press.

Fransella, F. (1995). *George Kelly*. London, England: Sage.

The Gift of ADHD. (2007). Retrieved December 29, 2013 from http://www.visionarysoul.com/gift.html

The Gift of Depression. (2007). Retrieved December 29, 2013 from http://www.visionarysoul.com/depression.html

Gillies, J., & Neimeyer, R. A. (2006). Loss, grief, and the search for significance: Toward a model of meaning reconstruction in bereavement. *Journal of Constructivist Psychology, 19,* 31–65. doi:10.1080/10720530500311182

Glasersfeld, E. von. (1995). *Radical constructivism: A way of knowing and learning*. London, England: The Falmer Press.

Hawley, M. (2007). The repertory grid: Eliciting user experience comparisons in the customer's voice. Retrieved from http://www.uxmatters.com/mt/archives/2007/12/the-repertory-grid-eliciting-user-experience-comparisons-in-the-customers-voice.php

Henderson, G., Iacobucci, D., Calder, B. (2002). Using network analysis to understand brands. *Advances in Consumer Research, 29,* 397–405.

Hodgkinson, G. P. (2002). Comparing managers' mental models of competition: Why self-report measures of belief similarity won't do. *Organization Studies, 23,* 63–72.

Honos-Webb, L., & Leitner, L. M. (2001). How using the DSM causes damage: A client's report. *Journal of Humanistic Psychology, 41*(4), 36–56.

Honos-Webb, L., Sunwolf, & Shapiro, J. (2004). The healing power of telling stories in psychotherapy. In J. D. Raskin, S. K. Bridges (Eds.), *Studies in meaning 2: Bridging the personal and social in constructivist psychology* (pp. 85–114). New York, NY: Pace University Press.

Kelly, G. A. (1969). Ontological acceleration. In B. Maher (Ed.), *Clinical psychology and personality: The selected papers of George Kelly* (pp. 7–45). New York, NY: Wiley.

Kelly, G. A. (1977). The psychology of the unknown. In D. Bannister (Ed.), *New perspectives in personal construct theory* (pp. 1–19). London, England: Academic Press. (Original work published 1955)

Kelly, G. A. (1991a). *The psychology of personal constructs: Vol. 1. A theory of personality.* London, England: Routledge. (Original work published 1955)

Kelly, G. A. (1991b). *The psychology of personal constructs: Vol. 2. Clinical diagnosis and psychotherapy.* London, England: Routledge. (Original work published 1955)

Kleinrock, L. (n.d.). *What is emergent behavior?* [Video file]. Retrieved from http://curiosity.discovery.com/question/emergent-behavior

Mackay, S. (2004). The role perception questionnaire (RPQ): A tool for assessing undergraduate students' perceptions of the role of other professions. *Journal of Interprofessional Care, 3,* 289–302.

Napier, N., Keil, M., & Tan, F. B. (2009). IT project managers' construction of successful project management practice: a repertory grid investigation. *Information Systems Journal, 19,* 255–282.

Neimeyer, R. A. (1985). *The development of personal construct psychology.* Lincoln, NE: University of Nebraska Press.

Neimeyer, R. A. (1997). Problems and prospects in constructivist psychotherapy. *Journal of Constructivist Psychology, 10,* 51–74.

Neimeyer, R. A. (2001). *Meaning reconstruction and the experience of loss.* Washington, DC: American Psychological Association.

Neimeyer, R. A. (2004). Fostering posttraumatic growth: A narrative elaboration. *Psychological Inquiry, 15,* 53–59.

Neimeyer, R. A. (2005/2006). Complicated grief and the quest for meaning: A constructivist contribution. *Omega: Journal of Death and Dying, 52*(1), 37–52. doi:10.2190/EQL1-LN3V-KNYR-18TF

Neimeyer, R. A. (2006). Complicated grief and the reconstruction of meaning: Conceptual and empirical contributions to a cognitive-constructivist model. *Clinical Psychology: Science and Practice, 13,* 141–145. doi:10.1111/j.1468-2850.2006.00016.x

Quote Investigator. (2011, April 18). I don't want to belong to any club that will accept me as a member. Retrieved from http://quoteinvestigator.com/2011/04/18/groucho-resigns/

Pavlović, J. (2015, this volume). Imagining possible futures: Scenarios for constructivist psychology. In J. D. Raskin, S. K. Bridges & J. S. Kahn (Eds.), *Studies in meaning 5: Perturbing the status quo in constructivist psychology.* New York, NY: Pace University Press.

PCP Portal (2010). Computer programmes for analysis of repertory grids. Retrieved from http://www.pcp-net.de/info/comp-prog.html.

Ralley C., Allott, R., Hare, D. J., & Wittkowski, A. (2009). The use of the repertory grid technique to examine staff beliefs about clients with dual diagnosis. *Clinical Psychology & Psychotherapy, 16,* 148–158.

Raskin, J. D. (2015, this volume). An introductory perturbation: What is constructivism and is there a future in it? In J. D. Raskin, S. K. Bridges & J.

S. Kahn (Eds.), *Studies in meaning 5: Perturbing the status quo in constructivist psychology*. New York, NY: Pace University Press.

Raskin, J. D., & Debany, A. E. (2012). The inescapability of ethics and the impossibility of "anything goes": A constructivist model of ethical meaning-making. In S. Cipolletta & E. Gius (Eds.), *Ethics in action: Dialogue between knowledge and practice* (pp. 13–32). Milan, Italy: LED.

Schweinsberg, S., Wearing, S. L., & Darcy, S. (2012). Understanding communities' views of nature in rural industry renewal: The transition from forestry to nature-based tourism in Eden, Australia. *Journal of Sustainable Tourism, 20*, 195–213.

Speed Demos Archive. (n.d.). In *Wikipedia*. Retrieved December 29, 2013 from http://en.wikipedia.org/wiki/Speed_Demos_Archive

Strong, T. (2015, this volume). On being a social constructionist in a more than human world. In J. D. Raskin, S. K. Bridges & J. S. Kahn (Eds.), *Studies in meaning 5: Perturbing the status quo in constructivist psychology*. New York, NY: Pace University Press.

Winter, D. A. (2015, this volume). What does the future hold for personal construct psychology? In J. D. Raskin, S. K. Bridges & J. S. Kahn (Eds.), *Studies in meaning 5: Perturbing the status quo in constructivist psychology*. New York, NY: Pace University Press.

Zinkhan, G. M., & Biswas, A. (1988). Using the repertory grid to assess the complexity of consumers' cognitive structures. *Advances in Consumer Research, 15*, 493–497.

About the Editors

Jonathan D. Raskin is a professor of psychology and counseling at the State University of New York at New Paltz. His scholarship focuses on constructivist theory, particularly as it pertains to the practice of psychotherapy and conceptions of abnormality. Dr. Raskin's published work includes five co-edited books, including the previous *Studies in Meaning* volumes. In addition to being a past president of the Constructivist Psychology Network, he currently serves as managing editor for the *Journal of Constructivist Psychology*. Dr. Raskin is licensed as a psychologist in New York and is a fellow of the American Psychological Association.

Sara K. Bridges is an associate professor of counseling psychology at The University of Memphis. Her scholarship examines constructivism, sexuality, and depth focused approaches to psychotherapy. In addition to publishing extensively on constructivism, Dr. Bridges has co-edited all four previous *Studies in Meaning* volumes. She is a past president of both the Constructivist Psychology Network and the Society of Humanistic Psychology (Division 32 of the American Psychological Association). Dr. Bridges is a licensed psychologist and co-director of the Coherence Psychology Institute.

Jack S. Kahn is the Dean of Social and Behavioral Sciences at Palomar College. His scholarship focuses on masculinity and gender, particularly in examining the negotiation of diverse masculinities utilizing dialogical self theory. Dr. Kahn's published work includes a text, *An Introduction to Masculinities*, and several articles providing support for a new model of masculinity analysis and measurement entitled dialogical masculinity. Dr. Kahn has served on the steering committee of the Constructivist Psychology Network, is a member of several professional organizations, and is a contributing editor to two academic journals. He is licensed as a psychologist in California and has an active consultation practice.

Appendix:
About the Constructivist Psychology Network

Studies in Meaning is the official book series of the Constructivist Psychology Network (CPN). CPN is a network of persons interested in constructivist approaches to psychology, relationships, and human change processes. It is largely comprised of psychologists, but there are also members from related disciplines. Those interested in personal constructivism or related areas of constructivist, constructionist, narrative, or postmodern approaches to psychology are encouraged to join. CPN officially became a non-profit organization in July 2005. Up to date information about CPN is maintained on the organization's website: http://www.constructivistpsych.org

CPN membership is open to anyone. An annual membership includes a subscription to the *Journal of Constructivist Psychology* (4 print issues per year plus full electronic access to all back issues) and receipt of the electronic CPN newsletter, the *Constructivist Chronicle*. Members often receive discounted rates for the biennial CPN conference held in even numbered years. CPN membership rates at the time of this volume's publication are as follows:

Professional memberships: $70
Student memberships: $40

This is an excellent deal, especially when you consider that the current non-CPN member price for an individual print subscription alone to the *Journal of Constructivist Psychology* is over $300 US per year, while an online subscription alone is over $575 per year. Further, no matter where you live or what currency you use, you can pay your dues quickly and easily online using our secure online payments option.

How to Join CPN

The easiest way to join CPN is via our secure website using a credit card or PayPal account. Go to http://www.constructivistpsych.org and click the membership link. Then follow the easy instructions. Dues payments can also be made by check or money order (in US dollars made payable to CPN); instructions for paying by mail are available on the CPN website.

Index of Proper Names

[numbers in bold refer to listings in reference sections.]

Subject Index

www.ingramcontent.com/pod-product-compliance
Lightning Source LLC
Chambersburg PA
CBHW061000280326
41935CB00009B/775